The Sanitation of Brazil

The Sanitation of Brazil

Nation, State, and Public Health,
1889–1930

GILBERTO HOCHMAN

Translated by
Diane Grosklaus Whitty

UNIVERSITY OF
ILLINOIS PRESS
Urbana, Chicago, and Springfield

Funds for the publication of this translation were provided
by the Lemann Institute for Brazilian Studies, University
of Illinois at Urbana-Champaign, and by the Ministerio
da Cultura do Brasil / Fundação Biblioteca Nacional.

 MINISTÉRIO DA CULTURA
Fundação BIBLIOTECA NACIONAL

Originally published in 1998 by Editora Hucitec
(São Paulo) as *A Era do Saneamento: As Bases da
Política de Saúde Pública no Brasil*

The first edition of this book in Portuguese (1998)
was coedited by the Associação Nacional de Pós-
Graduação e Pesquisa em Ciências Sociais (ANPOCS)

Manufactured in the United States of America
1 2 3 4 5 C P 5 4 3 2 1
∞ This book is printed on acid-free paper.

Library of Congress Control Number: 2016947897
ISBN 978-0-252-04061-0 (hardcover)
ISBN 978-0-252-08211-5 (paperback)
ISBN 978-0-252-09905-2 (e-book)

For any and all reasons,
I dedicate this book to my parents,
Samuel and Clara

Contents

Preface

Released in 1998, the first Brazilian edition of this book was made possible by the Associação Nacional de Pós-Graduação e Pesquisa em Ciências Sociais (ANPOCS), which granted my political science dissertation the José Albertino Rodrigues Award for the best social science dissertation of 1996. The book was republished in Portuguese in 2006 and rapidly sold out. A third edition was released in 2012, followed by a number of new printings. For nearly two decades, the book has made the rounds of various fields in Brazilian and Latin America academia, including the social sciences, history, collective health, education, and environmental engineering. It seems clear that it also helped cement an original interpretation of the relations between health policy and the formation of the state and nation in Brazil while pointing the way for a mounting new body of scholarship in the social sciences, history, and public health.

This book endeavors to understand the formation of national public health policies through a focus on rural sanitation policies in Brazil over the final two decades of the First Republic (1889–1930). During this time frame, public health moved to the top of Brazil's political agenda, propelled by a distinctively nationalist ideology. A nationwide state health and sanitation policy was built on the foundation of this privileged position. The 1910s and 1920s afforded unique political opportunities for wide-ranging public health reform. The book is about these opportunities, this reform, and some of the reform's successes and failures. Its guiding questions concern when, why, and how health became public. The only other occasion in Brazilian history that presented similar prospects was the late 1980s, when the country's new democratic constitution not only declared health a citizenship right but also charged the state with its provision.

Health and sanitation policies played a major role in significantly extending the state's reach across society and across the nation's territory. As a study of the collectivization of protection against human destitution or of the beginnings of social policies, *The Sanitation of Brazil* suggests that this process depended on how the Brazilian elites addressed the dilemmas and impasses engendered by health interdependence. Social protection policies arose when the elites' social consciousness converged with their material interests and they saw that benefits could be gained by collectivizing welfare. In addition, the organizational format and substance of these policies were the objects of calculations and bargaining involving the costs and benefits of tasking the state with health vis-à-vis the costs imposed by disease.

A nationwide public health policy became possible and viable in Brazil thanks to this intersection of the elites' consciousness and interests, and its foundations grew out of negotiations between the states and central power within the political and institutional framework of federalism. This convergence was fostered by the Brazilian public health movement, which strove to redefine the borders between *sertões* and coast, interior and city, and rural and urban Brazil in light of the issue the crusaders chose as the top national priority: public health. The movement worked tirelessly to promote an essentially political understanding of these demarcations; the *sertões* painted by public health doctors and hygienists were characterized by the simultaneous absence of public power and the ubiquity of communicable diseases, especially Brazil's major rural endemic maladies. Through a fierce public opinion campaign, the movement for rural sanitation sought to convince the political elites that the *sertões* (government neglect and disease) were all much closer and more menacing than these advantaged sectors might imagine. Thus, the first steps toward a national health policy were taken during the First Republic. The central arguments of the book gave birth to a gamut of interpretations, some of them surprising in relation to my own original thoughts. Much scholarship on the history of health and on health policy in Brazil has come out since this book's initial publication in 1998. Just as children must be rebels at a certain point in their lives, books march down their own paths, independent from their authors and even at times in disagreement with them. In offering this English-language edition to a new set of readers, very few changes have been made to the arguments put forth in the original or in subsequent editions. The book was warmly received across broad sectors of academia and has been cited abundantly, indicative of how its groundwork has held its own and its interpretation has been incorporated into scholarly reflections on public policy, the history of health, and social and political thought in Brazil; further, it has enabled comparisons with other national experiences. Still, like all academic work, the book in Portuguese and now in English must be the constant object of new questioning, and my later articles and book chapters have reworked some of its viewpoints and perspectives. The translation process itself led certain material to be updated, bits of the narrative to be revised, and some lines of reasoning to be further explicated without altering my arguments. The publication of this title in English by the University of Illinois Press allows me to renew my intellectual and political commitments to people's health in Brazil and elsewhere and to again highlight the central role of the state and government in the provision of social protection from a historical and sociological perspective. This contributes to a wider debate of the past, present, and future of health, an increasingly global issue.

While the book is in essence the same, the author's life has seen great changes, not just intellectually. John Lennon tells us that "life is what happens to you while you're busy making other plans," and life went on happening while people read *A Era do Saneamento*—new friends (some made through the book), students, and colleagues; countless trips, projects, and conferences; fresh personal and intellectual challenges; renewed joys; some deep sorrows; and a powerful new love and family life.

But let's get down to the essentials. Jerry Dávila took the initiative to submit the book to the University of Illinois Press for evaluation, setting in motion this English translation. Jerry has always been an enthusiastic force in expanding and deepening the conversation between U.S. and Brazilian historians. The press embraced the proposal and, when translation was already under way, Brazil's Fundação Biblioteca Nacional selected the title under its Support Program for the Translation and Publication of Brazilian Authors. Editora Hucitec publishing house, with the intercession of Flávio Aderaldo, ceded English rights. The enterprise was also possible only thanks to the dedication, skill, and zeal of Diane Grosklaus Whitty. More than a translator, Diane was at many moments editor and coauthor. Not coincidentally, she translated my first article in English in 1993. My special thanks to Jerry and Diane.

Through the Oswaldo Cruz Foundation's Graduate Program in the History of Science and Health, established in 2001, I have engaged in rewarding intellectual exchanges with master's and doctoral candidates that have profoundly affected my analysis of the history of health policies in Brazil. Interactions with my students have contributed decisively to the further development of the line of research into health policy from a historical perspective that I began in the 1990s. This new edition is in part a by-product of ongoing, fruitful dialogue with my students in my capacity as teacher and adviser.

I extend a general round of thanks to the early supporters of my doctoral work and its publication in Portuguese. First, my gratitude goes to the Casa de Oswaldo Cruz, the division of the Fundação Oswaldo Cruz where I have worked since 1987 and where I conducted my PhD research. There I never lacked for intellectual freedom, fine working conditions, and support for my work. I am grateful to the other researchers, librarians, administrative staff, and directors for the challenging and creative environment that has become the Casa's trademark. I also acknowledge special gratitude to Nísia Trindade Lima, dear friend, colleague, and coauthor of many articles and chapters. I credit my intellectual training and professional identity to the Instituto Universitário de Pesquisas do Rio de Janeiro (now the Instituto de Estudos Sociais e Políticos): if I am a social scientist, I owe it to this institution. I thank its professors, librarians, staff, and students for the years of intellectual and personal camaraderie that I enjoyed from 1983 to 1996. Very special thanks go to Elisa Pereira Reis, my doctoral adviser, and Wanderley Guilherme dos Santos, my adviser during my master's program.

The Sociology Department at Boston College received me as a visiting scholar in 1994 and provided me with all the resources and facilities I needed to concentrate fully on reading, researching, and writing. For this I am indebted to Professor John B. Williamson, with whom I had the privilege to work. My thanks as well to CAPES and CNPq for the funding I received in Brazil and the United States during my PhD studies and to ANPOCS for recognizing my work and making its publication in book form possible.

My mother, Clara Cohen Hochman, public health educator and champion of my career, left us in November 2010. She would have loved to see this book in English. I will miss her always, and I rededicate the book to her and my father, Samuel. I am grateful for my bond with my brother, Rogério, which has grown ever deeper. Last, and most important, I have been taking the journey into the twenty-first century hand in hand with my darling Simone Kropf and our daughter, Ana Clara. Nothing would be possible without their love and affection. As our Natalie Merchant sings in "Kind and Generous," Simone, "For everything you've done, you know I'm bound, I'm bound to thank you for it . . ."

Translator's Note

It is my privilege and honor to provide English readers direct access to Gilberto Hochman's seminal exploration of the development of public health policy and the growth of the State in early twentieth-century Brazil, a topic that at its core retains great relevance today.

This translation is not a completely faithful rendering of the original Portuguese. Rather, the author and I agreed that this would be an opportunity to update and further polish a text written seventeen years ago and tailor it to an English-speaking audience. That said, as Gilberto emphasizes in the preface, none of these minor changes have modified the key arguments, and this edition should not be considered in any way a rewrite. Collaboration with the author notwithstanding, any inaccuracies in the translation are fully my responsibility.

Gilberto has in places introduced new information to reflect scholarship produced since original publication in Brazil, including a good number of more recent references. Furthermore, as any translator can tell you, no form of revising or editing is more thorough than translation, leaving (virtually) no ambiguity or misinterpretation unturned; where necessary, Gilberto and I worked together to enhance clarity, particularly with the non-Brazilian reader in mind. This means small stretches of text were reorganized; certain time periods, dates, and other facts were explained with greater precision; and subjects hidden by the Portuguese language's heavy reliance on the passive voice were coaxed out of the shadows.

Other alterations and additions spoke directly to the shift in audience. For example, pursuant to U.S. publishing practice, footnotes were changed to less visible endnotes, so in a few cases information found in the notes has been relocated to the actual body of the text. In addition, facts and allusions that go without saying for Brazilians but that would most likely be lost on many English readers have been made explicit. Such direct intervention—always with the author's collaboration and consent—precludes the need for the cumbersome stutter of Translator Notes in the text.

Likewise with smoother reading in mind, I chose to eschew the hurdle of parentheticals and present the names of agencies and institutions solely in their English translation, with the original Portuguese name available in an appendix at the back. However, when the name of a body appears only a single time in an endnote, a parenthetical translation does accompany the English. Portuguese loves acronyms, and I also wanted to avoid a confusing jumble of DNSPs, DGSPs, DSPRs, and the like; I therefore opted to use only one such abbreviation, preferring instead to employ English short forms for recurring organizational names.

English-language quotations that appeared in Portuguese translation were traced back to their English originals and the corresponding bibliographical data replaced. In other cases, where I was unable to pinpoint corresponding page numbers in Portuguese translations and English editions, I supplemented the bibliography with the English-language reference—for example, page numbers are cited from Norbert Elias's *Introdução à Sociologia*, but publication details are also provided for the English version, *What Is Sociology?*

In closing, I am deeply indebted to the University of Illinois Press and Gilberto Hochman for entrusting me with this task. Working with Gilberto was, as always, a rich learning experience. I also recognize Christopher J. Ballantyne, who translated a summarized version of chapter 2 for a presentation by the author; this proved a valuable reference during my rendering of that chapter. My gratitude as well to the members of our Madison translators group, whose camaraderie and support keep my batteries charged. Last, boundless thanks to my husband, Michael, a first reader, kind and thoughtful critic, and consummate chef, for showing me how to rejoice in every day. Misha, you are my *tov meod*.

CHAPTER 1

When Health Becomes Public

State Formation and Health Policies in Brazil

> All human activity, political and religious, stems from
> an undivided root. As a rule, the first impulse for . . .
> social action comes from tangible interests, political or
> economic. . . . Ideal interests elevate and animate these
> tangible interests and lend them justification. Man
> does not live by bread alone; he wants to have a good
> conscience when he pursues his vital interests; and
> in pursuing them, he develops his powers fully only
> if he is conscious of simultaneously serving purposes
> higher than purely egotistical ones. Interests without
> such spiritual elevation are lame; on the other hand,
> ideas can succeed in history only when and to the
> extent that they attach themselves to tangible interests.
>
> —Otto Hintze, 1931

I begin this analysis of the formation of public health policy in Brazil with the words of German historian Otto Hintze because his linkage of ideas and interests bears greatly on the topic at hand. The convergence of the two ultimately bolstered the decision to make health in Brazil not just a public matter but also a nationwide, state-led one. These pages explore how Brazil responded to its public health problems and examine the consequences of its decision to collectivize health nationwide, identifying the specific circumstances under which consciousness met interests, prompting relevant parties to act and permitting the genesis of state provision of public health.

I seek to construct a plausible interpretation of when, why, and how compulsory, nationwide, collective health care arrangements emerge within a given historical context and to examine the political consequences of this process. When does health become public? Or, to put it another way, why does health become a matter of public interest and the target of political initiatives? The second line of inquiry explores the circumstances under which public interests can be transformed into actual public policy—that is, what conditions prompt individuals to transfer responsibility for health to the state? A third question concerns the relations between the substance of the policies that are made public and the legal and institutional arrangements designed for policy enforcement. In other words: how do public policies reflect and/or alter relations among public power, political elites, and society at large? Finally, how does the process of collectivizing health nationwide relate to state building? Working within a particular historical and sociological framework that contextualizes and constrains choices and decisions, I answer these questions by analyzing the crucial decision-making processes that placed more power in the state sphere and the effects of these decisions on this framework.

Specifically, I explain why, at a given moment, individuals or groups collaborate in the creation of a public compulsory arrangement to address issues that do not necessarily affect them. This decision is in part connected with the rules governing how responsibilities are transferred to the state, or how public health authority takes shape. Furthermore, the decision to increase and expand state action affects both the framework of the initial decision and the decision makers themselves.

To this end, I present a formal logical argument that accounts for the decision to collectivize health care and connect that decision to the historical nature of the process of fashioning public authority. This interpretation is compatible with explanations for the emergence of social policy found in the vast literature on the topic. Combining logical and historical arguments allows us to observe both the conditions that induced a convergence of interests and ideas, thereby impelling actors to intervene, and the impact of this convergence. And by focusing on the collectivization of welfare within a given society at a given time, we can see why and how certain choices and decisions are made and subsequently produce laws, policies, institutions, bureaucracy, and so on. These choices and decisions not only are shaped by broad historical processes but also shape history. Historical processes thus form the backdrop and substance of my formal theoretical argument.

I also highlight the political backdrop, national context, and era when public health and rural sanitation policies emerged in Brazil under the so-called First Republic (1889–1930) because doing so permits me to evaluate two general interpretations that challenge some of the research as well as the conventional wisdom. First, the First Republic (also known as the República Velha [Old Republic]) was not an interregnum in the process of state building, running from the close of the empire through the post-1930 period, nor was the state fully formed at the end of the Brazilian Empire (1822–89). Second, the oligarchic domination characteristic of the First Republican period did not impede a process of mounting centralization and government intervention but was compatible with that process.[1] According to the alternative interpretations offered by Elisa Reis, the state-building process is not a discrete event with a firm endpoint and does not proceed solely in one direction. Further, the creation of public power is not necessarily incongruent with the strengthening of private interests.[2] To guarantee their interests, Brazil's oligarchies—especially the coffee sector—turned to public authority rather than the market to regulate economic activities, and this decision affected the construction of the state and the laying of its authoritarian foundations.[3] This period indeed witnessed the effective creation of public power rather than a pure and simple freezing of the administrative and regulatory abilities of the nation-state under the might of coffee planters.

In his work, Luiz Antônio de Castro Santos takes up three main questions: the significance and impact of the movement for the sanitation of Brazil and public health policy under the First Republic, especially in the 1910s and 1920s; the construction of an ideology of nationality; and state building through the emergence of new public apparatuses charged with enforcing health and sanitation policy at both central and local levels.[4] In his view, contrary to what a number of public health studies have claimed, the First Republic saw no straightforward causal relation between economic interests and health policymaking. Furthermore, according to this author, the period can be favorably assessed if the benchmark is the creation of public authority and corresponding health infrastructure rather than the short-term performance of public power in the provision of health, an approach that usually yields negative evaluations.

Throughout Brazil's First Republican period, in response to a number of decisions and initiatives to which the political elites acquiesced, government activism in health and sanitation grew in tandem with the government's capacity to implement policies nationwide. We observe the development of public consciousness and greater governmental responsibility for public health conditions and the health of the population in Brazil—any judgment about the performance of public power or about any seemingly preferable alternative aside. Yet we should not deem this a historically inevitable process, for such a perspective would shed little light on the form and content of subsequent government institutions and policies. The latter are unintended results shaped by the goals, conflicts, strategies, and choices of defined actors caught up in networks of institutions and mobilized by a social awareness enmeshed with material interests.

State, Power, and Public Health:
On Theory and Methodology

This analysis of the transformation of health into a public good and the establishment of broad collective arrangements to produce this good draws associations between health issues on the one hand and the forging of public power and the associated emergence of public policies and government agencies on the other. Public power spread throughout the national territory in the form of newly created administrative structures, legal instruments, and personnel. The transformation of health into a public good interacted strongly with the shaping of a national community and state formation in Brazil.

Crucial choices and decisions transformed the approach to human deficiencies and adversity. According to Abram De Swaan, this process of collectivization of care can be analytically divided into three stages: care was first individual; became collective while preserving its voluntary, community, and local nature; and finally was shifted to the state.[5] Yet this process was not as linear, evolutionary, or inexorable as this division into stages may seem to suggest.

In De Swaan's view, formal theory has ignored the collectivizing process of health just as it has neglected the process of collectivizing poor relief, education, and social security—in other words, it has neglected the historical nature of collective goods. Using as his point of departure Norbert Elias's analysis of the sociogenesis of the state, De Swaan offers an analytical frame of reference and an interpretation of the rise of welfare states that I employ, critique, and expand in conjunction with the contributions of other authors.[6]

Key to understanding the collectivization of welfare is Elias's idea of figuration. A figuration can be defined as a structured yet fluid pattern of reciprocal dependence between individuals, groups, and institutions. As a conceptual tool with an emphasis on interdependence, Elias's notion frees us from the antagonistic juxtaposition of individual versus society.[7]

4

In Elias's formulation, the transition from the traditional to the modern world brought the rise of nation-states and the development of capitalism along with its corollaries of industrialization, urbanization, and secularization. Concomitant chains of interdependence became so much more complex that they grew opaque and could not be controlled by any one individual or group, making it impossible to explain figurations through the properties of their individual components.[8] In this interpretation, the development and historical dynamics of these chains of social interdependence wrought unplanned and even undesired social consequences independent of any component individual or group. Yet the chains also were the product of the interweaving of the motives and actions of these individuals and groups.[9] In addition, complex figurations can be characterized and analyzed only by reference to their constituent bonds of interdependence.[10]

For De Swaan—still drawing from Elias—the analysis of the emergence of social policy is also an analysis of both the historical process by which human interdependence is generalized and the responses to the problems that accompany the ascent of nation-states and the development of capitalism.[11] The collectivization of welfare and state formation are more specific processes whereby the bonds of human interdependence change and lead to new arrangements as part of a broader, lengthier process. The collectivization of social provision thus breeds not only public power but also human collectivities. The formation of a national community is associated with the extension of chains of reciprocal dependence.

The bonds of interdependence that instill the need to collectivize care of the poor, destitute, malnourished, infirm, illiterate, and any other individuals suffering from temporary or permanent adversity are called external effects or externalities. They are, De Swaan tells us, "the indirect consequences of one person's deficiency or adversity for others not immediately afflicted themselves."[12] For example, the poverty and destitution of some members of society brings the threat of illness, crime, unproductivity, or revolt for others.

De Swaan proposes to entwine formal theory on collective action—which he assigns to "welfare economics"—with historical sociology. Welfare economics endeavors to identify and analyze the circumstances requisite to state intervention and regulation in situations of human interaction and interdependence—that is, vis-à-vis public goods, negative externalities, and the dilemmas of collective action. Historical sociology, conversely, analyzes how interdependence affects the development of society. De Swaan introduces the idea of process to the analysis of individual interactions and choices.[13] While following different routes, both approaches suggest that individual actions and choices yield unexpected aggregate results. I explore this idea of conjoining formal and historical arguments by discussing the negative effects of human interdependence and its possible remedies as part of a broader historical, sociological process.

Increased human interdependence expanded and intensified the external effects that the actions or existence of some (the poor) had on others (the established in society). By heightening problems of mutual dependence, the shift to an urban, industrial society compelled the gradual abandonment both of individual solutions (for example, fleeing contact with the destitute and/or leaving them to their own devices or the devices of the market) and of voluntary remedies (such as philanthropic, charity, or mutual aid associations) because neither approach could cope with the problem in its entirety. Contemporary welfare policies, like the state that produces them, are the unintended historical products of efforts by the elites (and of their internal conflicts) to exploit, administer, control, and remedy the progressive external effects of poverty in the face of the mounting failure of individual solutions and the fragility of voluntary solutions.

Based on the work of Mancur Olson Jr., De Swaan points out that in ever more complex societies, voluntary associations become unstable as a consequence not only of the challenges of coordination but also of the dilemmas of collective action—the problem of controlling the free riders who benefit from these arrangements or public goods without helping produce or maintain them.[14] The issue is how to produce a collective good and distribute attendant costs when no member of the collectivity can be excluded from using or enjoying the good. The solution tends to be mandatory contribution and social provision through public authority. In the course of this process, a social consciousness of interdependence emerges. De Swaan defines this phenomenon, which is essential to the formation of a collective national identity, as an "awareness of the generalization of interdependence . . . coupled with an abstract sense of responsibility which does not impel to personal action, but requires the needy in general to be taken care of by the state and out of public tax funds."[15]

This sense of responsibility did not end voluntary action but rather dictated ever greater reliance on state care and demanded ever greater resources, which are coercively extracted from society and benefit everyone, whether or not they contributed. Through the formation of this social consciousness, the state affirmed itself as a legitimate organization capable of regulating the negative effects of social interdependence, which, over time, tend to be reduced to legal, administrative solutions in the hands of a bureaucracy.[16]

According to De Swaan, this process of public collectivization of remedies for poverty, deficiency, and adversity has displayed three dimensions:

1. The scale of arrangements shifts from the level of some individuals to encompass groups of citizens or entire nations.
2. Arrangements grow more collective in nature as access to benefits grows more independent from the contributions of individual users.
3. The state becomes increasingly involved as there is greater agreement about allowing government to exercise authority and coercion and boost the level of bureaucratization.[17]

De Swaan says that the development of this process depends on three conditions. Two of these conditions promote collectivization but not necessarily the shift to government control: escalating *"uncertainty* as to the *moment* and the *magnitude* of the adversity [and] as to the *efficacy* of remedies against adversity or deficiency." The third condition is a tendency for an increase in "the extent and reach of the *external effects* of adversity and deficiency," which promotes a transfer of control to the state because problems have attained such magnitude and involve so many people that the successive dilemmas of collective action thwart any market solution or cooperative arrangement.[18]

In specific relation to public health, migration from country to city in conjunction with urbanization and industrialization engendered unprecedented levels of adversity and deficiency, affecting established urban dwellers and new arrivals alike. Urban density and tightening economic links between the healthy well-to-do and the infirm poor intensified, multiplying the external effects of individual adversity to such an extent that it was almost impossible to isolate the threats posed by urban life through, for example, spatial segregation or by excluding some parties from the benefits of services that could be rendered under private contract, like garbage collection or water supply. Health—or disease—thus affords one of the best examples of the problems of human interdependence and their possible remedies. An epidemic in fact constitutes a paradigm of interdependence in that it illustrates both the external effects of individual adversity that impinge on all of society as well as uncertainty about the efficacy of any individual, local remedy.[19] From this perspective, I suggest that epidemics and communicable diseases be treated as social evils because they strike all members of various collectivities, whether or not a collectivity has contributed to the emergence and spread of the disease. In the words of Wanderley Guilherme dos Santos, if "no one can be kept from consuming a collective good if he so wishes ... no one can abstain from consuming a collective evil, even if unwillingly."[20]

During the nineteenth century, cholera epidemics in Europe and the United States assaulted both rich and poor and ignored all borders in their march across cities, regions, and countries. The experience impressed on the elites the dilemma of social interdependence and the need to combat the risks of mass infection and contagion by devising permanent, broad, collective, compulsory, and supralocal organizations and policies for the purposes of prevention. With the political and intellectual elites motivated to action, the topic of urban sanitation thus made its way onto the public agenda, producing concrete political results.[21]

The increasing complexity of social figurations—more individuals, increased interdependence, more externalities—bred a consciousness of mutual dependence and of the need to contribute to remedying negative effects. Accordingly, overcoming the problems of organizing and funding the provision of collective goods demanded the creation of public authority capable of coercively extracting resources from society and crafting comprehensive policies to solve or correct the effects of social interdependence. The critical stages in establishing social provision policies were a function of disputes among the elites over how to manage external effects, control the dispossessed, and exploit the opportunities generated by these policies. While this concern was not limited to the elites alone, it did begin with them, and they were the main actors in the discussions surrounding solutions and opportunities. The contemporary state is thus the product of the need to regulate negative externalities, produce public goods, and administer the opportunities arising from the collectivization of health care, education, and income maintenance.

De Swaan views social policy development as an evolutionary, cumulative process that grows ever less differentiated. He points to an exponential expansion in welfare policies as countries increasingly adopted such policies. In his thinking, historical and social processes made external costs unbearable, collectivization inexorable, and the results unintended yet quite similar across national experiences.[22] This interpretation of the process by which responsibilities were transferred to the federal government muddies the fact that each stage in collectivization, with its particular institutional arrangements, coexisted alongside other arrangements over long periods during which neither individual nor voluntary arrangements were wholly eliminated. Furthermore, these combinations differed in accordance with national experience. The variability of the state phenomenon as posited by J. P. Nettl serves as a warning about the limits of De Swaan's perspective.[23] The features of contemporary state policies depend essentially on the specific decisions and choices made during the passage from one arrangement to another and on the ways in which these arrangements coexist.

The historical background of the process (urbanization, industrialization, population growth, and so forth) feeds the inference that collectivization is inexorable and its results convergent. The assumptions behind De Swaan's formal argument, grounded in rational choice approaches, likewise underpin the assumption that the key motivation for the collectivization of welfare is the perception of the presence and extent of external effects or consciousness of interdependence. As the number of externalities climbs and more people are concerned, society becomes more complex and encounters the dilemma of collective action in its need to provide for welfare. Selective incentives and coercion are seen as tools for fostering cooperation and thus producing a public good, while public authority is seen as legitimately capable of coercing all individuals within a given society, offering incentives through its activities, and thus countering the collective temptation to catch a free ride (since it is impossible to exclude any one person from consuming a public good).[24] Thus, according to De Swaan, the extension of bonds of interdependence through historical, economic, and social processes would necessarily lead to the collectivization of welfare and its transfer to the state.

This caveat applies to the same assumption behind the formal model used by De Swaan, in that a consciousness of externalities and incentives is not enough to trigger the collectivization or transfer of an activity to the public sector. However, based on the arguments of J. M. Buchanan and G. Tullock, we can postulate that individuals might tolerate the external costs imposed on them. For these two authors, externalities "are neither a necessary nor a sufficient condition for an activity to be placed in the realm of collective choice."[25] Rather, shifting action from the individual to the voluntary collective realm and then to the public, collective realm depends on how each decision-making unit assesses external costs, the costs of achieving agreement on this transfer, and the costs that would presumably follow from any adverse collective decisions. This third cost is highly relevant because it can alter the fundamental rights of the decision-making units, such as freedom and property rights. Ergo, the decision to shift an activity to the public sector and its attendant price will depend on the selected decision-making rules. The sum of these costs is designated "interdependence costs."[26]

The individualist postulate underlying the formal dimension of De Swaan's interpretation does not allow us to assert that after social interdependence (or consciousness) has generalized, welfare provision will become a public matter or that transferring the matter to the state and relying on its coercive power and on relative benefits would be the only way to eliminate free riders. This assertion stems from the historical basis of De Swaan's argument. Relying on this same logic of collective action, there is at least one case in which it would be rational for an individual to foot the bill for the production of a public good even if free riders stood to gain: when the cost of nonproduction (and consequent consumption of a social evil) would be more costly than production.[27]

Anchored in Buchanan and Tullock and taking into consideration the problems of interdependence highlighted by De Swaan, I suggest that the decision to shift an activity or a good to the realm of the state depends on a comparison between the external costs of maintaining the activity within the individual or local realm and the costs and constraints associated with turning these activities over to public power. The calculus of the costs and benefits of collectivization and of its organizing rules is highly relevant when developing an analysis of crucial choices and decisions. Rather than simply identifying increased state intervention, I analyze the substantive content of these decisions, the ideas and strategies of the decision-making units, and the effects of their choices on the collectivized activity, on decision makers, and on the relations between state and society.

My approach differs from some rational choice literature in that I do not define the interests or preferences of the actors in abstract or theoretical terms. Institutions are not merely a strategic context in which rational, utility-maximizing individuals strive toward their goals. The actors are embedded in broader institutional contexts where interests and preferences are shaped, as indicated in the neoinstitutionalist literature.[28] Therefore, when investigating the Brazilian experience of shifting health to the state, I suggest that consciousness, interests, cost calculi, and decision making as well as the actors themselves can be understood only within specific historical contexts—in this case, within the political and institutional framework specific to the First Republic period.[29]

Another important consideration when discussing the collectivization of welfare is the concept of the state as the product of long-term societal processes that account for the emergence of government agencies and public policy (although not for their continuation or further development). The attributes of the state must be distinguished from those of society so that we can also understand why the state offers an efficient response when problems prove unsolvable by society. After all, why is public power the alternative to other societal arrangements? What distinct attributes of the state elect it to this position?

Beginning with a rather broad definition, Michael Mann says that the state is a place of differentiated autonomous power that is not irreducible to a simple product or instrument of social conditions, preferences, or claims.[30] While avoiding a wholly functional definition—that is, a characterization of the state in terms of what it does—Mann puts forward an institutional definition, drawing from Max Weber: "The state is a differentiated set of institutions and personnel embodying centrality, in the sense that political relations radiate outward to cover a territorially demarcated area, over which it claims a monopoly of binding and permanent rule-making, backed up by physical violence."[31]

As Mann sees it, the means of power employed by the state are no different from the resources employed by society. The key element in this definition is territorial centrality, the distinctive attribute from which the state derives its autonomous power. Thus, "territorial-centralization provides the state with a potentially independent basis of power mobilization . . . uniquely in the possession of the state itself."[32] This characterization follows the tradition of thought that posits the state as a differentiated set of institutions that claim centrality, sovereignty, and coercive control over a territory and its population, seeking to defend and extend it in competition with other social institutions and other states.[33] State formation thus entails concentration of power in the center, institutional penetration into the territory from the center, and the centralization of nationwide authority and its specialized function.

Power/coerciveness and penetration/territoriality define the state and endow it with autonomy. In discussing the specific nature of the autonomous power of the state vis-à-vis society, Mann separates two analytically distinct types of power, which do not necessarily reinforce or represent alternatives to each other. One is distributive in essence (power/coerciveness), while the other is collective (penetration/territoriality). The first is despotic power, encompassing "the range of actions which the elite is empowered to undertake without routine, institutionalized negotiation with civil society groups," and it derives from the fact that only the state is territorially centralized.[34] The second, infrastructural power, equates to "the capacity

11

of the state to actually penetrate civil society and to implement logistically political decisions throughout the realm."[35] It reflects the state's ability to coordinate social life through state infrastructure, while the state may then in turn be controlled by society.

Given territorial centrality as a distinct resource, the process of state formation harbors tensions between public power and the social elites that can find expression in an ongoing endeavor by the state to convert its infrastructural capacity into despotic power and by society to control government infrastructure. The central question is how these two dimensions of power have varied and combined during the process of state building and development. The particular ways in which these variations and combinations have been organized suggest hypothetical paths in the formation of modern states and their political systems. Based on the table presented by Mann, adapted for the purposes of this discussion, table 1 shows four ideal types.

The emergence of modern nation-states brought the growth of infrastructural power. However, the intensity of despotic power is a matter of dispute that defines the political form acquired by the state. Starting from a hypothetical stage 1—a world of autonomous organizations—conflicts and negotiations between public power and the social elites (and among the elites) revolve around the combination in question. When increased state intervention occasions greater despotic power, authoritarian forms may arise (sequence 1–2–3). The tendency for infrastructural coordination to

Table 1. Dimensions of State Power

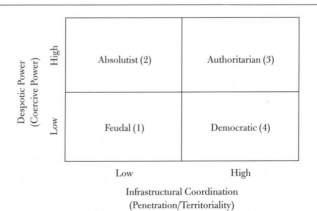

	Low	High
High (Despotic Power / Coercive Power)	Absolutist (2)	Authoritarian (3)
Low (Despotic Power / Coercive Power)	Feudal (1)	Democratic (4)

Infrastructural Coordination
(Penetration/Territoriality)

Source: Based on Mann, *Sources of Social Power*, 60–61.

be converted into despotic power stems from "the inability of civil society forces to control those forms of territorial centralization."[36]

Crucial decisions and choices made during the process of tasking the state with welfare have a significant bearing on the relations between public authority and society. The weighing of external costs against the benefits and costs of collectivization, which frames the decision to transfer activities to the state, has much to do with the reigning combination of state infrastructure and coercive power—that is, with external costs plus the benefits of collectivization versus the costs of collectivization. At the same time, in the long run, the consequences of this calculus produce combinations unforeseen by actors at the decision-making moment.

The relations between the central and local spheres of government during the collectivization process are important to any analysis of choices in a historical experience. Especially regarding poor relief, De Swaan's analysis indicates that the local sphere is equivalent to the initial, "natural" stage (analogous to the individual in the market) and that the challenges inherent in coping with external effects via cooperative means can lead health to be assigned to the central realm.[37] If welfare policymaking requires the development of state infrastructure, it would seem reasonable for us to ask in what realm this infrastructure is established, given that a substantial share of the process of building modern states has involved conflicts between central and local powers. Just as externalities do not automatically bring about collectivization, collectivization does not necessarily mean that activities will be transferred to the central public authority.[38]

Whether the distribution and localization of state infrastructure expands along path 1–2–3 or 1–2–4 depends on the cost-benefit analysis undertaken by decision-making units and on the rules governing the decision to collectivize. However, the expansion path also depends on the broader institutional context framing this decision. Table 2 illustrates the importance of the distribution of infrastructural power among the different spheres of government during state formation.

The development of state infrastructural capacity along path 1–2–3 or 1–2–4 leaves cell (a) empty. Forms of state organization (b), (c), and (d) result from the way infrastructural power develops and is distributed between the local and central spheres. Furthermore, the allocation of these public activities is determined through political conflicts and agreements driven by religious, ethnic, economic, and other interests.[39] Some nations—the United States, for example—made the transition from (b) to (c). In my analysis, what matters most are not the organizational formats represented

Table 2. Infrastructural Coordination

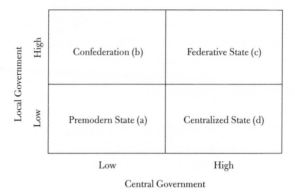

	Confederation (b)	Federative State (c)
	Premodern State (a)	Centralized State (d)

Local Government — High / Low

Low · High
Central Government

Source: Mann, *Sources of Social Power*, 85.

by each cell but the hypothetical sequences (a)–(c) or (a)–(d), where these formats are understood as the institutional context. The relation between local and national infrastructure is especially important when analyzing public policymaking in federative orderings such as Brazil's First Republic.

A final consideration crucial to any explanation of the further development of social provision policies concerns the impact of state policy on three things: the state's capacity to continue implementing policies, the existing political system, and the groups concerned.[40] Concordant with the general definition of state, Theda Skocpol takes up a "'structured polity' approach" to the development of social provision that "views the polity as the primary locus of action, yet understands political activities, whether carried on by politicians or by social groups, as conditioned by the institutional configurations of governments and political party systems."[41]

Skocpol's institutionalist approach requires us to examine certain processes, foremost among them the perspective that "policies . . . remake politics." The implementation of new government activities can transform and augment the capacities of the polity, affecting further policy development and the possibilities for future initiatives. This process also affects "the social identities, goals, and capabilities of groups that subsequently struggle or ally in politics." In the eyes of the author, a public policy succeeds when it enhances the ability of the state and political system to foster its future development, prompting individuals, groups, and alliances to defend the policy's continuation and expansion and thereby shaping and politicizing interests and identities. Skocpol proposes that public policies be assessed on the basis of "policy feedbacks"—that is, in keeping with ongoing political processes—rather than "some external economic criterion or . . . moral worth according to a given normative standard."[42]

The institutional impact of public policy implementation is key. To be clear, this is a matter not of transforming public policy effects into causes— a criticism posed by Paul Pierson—but of ascertaining the institutional constraints that policy enforcement places on relevant actors and the state since policy implementation can modify factors fundamental to the original calculus.[43] Assessing performance in terms of how a policy reinforces its own continuity is an approach that derives from the structured polity perspective. However, such an assessment is in fact overly endogenous, for it not only considers state centrality as a theoretical and analytical instrument and/or historical fact but assigns state action a positive worth. In practice, this approach makes no clear distinction between identifying growth in government activism and making an inherently favorable judgment on the benefits of this growth. This book seeks precisely to balance the topic of state power creation against assessments of state performance.

The Pathways of Public Health in Brazil

In my interpretation of the Brazilian experience, the phrase *sanitation of Brazil* denotes a historical process that has two interwoven meanings. First, it refers to the particular era of Brazilian history that is the subject of my analysis—from the 1910s to the twilight of the First Republic. During this period, the Brazilian elites grew increasingly aware of the serious public health problems plaguing their country and a generalized feeling developed that the nation-state should assume greater responsibility for the health of the population and salubrity of the territory. Taking on this responsibility would mean broadening the duties of the federal government, which until then were limited to the Federal District and maritime sanitary defense. A robust, nationalist movement in favor of the sanitation of Brazil came into being and tied the forging of nationhood to the vanquishing of endemic diseases; at the same time, heated discussions and major political decisions centered on how to remedy Brazil's public health problems against the backdrop of the constitutional and political order established in 1891. The denouement was the reformulation and expansion of public health services.

Under these reforms, states could obtain federal aid via formal health and sanitation agreements with the federal government, allowing central power to act inside the states while still safeguarding their autonomy.[44] Over time, public activities in health and sanitation proliferated countrywide, not only centrally but also locally, as states began developing their own agencies and services. São Paulo was practically the only state actively committed to enforcing a broad public health policy right from the dawn of the republic and to preserving its autonomy from federal agencies. The movement for the sanitation of Brazil did not remedy Brazil's complex gamut of health problems, but it did bequeath state infrastructure and public health authority across a large part of the land.

Second, the notion of the sanitation of Brazil constitutes the logical construct that organizes this historical narrative. On its stage stand the countless actors who engage in health matters: members of medical, scientific, and professional circles; sanitation service personnel; intellectuals in general. By educating society about the public nature of disease and diagnosing the country's public health status, these actors transformed the external effects of disease into a consciousness of social interdependence. As politically relevant figures, they could exert pressure, advance convincing arguments, and devise health policies, but they lacked the power to decide whether an activity should pass to the state sphere. The relevant calculus- and decision-making units were the states and central power, while the federal government and Congress constituted the decision-making loci. The formal institutional context was set by the constitution of 1891, which specified the duties of the central and state governments and the federal legislature and stipulated the nation's political arrangement. The informal context was defined by the politics of state bosses and the unequal distribution of political and economic power among the states.

The tension between state autonomy and the national and interstate problems caused by endemic and epidemic diseases presented a dilemma for the decision-making units. Under the formal arrangement of 1891, each state was supposed to look out for itself, while the federal government would see to relations with the world abroad. This cooperation between autonomous bodies ideally would result in a healthy country. In a nation of surging complexity, the communicability of disease was perceived as a national problem that surpassed the bounds of the constitutional framework. Reliance on the central government's territoriality offered a way of controlling public health interdependence, while coerciveness afforded a route for coping with public evils, thwarting free riders, and dealing with the inept.

Why, when, and how duties were transferred to Brazil's central power depended on how the states weighed three things: external costs (that is, the costs that the horrific public health conditions of some imposed on others), the costs of transferring duties to the state (that is, the costs of constraining state autonomy through federal interference), and the benefits of this transfer (that is, the direct and indirect benefits of federal initiatives). When external costs surpassed the costs of transferring health to the state and the benefits of this transfer outweighed its costs, public health in Brazil became collectivized. Moreover, both this calculus and the ensuing decision depended on the rules governing the collectivization arrangement and on the substance of what was to be collectivized. As it turned out, both rules and substance spelled the success of negotiations: each state could accept or veto a bilateral agreement, depending on whether it felt the costs of letting the federal government step in outweighed the external costs of not doing so and the benefits of doing so. The resultant decisions were then transformed into policies, whose implementation and enforcement modified both the institutional context and the decision-making units themselves. The direction of these changes was largely determined by the substance of the policies.

The First Republic represented a period when health policy began to be transferred to the central government. The first stage, ruled by the 1891 constitution, was characterized by the saliency of the coercive power of public health authority combined with territorial or infrastructural frailty.[45] The second stage (1910–30) represented the continuity of state accrual of despotic power but combined it with the territorial expansion of public power or with an increase in infrastructural power, especially in the 1920s. The process by which health was collectivized and shifted to the federal government nationwide during the First Republic ultimately created both infrastructural and despotic power.

Table 3 illustrates my interpretation of the path by which public health authority took shape and in what combinations during Brazil's First Republic. The efforts to achieve the sanitation of Brazil basically corresponded to a journey from (1) to (3) to (4), entailing the expansion of the territorial reach of public authority and the conversion of infrastructural power into coercive power.[46]

During this 1–3–4 journey, decision-making units made choices about whether to develop public health policy on their own and/or transfer some duties (beyond those enumerated in the constitution) to the central government. The development of public authority in this case implied forging public health infrastructure and coercive capacity. Table 4 depicts the possible results of these choices.

The calculi made during this period prompted most states to decide to move from (a) to (b) because they perceived the external costs as higher than

Table 3. Public Health Authority

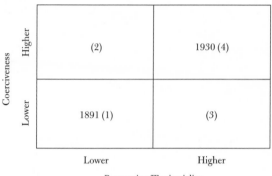

Table 4. Infrastructure Plus Coerciveness

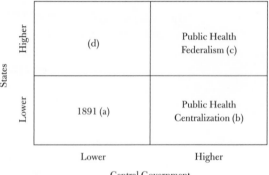

the costs of transferring activities to the state and the costs of transferring activities as less than the attendant benefits. São Paulo was the only state that insisted on solution (c), building its own public health infrastructure while the federal government did likewise. Because São Paulo believed the costs of central government interference too high, a decision to pass responsibility for health to the state would be possible only if São Paulo occupied cell (c), whereas the other nineteen states occupied (b). Reorganizing table 4, table 5 shows the interactions between São Paulo and the other states regarding the transfer or nontransfer of health and sanitation to the central power.

Table 5. Interactions between São Paulo and Other States Regarding the Transfer of Health

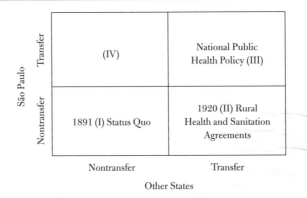

Brazil's public health physicians pursued the ideal of a centralized policy that would solve the impasses of public health interdependence engendered by the federative status quo. That ideal also provided states with a rational solution, since the vast majority of them were resource-poor and problem-rich. For most states, the benefits of collectivizing health would outstrip the costs of any lost political autonomy, but for São Paulo—a powerful state protective of its autonomy—the costs of a more centralized policy were perceived as potentially much greater than any possible benefits. Nevertheless, São Paulo's best interests required it to cooperate with a solution that decreased the external costs imposed by other states.

Between a world that was becoming ever more unworkable (I) and the idealized world sought by the majority (III), a negotiated, cooperative formula rendered arrangement (II) politically viable by allowing São Paulo to exempt itself from the costs of collectivization while taking advantage of the decrease in negative externalities. In other words, the shift of health to central power was not a "natural" process but was the product of conflicts and political bargaining. Arrangement (II) was the outcome of discussions and decisions between 1916 and 1919, with implementation starting in 1920. It represented the beginning of federal public health and rural sanitation policy in the states and framed the path of public power in this arena.

Understanding these calculi, choices, negotiations, and institutional arrangements is vital to understanding the genesis and features of public health policy in republican Brazil. The broader process of state formation lay in solution (II), table 5, and in the pathways suggested in tables 3 and 4, which explicate the foundations of the country's public health policy. The model presented in this chapter allows us to arrive at a plausible interpretation of why and how health became public, collective, and nationwide.

Structure of the Book

The next four chapters explore the literature on public health and health policies in Brazil under the First Republic; a brief chapter with concluding comments closes out the book. Because scant quantitative data or organized information is available on federal health and sanitation policies between 1919 and 1930, I use a wide array of primary sources and rely on the analyses of other scholars.[47]

Chapter 2 shows how public health conditions during the First Republic and the sad state of people's health awoke a consciousness of negative externalities among the elites, and health issues were increasingly perceived as one of the main bonds of interdependence in Brazilian society. This burgeoning awareness of social, political, and territorial interdependence constituted a stage in the formation of a sentiment of nationhood. The main focus is on the 1916–20 campaign for the sanitation of Brazil and its concepts, evaluations, and proposals for reform born from the relations between communicable disease, society, and public authority that strained the boundaries of the constitutional order ordained in 1891.

Chapter 3 analyzes the political process that in 1920 resulted in the first major change to federal public health agencies since the dawn of the twentieth century. It begins by describing the development and analyzing the main features of the federal public health structure from the early Republic through the mid-1910s. Broad sectors of the political elites came to embrace an awareness of public health interdependence. The chapter covers the main health reform proposals; discussions in professional arenas, the press, and the legislature; and decisions to create and extend federal responsibility in health and sanitation from 1918 to 1920.

Chapters 4 and 5 test the analytical performance of the proposed model and the plausibility of this interpretation. Chapter 4 engages in a detailed analysis of the decisions surrounding the expansion of health and sanitation policies during the 1920s and the content and impact of the selected policies. A further point of focus is subsequent implementation of these policies and interactions between the state and federal governments. Chapter 5 is devoted to an analysis of the state of São Paulo as a case of so-called exceptionalism in the realm of health during the First Republic. However, the São Paulo experience should not be interpreted as a case apart but as integral to the formation of public health policy at the federal level. Chapters 4 and 5 thus explain why and how health became public and national, rounding out my central argument. Chapter 6 is devoted to general considerations concerning the relations between the analysis of public health policies and the process of state building and health reform in Brazil.

The Microbe of Disease and Public Power

The Public Health Movement and a Growing Consciousness of Interdependence

My neighbor fell sick of his own free will; he went to a laboratory and injected himself with a live culture of cholera bacilli. If
he had simply thrown himself off the roof and onto the street,
or blown his brains out with a bullet, or swallowed a gram of
strychnine, it would affect no one but him, and I could do no
more than lament the incident. But it is another matter in the
case of the cholera bacilli—millions and millions of them will
spread across objects that I have to touch, into the pipes from
which I have to drink water, into the sewer systems passing
by my home. And I will have to resign myself, for no effective
measures lie within my isolated grasp; they are so major and so
complex that only the state could carry them out. But the state
must not obstruct my neighbor's freedom to wish to fall ill and
die, even if it is to protect my own freedom to aspire after health
and life. And this bane will spread throughout the city, and
neighboring cities and the countryside will be contaminated;
the entire country will suffer from this scourge, and thousands
upon thousands of lives will be lost.

—Sebastião Barroso, 1919

Sebastião Barroso, a native of the state of Rio de Janeiro, was a physician,
politician, and head of the federal rural sanitation agency in the northeastern
state of Bahia in the early 1920s. His observation captures the essence of the
links between communicable disease and the role of government. Cholera
fueled ties of mutual dependence between individual people, neighbor-

hoods, cities, and regions, precluding any reliance on isolated solutions. Grounded in the contagious nature of disease, this figuration required an authority with nationwide jurisdiction, capable of stretching to all corners and inhabitants of the nation and preventing some places and people from imposing costs on others. The situation implied curtailing individual freedom, altering property rights, and violating political autonomy. Barroso's tongue-in-cheek commentary is a direct reference to the many who balked at the idea of greater state power in public health. As Barroso saw it, once people understood that communicable disease engendered a new form of sociability, greater public power would be inevitable.

This chapter demonstrates how health—and more to the point, its absence in the form of disease—was increasingly viewed as one of the main threads weaving together Brazilian society during the First Republic, an interpretation that made steady headway and was shared by important segments of the elites. The chapter also suggests how the elites became ever more cognizant of the negative effects occasioned by the country's appalling sanitary conditions and its sickly population. This newfound awareness of social, political, and territorial interdependence helped mold a sentiment of national community and sparked reflection and debate about Brazil's institutional arrangements and its policies to effectively address the negative effects of interdependence. Understanding the relationship between communicable diseases and society means first understanding the capacity and scope of public authority.

This process can best be comprehended by analyzing the concepts and proposals espoused by a broad movement known as the rural sanitation campaign (*campanha pelo saneamento rural*) or the campaign for the sanitation of Brazil (*campanha pelo saneamento do Brasil*). From 1910 to 1930, the Brazilian public health movement promoted its interpretation of the foundations of the national community and political and institutional proposals for transforming a community grounded in the negative effects of communicability into a community grounded in the health and hygiene of its people. Movement proponents argued that this transformation could be accomplished by adopting and extending sanitation and public health policies to all members of the community. Under the First Republic, the rural sanitation movement held that communicable disease both reflected and shaped Brazilian society and that this situation, which challenged the elites as well as the country's political institutions, demanded greater government responsibility for health. This process ultimately meant revisiting the political and legal framework defined by the constitution of 1891.

The chapter first discusses analytical aspects of the relations between disease contagion, social interdependence, and government, with special attention to an emerging social consciousness—essentially a consciousness of the negative effects of disease in Brazil. This process resulted in the forging of a feeling of national community accompanied by the conviction that the relations of reciprocal dependence within Brazil's newly expanded community could be addressed only by public power. The chapter next investigates the Brazilian public health movement under the First Republic as a vehicle for expressing, developing, and propagating an awareness of interdependence. This section focuses on the broad-based rural sanitation campaign's "diagnosis" of the country, submitted in the 1910s when the newly recognized ubiquity of disease prompted a so-called rediscovery of Brazil. Against the backdrop of this diagnosis, the third section of the chapter discusses the underpinnings of the proposals for sanitation services reform and how these proposals defied the boundaries of public authority established in the 1891 constitution and tested the prevailing political order. The chapter closes with a summary of these arguments.

The Social Nature of Disease:
Externalities, Consciousness, and Community

In 1895, Dr. Cyrus Edson, New York City health commissioner, published a paper with the suggestive title "The Microbe as a Social Leveler." An enthusiast of the new conquests in the field of bacteriology, Edson asserted that the equality among humans so desired by socialists was becoming a reality not through political projects or revolution but through "infinitely tiny" organisms invisible to the naked eye: microbes, the cause of communicable disease. Human beings stand as equals before the menace of disease, he wrote, because "the microbe of disease is no respecter of persons" and pays scant heed to the status, class, race, or gender of its prey. Disease thus equalizes people and "binds the human race together as with an unbreakable chain" of mutual dependence.[1]

Edson further argued that the prospect of contagion inextricably bound poor and rich, healthy and ill, mansions and tenements, diverse regions within a country and across the planet. No one anywhere was safe from the threat of disease, and for this reason, no one could be indifferent to the fortunes or misfortunes of other people, wherever they might live—on the same street, in the same city or country, or in some other, far-off place. What,

Edson asked, do a prosperous American and a poor Russian peasant have in common? The disease-causing microbe.[2]

For Edson, public health initiatives would have to reach all communities as a necessary consequence of this endless chain of humans and societies. Herein lay the "socialistic side of the microbe."[3] When confronted by the revolutionary action of these invisible beings, people seemed to have more in common with each other or at least to be equally fragile, interconnected in a vast web of interdependent relations, leading to an awareness of community at both the national and international levels.

Public health professionals, political reformers, and observers of everyday life had been keenly aware of the phenomenon contemplated in Edson's brief article since the mid-nineteenth century, well before bacteriology and microbiology stepped onto center stage thanks to the work and discoveries of scientists such as Louis Pasteur and Robert Koch.[4] Industrialization, urbanization, and population growth had created a society where disease formed one of the primary bonds between people, especially when it struck in epidemic fashion. Once nation-states had formed, these problems were perceived to be circumscribed within specific political and territorial spaces, and their solutions were deemed the responsibility of these nations. Moreover, there was a rising conviction that the individual, local solutions of the day were no longer effective against an ever more collective, national problem.

In keeping with this interpretation, the wealthy and healthy showed concern for the less fortunate and the ailing and combated the status quo not solely out of ethical or moral concern but primarily because they realized the threat of disease had fashioned bonds of solidarity and reorganized society (no doubt to the dislike of many). The elites now understood that they no longer enjoyed social immunity from what was largely an inescapable problem for everyone. In other words, the elites recognized they were no longer exempt from the negative effects generated by the less fortunate, leading to the development of a social conscience—or, in the terms to be used in this book, an awareness or consciousness of social interdependence.[5]

From a historical standpoint, the awakening of this social consciousness formed a significant chapter in Brazil's discovery of national community or of nation-state building. The recognition of this generalized interdependence and its effects bred an abstract sense of responsibility and sparked debate about how to improve the plight of the underprivileged and consequently attenuate the threats felt by the powerful, well-to-do, and healthy. If consciousness of social interdependence is bound up with the emergence of a national community, addressing its external effects is bound up with the role of public authority.

Over time, as voluntary, individual solutions proved highly ineffective in attending to the direct and indirect consequences of individual and group deficiencies or adversities—whether or not their impact on others was immediate—the need to manage these externalities generated mounting demand for collective, compulsory care. Microbes and epidemics wove a vast web of individuals and regions and thus collectivized the health problem, hindering any attempt to foster localized, individualized protection schemes. If, as Norbert Elias suggests, complex figurations should be understood indirectly, through an analysis of their bonds of interdependence, then analyzing the birth of this consciousness can be instrumental when studying the process of shaping a national community and public power.[6]

Once the bond that rendered people socially and politically interdependent had been perceived and an awareness of interdependence acquired, negative effects might be controlled. Edson identified this bond as the disease-causing microbe. But the elites identified this bond of interdependence less with the microbe (or germ) and more with a very blatant feature of the diseases induced by these invisible pathogenic agents: communicability. Disease transmission thus displays analogies to the external effects of individual behavior in society.

Leaving aside any attempt to precisely define the terms *contagion* and *infection* or to trace their historical development, both have acquired commonplace meanings far looser than their strictly medical and scientific senses. For centuries, even their medical and scientific denotations could not be separated from their religious, cultural, political, and economic overtones in Western society.[7] Roughly put, *contagion* involves the idea that diseases can be transmitted directly, from one person to another, or indirectly, through air, water, living organisms, or other contaminated media or objects.[8] An *infection* can be defined as "the invasion of the body by pathogenic microorganisms that reproduce and multiply, causing disease."[9] Distinguishing between the agent that is transmitted via people or the environment (a process more readily associated with contagion) and the transmission process itself (more readily evocative of infection) has always presented something of a challenge.[10]

Many authors agree that laypersons have by and large come to use these terms loosely and interchangeably.[11] The popular connotations of the two words have less to do with characterizing the causal agent or means of transmission and everything to do with the idea that some diseases are communicable. To cite one example in Brazil, in a book on public health education, Barroso describes the popular criterion for identifying what he termed "diseases that can be caught": "the healthy catch diseases from the ill, and the happenstances that may have prompted this matter little."[12]

According to some authors, the nineteenth century saw the close of a long process begun during classic antiquity—that is, the secularization of the concept of infection. As religious interpretations were superseded, so too were the beliefs nourishing the first public health reforms: that epidemics were the product of environmental conditions such as atmospheric factors and weather, local circumstances, untreated sewage and garbage, unsafe water supplies, and unventilated, overcrowded housing.[13] According to the miasma theory, diseases were transmitted through humors that arose from rotting organic (plant or animal) matter and consequently were a by-product of specific environmental conditions, not of microbes.[14]

Through the nineteenth century (at least until bacteriology stepped in to provide scientific proof), the controversy over the germ theory of disease—that is, the idea that infection and contagion occurred via microorganisms—always came hand in hand with heated debates and invariable clashes over disease prevention measures, particularly those intended to combat and avoid the spread of epidemics. Sowing panic and producing scenes of great human drama, epidemics afford privileged opportunities for analyzing issues of interdependence. In the literature on the social, cultural, and political impacts of disease from the mid-nineteenth century through the first two decades of the twentieth, the major yellow fever epidemics, cholera epidemics (an illness many authors see as the paradigm of urban social interdependence), and the Spanish flu pandemic are the most often cited examples.[15]

The measures taken to beat back epidemics had serious implications in the realm of trade, public authority, individual liberty, and political order, and the contagionist and anticontagionist camps espoused divergent views in this regard. In brief, the anticontagionists championed concrete local measures to improve the social and environmental conditions that bred epidemic-causing miasmas. This "environmentalist" or "ecological" approach was the driving force behind the first nineteenth-century sanitary reforms in Europe and the United States. Public health policies based on anticontagionist views, which rejected the germ theory, denounced the local agents believed to spread epidemic diseases—garbage, sewage, polluted water, crowded and poorly ventilated housing—and promoted an agenda to ameliorate them.[16] Implementation of this agenda began in the mid-nineteenth century, and although the effort was bolstered by medical and scientific ideas disproven in later decades, it made two valuable contributions: it tied illness to the wretched living conditions then prevalent in urban areas, and it occasioned creation of the first urban public services, including sanitary sewers, water supplies, garbage collection, the regulation of dairy products and other food items, and so on, ultimately recording a victory for the collectivization of welfare.[17]

Until the late nineteenth century, no clear scientific evidence supported the contagionist perspective, which blamed microorganisms for spreading disease. The contagionist action plan centered on impeding contact between sick and healthy. This approach thus reinforced the role of public authority in the regulation of countless activities, especially forced isolation and regional or nationwide quarantines, which were imposed particularly to keep ships suspected of carrying sick passengers from making port.

Since the enforcement of quarantines interfered with business, international trade, and freedom of movement, an apparently scientific debate morphed into a political one. Granting more power to government and bureaucratic agencies also stirred unease at a time when liberalism was spreading. This has led some authors—most importantly, Erwin Ackerknecht—to suggest that the conflict between proponents and opponents of the theory of contagion was at the same time a conflict between autocracy and liberalism. According to these scholars, anticontagionism and the antiquarantine movement, in conjunction with nascent liberalism, found greater echo in the second half of the nineteenth century, just before advances in bacteriology dispelled the erroneous presuppositions underlying the anticontagionist stance and proved the germ theory.[18]

Simplified as it is, this overview highlights how the debates over the communicability of disease were never exclusively scientific. The concepts of contagion and infection could be seen in terms of the relationships between individuals within a society as well as between them and their surrounding environment, a notion that was not so far from the idea proposed by hygienists in the mid-nineteenth century and upheld for quite some time.[19] Despite being grounded in what would later be deemed false assumptions, many of these notions led to effective actions, since they sought to mitigate the negative consequences of the environmental background where social interactions transpired.[20] As J. I. Schwartz argues, an etiological hypothesis does not need to be correct to result in a public health program that sustains at least some success.[21]

Once bacteriology reigned supreme, the emphasis was placed on diagnostics and laboratories; efforts to attack specific diseases caused by specific but universal agents; the production of vaccines, serums, and medications; and initiatives aimed primarily at the individual patient. Above all, there was a tendency to eschew any nonscientific interventions—that is, modifications of social factors—as requisite to medical success. This attitude rendered society a mere contextual factor. Yet the reformulated environmental program still targeted living conditions favorable to microbe-human interaction. In other words, what remained in place was a disease model based on multiple causation in which social conditions could be treated as independent variables or at least be seen as constituting more than mere context.[22] For some authors, the environmentalist perspective is most clearly favorable to government responsibility in public health.[23]

The discovery that certain diseases have defined causes (that is, microbes) does not preclude recognition of other variables, outside the realm of the human-germ interaction, that might facilitate or obstruct this interaction. In addition, actors make decisions and behave in consonance with prevalent scientific knowledge, whether or not it will someday be judged erroneous or incomplete. Finally, society can still be regarded as an independent variable. According to L. Murard and P. Zylberman, public hygiene has historically combined the quest for a successful health program with the ambition of reorganizing society.[24] In other words, public hygiene has behaved like an applied social science.

The overriding question for society at large was whether an illness could be caught.[25] Here, the key challenge would be to keep people from coming into contact with the disease-causing microbe and keep the healthy from coming into contact with the sick.[26] Should contact be inevitable, then any negative consequences had to be managed and mitigated. The conviction that contact could be avoided or rendered less hazardous implied action on two fronts. First, carriers had to be cured of pathogenic microorganisms if possible or prevented from transmitting the agents to others. Second, the mechanisms by which these microorganisms infected people had to be addressed.

Individuals are inexorably linked by the communicability of disease, both because it constitutes a threat and because shared benefits can be reaped from prevention. The awareness of this reciprocal dependence effectively generated the idea of community, where responsibility for preventing and curing disease became a moral and political imperative.[27] Ample evidence indicates that this awareness of communicability and the role that microbes played in coupling people to people and places to places took root faster among the lay and society at large than within circles of sanitarians and physicians, at least in the United States and England.[28]

Awareness of the public threat presented by germs that "are everywhere" or by "the ill, who are everywhere," undoes the notion that individual self-sufficiency or reliance on voluntary, compartmentalized solutions to this public evil can prove effective.[29] This change in viewpoint, in turn, triggers an awareness of belonging to a broader community, which may be as large as a nation made up of beings, cities, and regions that see themselves as interdependent. These individuals and places are linked or equalized by germs, mosquitoes, flies, rats, untreated garbage, sewage dumped into rivers, travelers and immigrants journeying about bearing disease, the absence of any control over food that is produced in one place but consumed in many locales, and so on.[30] Thus developed the perception that sanitary conditions in a given location—via direct or indirect transmission, as a result of taking the wrong initiatives or failing to take any action at all, or for any other reason—could have a detrimental impact on other locations that had in no way contributed to this outcome. As the thinking went, established medical knowledge should forestall or eliminate the negative effects of communicable diseases. This awareness of social interdependence implied a consciousness of the need to manage the bonds of social interdependence. Responding to the scope and complexity of the issues associated with this new sense of community ultimately would require some supralocal arrangement. The most generalized by-product of the sociability kindled by microbes was a sense of a national community that came hand in hand with calls for increased government responsibility. Over time, voluntary, individual solutions proved highly ineffective in attending to the direct and indirect consequences of individual and group deficiencies or adversities, whether or not their impact on others was immediate. The need to manage these externalities consequently generated mounting demand for collective, compulsory care. Microbes and epidemics knit together a vast web of individuals and regions and thus collectivized the health problem, hindering any attempt to foster localized, individualized protection schemes. If consciousness of social interdependence is bound up with the emergence of a national community, addressing its external effects is bound up with the role of public authority.

The Public Health Movement Posits an Equation: Brazil = *Sertões* + Hospital

Luiz Antonio de Castro Santos has cast the public health reform movement of the final two decades of the First Republic as a pivotal element in the construction of an ideology of nationhood, with a significant impact on the formation of the Brazilian state.[31] A number of studies that speak either directly or indirectly to the topic have adopted the same outlook, which provides a starting point for any reflection on public health in Republican Brazil.[32]

Other authors similarly ascribe a nationalist character to the sanitation movement of the 1910s and 1920s but emphasize the health policies of these years primarily as a product of ruling-class strategies, with their development linked to the dynamics of capitalism both domestically and internationally. Moreover, proponents of this view argue that the chief public actors, especially sanitarians and public health leaders, were intellectuals subordinated to the interests of the dominant classes in Brazil and the rest of the world.[33] In his interpretations, Castro Santos explores a dynamic where diverse and complex policy determinants appear against the backdrops of differing times and spaces while rejecting the determinist or single-cause explanations so plentiful in the literature.[34]

Most studies divide the public health movement into two basic periods. During the first decade of the twentieth century, Oswaldo Cruz led federal health services (1903–9), which were essentially limited to the Federal District and ports.[35] The main features of this phase were the urban sanitation of Rio de Janeiro and battles against epidemics of yellow fever, bubonic plague, and smallpox. Castro Santos and most other authors hold that the period's public health policies were shaped by the need to reverse the appalling sanitary conditions in the city of Rio and its port because they were causing foreign trade to suffer.[36] In São Paulo, based on the same economic logic, the state government had undertaken sanitation initiatives in the port of Santos and the state capital and had enacted immigration policy in response to the needs of the coffee economy. All of these efforts preceded the sanitation work implemented in the Federal District.[37]

The prime feature of the public health movement's second phase (1910–30) was its stress on rural sanitation, especially the fight against three rural endemic diseases: hookworm (ancylostomiasis), malaria, and Chagas's disease (American trypanosomiasis). This focus was propelled by the "discovery of the *sertões*" (hinterlands or backlands) and their abandoned, ailing inhabitants and by the concomitant hope that these people could be cured and integrated into the national community. Unlike the previous period, sanitary reform during this phase expressed itself more as a path to nation building, riding the wave of a nationalist tendency averse to the notion that racial and environmental determinism could explain Brazil and Brazilians.[38] Under this interpretation, the measures taken as a result of the rural sanitation campaign account for the constitution of government agencies and public health and sanitation policies.[39]

The next section analyzes the sociological dimensions of the arguments advanced by the public health reform movement, builds an analytical bridge between these two periods of public health reform, and depicts the relations between disease, society, and government that were identified and publicized from 1916 to 1920. Considering health interdependence as a social and political dimension, this section evaluates arguments about public health's role in the process of nation-state building, suggesting that transmittable diseases helped mold a well-structured notion of national community, and tests the constraints on government defined by the Brazilian political order.

Since the dawn of the republic, physicians and a portion of the elites had shared this understanding of interdependence, and it still held true after federal health agencies began to be established in 1920, a sign of greater continuity over the first four decades of the republic than the literature suggests. The rural sanitation movement thus reflected Brazilian society's slowly but steadily rising identification of public health issues with the matter of interdependence. Yet one distinguishing factor justifies an analytical focus on 1910–30 and more specifically on 1916–20: at no other time were these relationships painted so clearly and so radically for Brazilian society. They were portrayed as part and parcel of a more global interpretation of Brazil that derived from a dramatic diagnosis of the population's living conditions, and this approach gave tremendous persuasive power to the portraitists—or at the very least, it gave them the promotional power typically fueled by major controversies.

One measure of the success of this effort is the fact that significant sectors of the political and intellectual elites eventually embraced this interpretation. Another is the fact that health and sanitation were assigned a place on the national political agenda. This brief period witnessed exponential growth in public awareness of government responsibility in health and hastened the rise of state action because communicable disease had become a political problem.

Disease and Abandonment:
A Diagnosis of Brazil's Woes

Brazil's debate over health and sanitation picked up pace in the 1910s amid the emergence of several nationalist movements. Indeed, both in Brazil and abroad, the years coinciding with World War I and its immediate aftermath witnessed the growth of nationalist movements that sought to unveil, affirm, and invoke the principles of nationality and to actualize them through the state.[40] Moreover, there are ample indications that warfare—and the attendant problems of recruitment, conscription, and military defeat—sparked public debate and controversy about eugenics, determinism, and "racial improvement," and the discussion of public health conditions featured prominent in those debates.[41]

The war in Europe also generated problems in areas such as immigration, hygiene, and sanitation controls on imports and exports. Several international conferences discussed health controls and devised regulations and strategies in this area, matters of no slight importance for Brazil, an exporter of primary goods as well as a receiver of immigrants. World War I also represented a watershed in terms of mortality rates among civilians and combatants alike as a consequence of health conditions on European battlefields. On the heels of the war, the Spanish flu pandemic proved remarkably lethal as well: in Brazil alone it is estimated to have caused between 30,000 and 160,000 deaths.[42]

Brazil's National Defense League and Nationalist League envisaged different routes for the foundation and/or recovery of nationality: health, education, civic-mindedness and national values, compulsory military service, and so on.[43] A similar movement, the Pro-Sanitation League of Brazil, was founded on February 11, 1918 (the first anniversary of Cruz's death), and sought to alert the political and intellectual elites about the country's tenuous health conditions and garner support for effective public action in the country's interior—that is, to "clean up the hinterlands [sanear os sertões]." In a context where the idea of national salvation was flourishing, proponents of public health proved finely attuned to the broad currents of nationalism sweeping Brazil.[44]

Three signal events set the key time frame for this chapter. The first was an October 1916 speech by Miguel Pereira before the National Academy of Medicine in which he likened Brazil to a "vast hospital." The speech is now viewed as inaugurating the rural sanitation campaign. Second, 1916 also saw the release of a report by the 1912 medical and scientific expedition into the interior of Brazil organized by the Oswaldo Cruz Institute and led by Arthur Neiva and Belisário Penna, who had encountered a country inhabited by backward, sickly, unproductive, and abandoned people who had absolutely no identification with their homeland.[45] The third event was public reaction to a collection of articles on health and sanitation by Penna. First appearing in the Rio press from 1916 to 1917, they were republished in book form in 1918 under the title *O Saneamento do Brasil* (The Sanitation of Brazil). The Pro-Sanitation League of Brazil also increased its activities between 1918 and the 1920s, when the federal government began to reform its health agencies.

Although the first event is often cited in the literature, the content of Pereira's address is largely overlooked except for his emblematic labeling of Brazil as a "vast hospital." The most relevant excerpt of his speech reads:

> Outside Rio or São Paulo—capitals that have been somewhat cleaned up— and a few other cities where Providence watches over hygiene, Brazil is still one vast hospital. In an astounding outburst of oratory in the Chamber, an honorable parliamentarian held forth that, should need be, he would travel from hilltop to hilltop to awaken the inhabitants of our *sertões*. Were he to go to such lengths of patriotic fervor, he would be gravely disappointed by his generous, noble initiative. Part—and no mean part—of these brave people would not even rise up; debilitated invalids, enfeebled by ancylo- stomiasis and malaria, maimed and massacred by Chagas's illness, eaten away by syphilis and leprosy, destroyed by alcoholism, withered by hunger, ignorant and abandoned, devoid of ideals and lacking any education, these forlorn and forgotten people would be unable to rouse themselves from their stupor at the resounding blare of a battlefield trumpet . . . or, should they awaken, ghost-like, they would be unable to understand why the Fatherland, which has denied them the saving grace of the alphabet, now asks of them their lives and lays in their hands not the book of redemption but, instead, a weapon of war.[46]

Pereira's talk was a tribute to Professor Aloysio de Castro, director of the Rio de Janeiro School of Medicine, but it was delivered in the context of a nationalist debate over military recruitment and conscription. Pereira also alluded to Olavo Bilac's exhortation to law and medical students.[47] But the brunt of Pereira's remarks targeted Carlos Peixoto, federal representative of the southeastern state of Minas Gerais, who had declared that if Brazil were invaded, he was willing to march into the *sertões* and convoke its deni- zens to defend the country. Decrying the deputy's naïveté and ignorance of Brazil, Pereira reminded his audience that Lassance, in the home state of this congressman, was where Carlos Chagas had in 1909 discovered the disease that came to bear his name and that had incapacitated millions of Brazilians and rendered them quite useless for menial labor and defending the fatherland.[48] How indeed could men ravaged by such a disease be enlisted to defend Brazil? In Pereira's view, the reality of public health and education in the Brazilian interior put the lie to any romantic, vainglorious rhetoric about the country's hinterlanders.[49]

As a consequence of Pereira's prestige as a professor at the Rio de Janeiro School of Medicine and president of the National Academy of Medicine, his words ignited tremendous controversy in the press and in medical and political circles. He drew motions of support and solidarity from one side and accusations of hyperbole from the other; his patriotism was even called into question.[50] The speech ranked disease as the top national issue, and the resulting groundswell in public opinion seized on the elites' indifference as the primary reason so little had been done about the problem.

Pereira had drawn inspiration for his address from Chagas's works and speeches and also from the report of the 1912 Oswaldo Cruz Institute expedition, which had traversed northern Bahia, southwestern Pernambuco, and southern Pará before marching the length of the central-west state of Goiás.[51] The report was a cornerstone for the campaign's diagnosis of Brazil—or, better put, for its veritable rediscovery of the country, which energized intellectuals and politicians alike and pushed forward the sanitation campaign. Moreover, the portrait of Brazil painted in the document was reproduced and commented on in the press and at academic and parliamentary debates, winning part of public opinion over to its harsh diagnosis.

Commissioned to draft preliminary studies for the construction of reservoirs by federal authorities, the Neiva-Penna expedition spent seven months journeying across vast stretches of the country, especially regions beset by seasonal drought, surveying and photographing climatic, socioeconomic, and epidemiological conditions.[52] The expedition's territory included certain areas between Goiás and the northeastern state of Piauí for which almost no prior documentation existed in the records of Brazilian or foreign naturalists.

The report stressed the need for prevention work to counter the perverse linkage between the availability of water and breeding grounds for disease, particularly malaria. The mission had also gathered information on climate, flora, and fauna, along with detailed records of the maladies afflicting the inhabitants of these regions and their living conditions and economic activities. Further, the report recommended a course of action for public authorities.[53]

The report contended that although some of the inhabitants of these regions—for example, in certain areas of the northeastern states of Bahia and Pernambuco—had been forsaken by the government and victimized by disease, they were nonetheless hardy and resistant. Still, the overall picture was described as "hellish," with an alarmingly high number of carriers of Chagas's disease, especially in Goiás. Physicians Neiva and Penna underscored the contrast between the prevailing romantic depiction of the hinterlander and what they had observed: people who were ignorant and abandoned, who employed primitive tools and were strangers to currency, and who clung to tradition and mistrusted progress. Their isolation, according to the report, accounted for their failure to display any feeling of national identity, the established symbols for which were altogether unknown to them. Indeed, "the only flag they [knew was] that of the Divine."[54]

According to Neiva and Penna, this overwhelming absence of any identification with Brazil was heightened by the neglect of the federal government, present only to tax the resources of a population that possessed barely any: "They live their lives bereft of any assistance whatsoever. [They have] no protection of any kind, knowing government only because it charges them taxes on their calves, steer, horses, and mules."[55]

Although often reiterating the negative images of hinterlanders typical of the day, the report's portrayal of these populations bore witness to an important shift in emphasis in such representations, laying blame for the hinterlander's apathy and backwardness squarely on government neglect rather than on nature, race, or the individuals themselves.[56] Public authorities at all levels were singled out as the true culprits behind the sad state of affairs in these regions, where neglect had left a legacy of rural endemic diseases and their grim consequences. At the height of the report's impact, Neiva recalled that he had found the inhabitants of Brazil's immense interior "left entirely to their own devices."[57] In short, the *sertões* came to symbolize abandonment, widespread endemic disease, and the absence of national identity, and the rural sanitation movement pointed the finger of blame at government authorities.

This diagnosis not only formed the basis for demands that the government take positive action to address deficiencies in sanitation and public health and boost its presence across vast neglected regions of the country but also held out the possibility of shaping a kind of Brazilian identity distinct from the one shaped by disease. In this diagnosis, the *sertões* were home to a vast hospital, representing neglect and its corollary, disease.

This attempt to establish a novel understanding of Brazil amounted to a rejection of both the romanticized view, with its self-aggrandizing nationalism, and the pessimistic view derived from climactic, physical, and racial determinisms, which saw the country sentenced to barbarism and fed the debates surrounding miscegenation and immigration.[58] This diagnosis dispelled the sense of impotence and resignation that surrounded the idea of an inalterable fate for people condemned to eternal backwardness. If these populations were afflicted by disease, they could recover through hygiene and public health measures based on medical knowledge implemented by public authorities. It was not enough to have found these "people whose time had yet to come"; the pressing task now at hand was to transform these "strange inhabitants" of Brazil into Brazilians.[59] The powers of medicine, together with the powers of the state, would provide the pivotal tools for achieving this transformation. Thanks to science, especially medical science, the intellectuals who had previously seen no alternatives for a country apparently condemned by its racial composition could now breathe a sigh of relief.[60]

As the setting for disheartening encounters with diseased compatriots, the *sertões* were not located solely in the north and northeast. Wherever their geographical backdrop, reports, descriptions, and prescriptions struck a similar note. Speaking before the Paraná Society of Medicine in August 1917, physician and public health activist Heráclides César de Souza Araújo read his report on a trip to the *sertões* of northern Paraná commissioned by the state's government. The report echoed Neiva and Penna's document in noting the ubiquity of rural endemic disease, but Paraná lay in southern Brazil, in an area of agricultural expansion and raging malaria, and Souza Araújo posited a clear causal relationship between the presence of disease and the absence of government. In his view, above and beyond the precarious living conditions, ignorance, environmental factors such as deforestation, and economic factors such as "anachronistic" methods of rice cultivation, the chief explanation for the sanitary situation in the *sertões*—whether in southern or central-west Brazil—was the local, state, and federal government's "criminal indifference" toward the endemic nature of malaria.[61]

Not only was the country inhabited by disease, but so too, were the bodies of its impoverished, abandoned people. According to the astonished testimony of a public health official involved in setting up federal rural sanitation agencies in the northeastern state of Paraíba in the 1920s, every Brazilian served as the host of multiple infections and/or infestations: "Every man is a zoological park unto himself; to each region of the body there corresponds a particular variety of fauna."[62]

For the sanitation campaign, the *sertões* and other rural areas were more a medical, social, and political construct than a geographical category.[63] Their location in space coincided with the twin conditions of abandonment and disease. In fact, the *sertões* were not so very distant from the sources of public authority under pressure to take action on the health front, and the concept was not merely a symbolic or geographical allusion to the country's enormous interior. In the thought-provoking vision of Afrânio Peixoto, a physician, man of letters, and professor, the Brazilian *sertões* began in downtown Rio de Janeiro, at the end of Avenida Central (today's Avenida Rio Branco).[64] Many observers saw disease as the real bond holding the federation together and believed that the map of the country itself could be redrawn in disease's image. According to historian and politician José Maria Bello, Brazil should be subdivided not into states and municipalities but into three regions—the outlying reaches of the Federal District, the coast, and the interior—whose contours were not defined by geopolitical criteria but by the presence of the three great rural endemic diseases: "At the doorstep of the capital, ancylostomiasis decimates the population in the lowlands, while farther beyond, malaria (all along the coast and on riverbanks) and American trypanosomiasis (in the *sertões*) harvest their victims."[65]

By equating the hinterlands with disease and neglect, this diagnosis stretched the rural frontier to the centralized seat of state power. From the standpoint of the rural sanitation campaign, these sickly slices of Brazil were neither so small nor so distant that public authorities could afford to leave them at the mercy of endemic disease. But if the consequences of neglect and disease were already nipping at the heels of the Brazilian elite—just at the end of the boulevard—they had yet to actually nip at its conscience.

Federalism, Disease, and Neglect:
An Interpretation of Brazil

Understanding how health moved onto the stage as a national issue between 1916 and 1930 requires looking at the arguments advanced by Belisário Penna, the chief spokesperson for the rural sanitation movement during the period. As leader of the Pro-Sanitation League of Brazil and as a "missionary" and polemicist, he spoke out wherever and whenever the opportunity arose. In his countless articles and lectures, reproduced and copied all over

Brazil, Penna ran riot with hyperbole and repetition, and his work was instrumental in articulating and propagating the movement's diagnosis about the health of the population. A sizable portion of the elites came to accept this assessment as the conventional wisdom. Furthermore, both his writings and actions played a vital role in calling attention to health issues and helping secure them a spot on the national political agenda, even though the elites might not have taken up the cause across the board.

Penna's *O Saneamento do Brasil* may well have been the most important and widely known book to spread the cause of Brazilian public health in the latter half of the 1910s and provides the most thorough exposition of the movement's propositions.[66] In the book's pages, Penna interprets the relations between disease, society, and politics in Brazil and proposes changes to the federal role in the fields of sanitation and public health. All of his analysis is grounded in a trenchant criticism of federalism and the neglect of the ruling elites. Penna's ideas, which he reiterated endlessly in other articles and lectures, won a considerable number of politicians and intellectuals, among them Monteiro Lobato, into the sanitarian fold, and they, in turn, extended the public impact of the campaign. At the same time, however, his work, especially his policy recommendations, spawned many opponents.

As a critic of the republic and especially of federalism, which he blamed for "all the evils that afflict" Brazil, Penna claimed that the country had been divided up among an unscrupulous lot of petty local tyrants, heedless of the interests of the populace. The republic amounted to little more than the union of "twenty fatherlands" dominated by "three or four" states with a central oligarchy that actually ran the country.[67] According to Penna, Brazil's "licentious" 1891 constitution had omitted two of the chief assets of the empire: unity of command and national solidarity.[68] Moreover, the abolition of slavery had been badly mismanaged, driving masses of unprotected and unskilled individuals onto the peripheries of big cities and thus creating dire education, housing, and sanitation problems. Concurrently, the countryside had suffered depopulation and a substantial decrease in the available agricultural workforce.

Following the tradition of conservative Brazilian thinkers such as Alberto Torres, Penna also attacked what he perceived to be the artificial character of the country's industry and urbanism and the subsequent neglect of its so-called natural industrial vocation: agriculture.[69] Rural populations, which Penna saw as the bulwarks of Brazilian nationality, had become the prime victims of disease, ignorance, and alcoholism and were being exploited by "contrived . . . urban industrialism," a national priority that was incapable of surviving without protectionism that benefited only a few.[70] In the final analysis, Penna argued, agriculture and rural populations bore the brunt of such artifices. Some rough indications of the type of agricultural economy envisioned by the rural sanitation movement are found in writings on agroindustrial modernization projects such as Delmiro Gouveia's experience in the northeastern state of Alagoas and Lobato's story about Jeca Tatu, a diseased and illiterate hinterlander who is saved by the rural health and education campaigns and becomes a U.S.-style capitalist rural entrepreneur.[71] Finally, given the absence of adequate public policies, intensified interactions between city and country spelled the worst of both worlds: the depopulation of the *sertões* as migrants bloated urban centers, triggering further poverty and disease, while the hinterlands were beset by syphilis, alcoholism, tuberculosis, and "immorality."[72]

Penna's argument shows us how disease fit into the broader panorama of Brazilian society. The country was facing two fundamental, interconnected problems: disease that was overwhelming inhabitants of both urban and rural areas, and the depopulation of a huge chunk of its territory. In tune with the agrarianist intellectual tradition, Penna felt that the rural population and *sertões* had been abandoned as a consequence both of policies designed to foment an "artificial industry" and of the federalist political framework imposed by the 1891 constitution. For Penna, autonomous federative units meant that distinct and incomplete legal, administrative, educational, and sanitation practices would be adopted in different regions, undermining any chance for solidarity and cooperation.[73] Proponents of the sanitation campaign held that disease was a product of an absent, ineffective government and decentralized government policies. At the same time, communicable disease was a potential force for national and territorial integration, since its presence or even its possibility could rebuild social solidarity. The apostles of sanitation believed that solving the problems they had identified required making Brazil's elites aware of the growing sanitary, social, and political risks and attendant costs of maintaining the health status quo. The centralization of public initiatives was seen as the way to tackle endemic diseases and promote health. One persuasive tactic was to evoke the examples of the Mexican and Russian Revolutions, still fresh in everyone's mind.[74]

Proponents of the sanitation movement believed that government action should focus on rural endemic diseases, with special emphasis on hookworm, malaria, and Chagas's disease. Such illnesses were believed to be preventable if not curable. From this viewpoint, the defining attribute of Brazilians and their low productivity was disease, caused by the negligence of public officials, rather than laziness.[75] Given the plausibility if not accuracy of the movement's diagnosis, advocates of public health reform felt sufficiently confident to reject out of hand explanations of the national character grounded in racial or climactic determinism.[76] Penna estimated that 70 percent of the rural population was infested with hookworm and argued that it should be the first target of a nationwide sanitation and health education campaign.[77]

In Penna's view, because hookworm advanced so slowly, neither killing nor even frightening anyone in its initial stages, it had led to the physical weakening of rural populations, diminishing their immunity to other diseases and thus compromising the health of the labor force while undermining the national economy as a whole. Human collectors of myriad diseases, Brazilians had become unproductive workers and obstacles to progress and development. Penna reckoned that six million Brazilians were producing only one-third of what they would be capable of producing under the optimal sort of health conditions enjoyed by laborers overseas, a loss all the more painful, in human and economic terms, because it was so eminently avoidable.[78] An unproductive economy in a place where disease ran rampant would hold little attraction for immigrants. In a grimly ironic aside, Penna suggested that immigrants immediately became "Brazilianized" by contracting parasitic worms.[79] Being Brazilian did not require birth on the country's soil or even naturalization: it merely required carrying the disease.[80]

The endeavor to show that sickness generated unproductive workers and thus fettered economic activity gave birth to the sanitation movement's best-known and perhaps most efficacious propaganda piece, the character of Jeca Tatu, chastised for his invincible sloth in Lobato's earliest renditions but later reformed.[81] By prioritizing the battle against rural endemic diseases, especially hookworm, the movement believed that Brazilians would come to realize how science and medicine could benefit Jeca and others like him. Moreover, Brazilians would be convinced that educational initiatives would prevent behavior that might lead to reinfection or further spread of the ailment and environmental initiatives would alter disease-breeding conditions.[82]

With Penna at the helm, the rural sanitation campaign sought to unify a broad spectrum of intellectuals and to persuade political elites and society at large of the gravity of the problem. Proponents presented a dramatic diagnosis of Brazil's illness while tendering a plausible interpretation of its causes. The most challenging task was generating the levels of consensus necessary to transform the movement's suggestions into policy. The campaign had to "instill in the spirit of the leaders" the need for a national sanitation policy.[83]

Once it had issued its diagnosis and stated its case for sanitation policies as an instrument for the recovery and unification of the country, the Pro-Sanitation League won the support of a large number of intellectuals who devoted their time to making speeches, demonstrating initiatives in prevention and health education, presenting statistics on the public health picture, writing books and articles on the topic, promoting the movement wherever they found a receptive setting, and publishing the League's journal, *Saúde*.[84] Above all, the movement pressured Congress to draft public health legislation and pushed to hold government at all levels more accountable for the health of the population.

League founders included members of the National Academy of Medicine, professors from the medical schools in Rio de Janeiro and Bahia, scientists with the Oswaldo Cruz Institute, National Museum anthropologists, employees of federal health agencies, military officers, educators, lawyers, journalists, and politicians, among them the acting president of the republic, Wenceslau Brás. In 1918–19, many across the country joined the movement, and regional delegations were established in nine states, reflecting the intellectual and political elites' support for more vigorous government action in the fight against disease, especially the "unholy trinity" of rural endemic maladies.[85] The Pro-Sanitation League and the São Paulo Eugenics Society released Lobato's book *Problema Vital* (1918) as a campaign tool.

Between 1918 and 1920, the League distributed twenty thousand copies of a brochure, *Opilação ou Amarelão* (two colloquial terms for ancylostomiasis), along with other educational pamphlets. In addition, members gave "more than one hundred speeches and hygiene demonstrations" at schools, military barracks, public squares, and elsewhere around the country and published "more than one hundred articles in magazines and daily newspapers." Further, the Pro-Sanitation League provided health care for the poor and rural workers, including free professional services on large estates in Rio de Janeiro.[86] League members also contributed to the movement intrinsically through their daily activities as physicians, teachers, and civil servants.

In addition to promoting education and raising awareness of the problem, the movement's efforts included using the country's meager public and philanthropic resources to create health posts on the outskirts of Rio de Janeiro to prevent and combat both malaria and hookworm. In April 1918, prompted by the persistent visibility of the sanitation campaign, Brás paid an official visit to one such post in the Rio neighborhood of Penha, where he was moved at the sight of "the cruel truth . . . of the morbid situation on the doorstep of the nation's capital" and "gained a pale idea of the havoc wreaked by rural endemic diseases."[87] Brás appeared to have been won over to the cause for greater action against rural endemic diseases.

As the organized expression of the rural sanitation movement, the League set as its overriding goal the establishment of a federal agency entrusted with nationwide delivery of standardized services and coordinated public initiatives. The agenda of such an agency would, however, exceed the constitutional strictures imposed on the center, whose theater of operations in public health was by law restricted to the Federal District and port areas. A nationwide health code enforced by this federal agency was thought to be the legal instrument that could achieve these aims. However, this measure would not preclude or supplant the need for states and municipalities to create their own services. The autonomy of these agencies, envisioned as purely technical in nature, would guarantee the continual triumph of science over political interests, which the rural sanitation movement saw as an obstacle or at any rate as a target of its critique.

In short, from the standpoint of the rural sanitation movement, Brazil was a diseased nation characterized by ubiquitous endemic maladies, and this was the price being paid for the absence or dereliction of public authority across great swaths of the country. The literature has branded the rural sanitation movement as nationalist in nature, but this nationalism must be understood as an awakening to a sense of nationhood born from a newfound awareness of social interdependence fostered by disease. The rural sanitation movement imbued Brazilian society with an interpretation of the country centered on two complementary, defining metaphors, the hospital and the *sertões*, where the former suggested the inescapable presence of sickness and the latter evoked neglect by an absent public authority. Within this frame of logic, as Brazilians developed a consciousness of the communicability of disease, proposals emerged to invert this characterization of the country to equate the presence of public authority with the absence of disease.

Communicable Diseases
Test the Limits of Public Power

Given what was then known about preventing and curing disease, the threat or constant menace of transmissible diseases—where human meets microbe—manifested itself essentially as a social phenomenon, resulting in the rural sanitation movement's clamor for public authority to arm itself with all the weapons of medicine and restrain some habits and practices. Because these habits might not only victimize their practitioners but also jeopardize the health and lives of other people, the public had to be taught to keep individual and collective behavior in line with medical knowledge. Such deeply ingrained social practices and customs as consuming alcohol, engaging in prostitution, going barefoot, not using latrines, dumping garbage in rivers and public streets, turning a blind eye to breeding grounds for flies, mosquitoes, rats, and mice, and selling unsafe milk and food would have to be transformed.

The public health movement of the First Republic had two significant outcomes. First, it gave voice to the feeling of interdependence stirred by communicable diseases while championing the idea that public health was the primary national issue, thereby constructing a powerful sentiment of national community—a community bonded by disease. Second—and this was the movement's most innovative achievement—it transformed the political order into an independent variable. The proposed reform solution would facilitate the unification and centralization of health and sanitation policies in the hands of the federal government. The reformist equation was public health consciousness + political and constitutional change = a national public health policy.[88]

From the rural sanitation movement's perspective, the constitutional framework of 1891 could not control the negative effects of the social, political, and territorial interdependence inflicted by microbes, which defied individual or local attempts to solve public health problems. The negative effects of disease consequently pitted individual freedom against the community and called into question the limits of public power. Out of this understanding of public health came a proposal for political reform that would defend what the movement believed to be the interests of the community by confronting institutional arrangements that went against these interests. Accordingly, public health proponents reframed their desired public policy and organizational goals as indisputable public needs, a testament to the movement's distinct authoritarian leanings.

The rural sanitation movement pointed out that the problems of social interdependence had been articulated on a number of occasions during the Old Republic. Based primarily on the perception that communicability placed special demands on government, many people had called for the centralization and unification of health services and agencies. At a lecture at the National Library in Rio de Janeiro, physician Carlos Seidl, head of the General Directorate of Public Health from 1913 to 1918, pointed out that the 1895 report of the Ministry of Justice and Internal Affairs had suggested that Congress unify and centralize public hygiene: "Stressing that a communicable illness, precisely because it is communicable, is not local in nature, insofar as it can invade territories lying outside the boundaries wherein it arose . . . the federal government would be justified in taking the necessary measures to ward off the spread of these illnesses, principally given that not all states of the Union have the capacity to establish hygiene services that might keep a contagious epidemic illness from moving beyond its borders to invade other states, in consideration of the most costly nature [of these services]."[89]

Starting in 1916, this argument reverberated nationwide as a challenge to the prevailing interpretation of the 1891 constitution. Illustrating how the movement viewed the scope of reciprocal dependence, Penna asked, "Given the hypothesis, for the sake of argument, that a certain municipality is impelled to act and rigorously enforces therapeutic measures against, say, ancylostomiasis and does manage to eradicate or reduce it to a minimal number of cases, will this be enough to remedy our great problem?"[90]

By definition, no merely individual, local solution could address health and sanitation issues. Even if individuals were to care for their own health or some local elites with a higher level of consciousness were to clean up their city, those citizens would remain in peril as a result of others who had failed to act, whether out of inertia, incompetence, or empty pocketbooks. From this perspective, health was a national, public issue, not because some politicians or government leaders and many physicians wanted it to be such an issue but because of the inexorable fact that countless maladies were communicable. Public health interdependence necessitated an authority that could cross state borders and implement policies applicable to the entire population, impinging on individual freedom and property rights when necessary. In other words, the movement and its sympathizers wanted to see the strengthening of distinctive, constitutive elements of state authority—territorial scope, territorial centrality, and coercive power.

The Pro-Sanitation League's program largely summed up the public health movement's proposals.[91] First, the program argued that "thirty years of autonomy" attested to the fact that states were incompetent with regard to health and sanitation.[92] Second, to mitigate the negative effects of interdependence, the federal government had to augment its ability to reach all corners of the country: "We do not agree with the notion of state and municipal autonomy in public health. . . . This matter is not strictly one of regional or local interest but is, rather, national, demanding one single direction and one single course of action."[93]

According to this argument, enforcing the constitutional principle of state and municipal autonomy in the realm of health would simply ensure that the country remain forever mired in a public health crisis. The proposed solution was the establishment of a federal agency with jurisdiction throughout the country, "independent from the petitions and excesses of the states."[94] Only a few states actually indulged in any "excesses," since most states and practically all municipalities lacked the funds to promote health and sanitation.[95] And even if some states could—or thought they could—attend to the health of their population and cleanliness of their territory, they would remain vulnerable to invasion by diseases and diseased people, since they lacked the legal power to force other units of the federation to take measures to combat the spread of disease.

Epidemics exemplified the perils of public health interdependence. In the most often cited study on the constitutionality of expanding federal services, Barroso strove to extend the concept of "public disaster" to include epidemics, thus empowering the federal government to wage war on them without authorization from state governments as prescribed under Articles 5 and 6 of the constitution.[96] Barroso argued that epidemics were a concern of the collectivity and therefore not the exclusive concern of states and municipalities, as Articles 65 and 68 contended.

> When such a disaster affects the state solely and exclusively, the federal government shall not intervene without a request from the state. This is not, as mistakenly believed, the case with an epidemic, which, while possibly limited to one state at first, nevertheless carries the risk of spreading into other states and posing a general threat to the interests of the entire Nation. And if it is in the general interest of the country, if it is not an exclusive concern of this one state, because it is shared by various others, then the federal government may take measures against it, decreeing laws that local governments cannot oppose.[97]

Communicable diseases had rendered the country's federative units "naturally" interdependent and its inhabitants unified, even against their will. Illness defied the political order born of the federative pact and would eventually reorganize it. To protect each of the units making up the nation and their populations and the country as a whole, the rural sanitation movement believed the obvious solution was to expand federal authority to advance nationwide public health policies.

The territorial dimension of the state was seen as intimately linked to its coercive power. Here again, the program of the Pro-Sanitation League is clear: "One cannot leave it up to the whim of the individual to spill his feces on the ground, when it is patently known that this constitutes a serious danger to health and the community."[98]

No matter how ostensibly obvious and how endlessly repeated, this line of argument has often fallen on deaf ears. The legitimacy of public health agencies within any sphere of government has long been a dubious matter. Opponents have raised questions, for example, when agencies have enforced the isolation of ships and passengers suspected of harboring contagious disease, forced people to be vaccinated, and battled disease vectors on private property. In the name of individual rights, resistance to the coercive power of public health authority in Brazil walked hand in hand with the evolution of pertinent legislation (though this resistance was even fiercer in other countries, among them France and England).[99] Such challenges to government power often wound their way through court systems—for example, petitions for habeas corpus relief in the case of compulsory vaccination or the violation of residences to combat the yellow fever mosquito. The notion of communicability was thus central to calls to increase the state's coercive power: "Every carrier of a communicable illness is a threat and danger to whomever comes in close contact with him. The state should exercise vigilance over him and endeavor to prevent him from contaminating those who are not yet carriers of the malady."[100]

As the awareness of social interdependence gained acceptance, it followed that an individual's state of health was not a private matter, much less a natural right, like individual freedom. The state had the obligation to intrude on personal liberty and property to protect the community. Public health authorities were vested with policing power because action had to be taken against those who polluted soil and water, sold contaminated or falsified products, and spread germs (wittingly or not) and against anyone else whose behavior produced negative external effects for whatever reason. The era's public health doctors saw health legislation not as an "intolerable tyranny" but rather as a form of coercion that was not only legitimate but indeed "necessary to protect the health of the greatest number."[101]

The various proposals for public health reform based on these arguments featured no consensus either about the best opportunity for implementing the reform or about its organizational format; they did, however, generally agree that government should enjoy greater coercive power and territorial scope of action at all levels. The most radical proposal envisaged a federal-level organization that would centralize all initiatives and services to fight epidemic and endemic diseases, including health and sanitation measures, and unify them within an exclusively technical agency that would encourage and help states and municipalities establish or amplify their own hygiene services. Another proposal called for legislation in the form of a public health code to define general guidelines applicable to the country as a whole and regulate all activities in any way perilous to health. These demands were presented primarily to Congress, which had virtually exclusive authority to legislate federal powers.

Because Brazil had been diagnosed as a diseased country and everyone from individuals to states stood equal before the menace of sickness, the rural sanitation movement assumed that this broader perception of mutual dependence and the ties between communicable diseases and society would compel the political elite to restructure the federative arrangement and enable it to effectively address serious health issues. Carlos Chagas, a preeminent Brazilian scientist and head of federal health services from 1919 to 1926, urged experts to recognize the absurdity of tying the hands of the federal government with "modifiable legal precepts" given the panorama of public health in Brazil and the technical and financial frailty of most states. The constitution and the laws of the land, Chagas contended, should be altered or reinterpreted in the light of this reality.[102]

The health movement's reform proposal carried further political heft because it was posited as the only feasible alternative for solving the nation's most dramatic problem. According to this logic, once the politics behind the notion of transmissible diseases were understood, the conflicts between individual freedom and community protection or between autonomy and centralization should fall by the wayside. Expansion of the government's ability to act would no longer be a matter of debate; instead, it would be an imperative mandated by the communicability of disease. The Brazilian political and institutional order should therefore adapt itself to the demands of nature.

Conclusion

Under the First Republic, the rural sanitation movement cast disease as a social evil that dictated public health and sanitation initiatives focused on the bonds of communicability, both between individuals within one community and between different communities. The movement's proponents felt that the notion that certain diseases are communicable would reframe perceptions of the relations between distinct groups: mutual dependence meant that depriving some could cost others a great deal. The attendant economic costs might likewise be stinging, since disease "squandered people"—to use an expression of that day—and thus jeopardized labor productivity and even national development. An awareness that the dire health conditions suffered by other slices of society presented real or potential hazards would spur healthy sectors of society to appeal for solutions that would necessarily reach into many different communities and territories and coercively impose laws and standards of behavior.

Against the backdrop of the rural sanitation movement and its diagnosis of a diseased Brazil emerged a social consciousness based on the identification of disease as a bond of social interdependence. Proposals sprang from the discovery that health, society, and politics were enmeshed by the communicability of disease, forging a national community and stirring feelings of union, fear, and responsibility. The rural sanitation movement drew an innovative parallel between the category of *sertões* and the image of a hospital, associating communicable diseases with the absence of government. Equally innovative was the movement's direct appeal to Brazilian politics and state power. From where the reformers stood, a modified political and constitutional order was a prerequisite for effective public health and sanitation policies, with public authority wielding increased power. Communicable disease had been definitively transformed into a political issue.

Accordingly, the diagnosis and proposals of the sanitation campaign challenged prevailing notions of individual freedom and the existing federative pact. The proposals to minimize the negative effects of interdependence saw administrative centralization and technical autonomy as the logical solution. Reformers saw Brazilian public health as in an extremely grave state but believed that the situation could be resolved or at least ameliorated with the aid of medical and scientific knowledge. Moreover, the elites had acquired social consciousness, meaning that the next step on the road to reform would be changes to the political order. Public health should be managed in consonance with the politics of communicable disease. The reformers believed that since this national tragedy had been exposed and publicized and a shared social consciousness had been constructed, so-called natural solutions would be adopted as a matter of course.

This conviction was so hardy among public health doctors that one federal health agency publication closed a text on public hygiene with lines from *Macbeth*:

> Alas, poor country,
> Almost afraid to know itself. It cannot
> Be called our mother but our grave, where nothing,
> But who knows nothing, is once seen to smile.[103]

Public Health Reform; or, Who Should Be Responsible for Communicable Diseases?

I indeed said that Brazil is one vast hospital. I did not say it is an enormous insane asylum. It is therefore our hope—and in this hope we take heart—that the director of this hospital, the Honorable President of our Republic, with the support . . . of all of us, simple, humble nurses, shall, based on his sound reasoning, begin treating this giant as soon as possible.

—Miguel Pereira, 1916

Shortly after his controversial proclamation that Brazil was a vast hospital, Miguel Pereira expanded his remarks to reflect the conviction shared by those intent on public health reform: once the country's critical medical condition had been diagnosed and remedies suggested, and if the resources were available to deliver those remedies, government leaders would take the appropriate, urgently needed measures. Yes, Brazil was a hospital, but, reformers believed, its elites were not madmen. Mad would be those who were aware that Brazil was diseased yet did little or nothing about the situation. Rather, they would use their position in the country's decision-making arenas to change the public health picture. And they would be crazier still if they failed to tailor the political and constitutional order to fit the exigencies of the new sociability bred by communicable disease. But the politics behind public health and sanitation policy reform during the oligarchic First Republic reflected a gap between the level of social consciousness produced by public health interdependence and the elites' willingness to do something to mitigate the negative effects suffered by their own group and by society at large. Social consciousness had not yet reached the point where it could foster nationwide, collective, and compulsory arrangements that would manage the negative effects of mutual dependence. The content and meaning of the public policies to be adopted and the organizational structure to support them were thus the object of disputes and negotiations, and politics bridged this gap. The politics of communicable diseases derived from the social nature of the microbe but entailed a process that involved actors, institutions, interests, and rules.

This political and decision-making process generated specific institutions, laws, and interests. While my analysis focuses on events within a specific time frame, the politics of public health reform played a significant role in the overall process of state building. The process ultimately engendered institutional formats that then framed future choices, decisions, and policies. Public health policy in Brazil has been the result of a number of reforms, some certainly more relevant than others, and understanding the progression of these reforms requires a thoroughgoing analysis of the political dynamics that yielded these early reforms.

Health was such a central issue on the Brazilian agenda from 1916 to 1920 that political positions, proposals, and events were concentrated in a short time, affording a prime opportunity for studying the political process that was an integral part of the reforms. The individuals mentioned in these pages are less important for who they are than for what they did as spokespeople for professional sectors, institutions, political groups, and even for public opinion (inchoate as it may have been). Since the public made no explicit demands, defining the content of health policies was the exclusive purview of the political elite and its representatives, participants in medical and public health circles, and members of government elites and the bureaucracy, groups that shared tight ties and had highly overlapping interests.

This chapter analyzes the political process that in 1920 led to the first major transformation in federal public health services and agencies since the dawn of the twentieth century. Broad sectors of the political elite came to share an awareness of the interdependence implicit to the revelation that Brazil was a diseased country with a negligent government. In concrete terms, a shift occurred from the view that health matters were a local, individual responsibility to the view that they were more collective and national. The chapter also describes the main reform proposals and the debates in professional arenas, the press, and the federal legislature as well as decisions regarding the creation and expansion of national public health agencies in the late 1910s. This process was not self-contained but rather formed part of a stream of prior and ensuing events that stretched into the 1920s. Also coming into play were the Spanish flu epidemic and the constant threat of new outbreaks of yellow fever from endemic breeding grounds in the north and northeast, both of which had a bearing on the political discussion about the directions of the reform. Further, the chapter looks at how the problems of interdependence challenged the way public health had been organized at the federal level in the early republic and how it prompted modifications over time. Each substantial change created public power and laid the foundations for future reforms and their potential and limitations.

The core of the chapter is divided into two parts. The first offers an overview of the historical evolution of public and federal responsibility for health over the first three decades of the First Republic. It also comments on the development of the original institutional and political design that was the butt of the criticisms highlighted in chapter 2 and the concern of the reform proposals analyzed here. The period witnessed the advance of public authority in the health arena, especially its coercive dimension. Starting in the 1910s, the territorial breadth of public health authority was in fact the prime subject of discussions regarding health service reforms.

The second part of the chapter shows how the elites began displaying an awareness of interdependence and analyzes the debates of the day, the proposed solutions to health and sanitation problems, and subsequent decisions. It also juxtaposes the arguments and proposals put forward essentially by members of medical and public health circles—which helped formulate ideas, exert pressure, and act as consultants—and those discussed in the federal legislature, where the real decisions about the direction of health reform were made. The Spanish flu and yellow fever epidemics provide a springboard for discussing the political impact of extreme experiences in health interdependence.

Both the territorial reach of public power and the government's ability to manage the effects of mutual dependence came under question. Moreover, although social consciousness and even paradigmatic experiences of interdependence such as epidemics drove the debate on the reform of health and sanitation policies, in and of themselves they defined neither the success nor the content of these policies. Awareness alone was simply not enough; the final outcome was ultimately a product of politics based on a preexisting institutional design. Moreover, this denouement constituted a departure both from the rural sanitation movement's centralizing proposals and from the proposals of those who simply wanted to stick with state and municipal autonomy. This outcome evinced a shift in the political and institutional order framing the debates on government responsibility in public health.

Government Responsibility in Health and Sanitation in the Early Decades of the Republic

There is a consensus in the literature that, starting in the mid-nineteenth century, the institutional design of public health under the empire moved slowly toward administrative unification as it worked to respond to frequent epidemic outbreaks of yellow fever, bubonic plague, and smallpox in coastal cities and regions of economic expansion and immigration.[1] These initiatives were not wide-ranging in territorial scope; rather, they were usually emergency actions that targeted areas surrounding the outbreaks. The last major reformulation of sanitation services under the empire came in 1886 as part of the Barão de Mamoré reform, when the Higher Council of Public Health was instituted and sanitation divided into the General Inspectorate of Hygiene, in charge of "inland hygiene" and concerned above all with the imperial capital, and the General Inspectorate of Port Health, in charge of "maritime hygiene." Although this arrangement was unified in the hands of the central government, the two inspectorates were restricted territorially and had limited powers. The provisional government of the republic inherited this structure and in 1890 attempted to bolster the power wielded over the states by the General Inspectorate of Hygiene and assign it more duties, effectively "demunicipalizing hygiene."[2]

The constitution enacted on February 24, 1891, reversed this trend. Although the charter itself makes no mention of health or sanitation, the interpretation took root, based on Articles 5 and 6, that these matters fell to the states and municipalities. In addition, under Article 34, Congress alone could legislate the exercise of federal power and the federal budget, meaning that any changes intended to augment central power would require the representatives of state oligarchs to form majority blocs within Parliament.

Approved in December 1891, the budget law for 1892 confirmed this interpretation when it stipulated that all expenses related to sanitation services in the nation's capital would fall to the government of the Federal District (Distrito Federal, or DF), while each state would assume all expenditures related to inland hygiene within its geographic jurisdiction. The federal government would retain responsibility for national sanitary defense, which amounted largely to maritime sanitation services.[3] To all intents and purposes, an official legal and technical affidavit handed down by the Higher Council of Public Health in January 1892 cemented this model, "in light of administrative decentralization and the sovereignty of local governments"—in consonance with the prevailing interpretation of the constitution.[4]

Thus, under the federative system, local powers were responsible for tending to the population's health. At the close of the 1890s, the national government was basically accountable for health initiatives within the DF, sanitary surveillance of ports, and aid to states in the situations foreseen under the constitution. Created in 1896 and regulated in 1897, the General Directorate of Public Health was the federal agency charged with rendering these services. Attached to the Ministry of Justice and Internal Affairs, the General Directorate had as its main duties managing sanitation services at maritime and river ports, overseeing the practice of medicine and pharmacy, fostering studies on infectious diseases, organizing demographic and public health statistics, and providing assistance to states in special situations, such as epidemics, when states requested such assistance.[5]

The first major changes came in 1902–4 under Francisco de Paula Rodrigues Alves's administration. Federal authority was extended at a time when pressures were being felt because of the epidemics of yellow fever, plague, and smallpox that perpetually menaced Brazil and its capital, exacting high death tolls, disrupting the national economy, and defiling the image of the city and the nation.[6] Signaling the incapacity and weakness of public health services in the capital, these problems were aggravated by what many deemed an inefficacious division of responsibilities between national and municipal hygiene services along with the near-nonexistence of such services at the state level.[7] Under the new public health legislation, the General Directorate was to pick up some of the slack, pursuant to an early 1904 regulation that incorporated into the agency defensive hygiene services in the DF—the sanitary police, general prevention, and household hygiene (Decree 1.151, January 5, 1904). The new legislation also established the Specific Yellow Fever Prophylaxis Service (Decree 5.157, May 8, 1904) and the Procedural Regulation of the Sanitary Justice (Decree 5.224, May 30, 1904). The new sanitary regulations were quite comprehensive, containing 316 articles that restructured and expanded services in the DF and at national ports (Decree 1.156, March 8, 1904).[8]

The provision for sanitary surveillance of the seas and ports is one of the best illustrations of the emergence and rapid evolution of a collective arrangement for coordinating public health control at ports and the flow of ships, passengers, and goods. The federal government was supposed to regulate and implement general policies rather than allowing local officials to decide whether to release passengers or goods that might jeopardize the health of the rest of the nation. For example, while a local authority might solve its own immediate problem by barring a ship from docking and unloading, it might also pass the buck by sending the ship on to another port. This dynamic could hold between port cities or between ports and noncoastal locales, which might thus suffer from the ineptitude of health officials on the seaboard. Harbors in different countries might also be affected, making international treaties necessary.[9] In the majority of nations, sanitation services at ports and aboard ships were among the oldest forms of government intervention in the field of health and among the sanitation initiatives that enjoyed fastest development, and Brazil was no different in this regard.[10]

Overall, the series of health decrees passed in 1902–4 left the federal government responsible for all hygiene services previously under the auspices of the DF, including municipal doctors, urban cleaning workers, and all infectious disease prevention. The legislation authorized negotiations with the DF, which was supposed to transfer to federal hands the Serum Therapy Institute (later the Oswaldo Cruz Institute). The facility, which produced serums and vaccines, would be responsible for supplying these materials to any state or municipality that requested them. At the national level, the General Directorate's duties would expand to include isolation hospitals at principal ports; oversight of official and private laboratories and their products, such as vaccines and serums; and preparation of a national sanitary code with enforcement at the local level.[11]

The federal government substantially expanded its public health role in the capital, ending the administrative separation between defensive and proactive initiatives, and increased its regulatory power over matters of public health and hygiene. In 1902, the government required the compulsory reporting of all cases of typhus, cholera, yellow fever, plague, smallpox, diphtheria, typhoid fever, tuberculosis, and leprosy (Hansen's disease) and instituted criminal penalties against anyone who failed to comply.[12] In addition, a health court was established and given jurisdiction over civil and criminal suits involving the enforcement of health and sanitary laws and regulations, thereby guaranteeing the work of public health officials.[13] Moreover, a compulsory, nationwide smallpox vaccination law was approved (Law no. 1.261, October 31, 1904), igniting civil unrest in Rio de Janeiro in November 1904 that became known as the Vaccine Revolt.

This was a period of intense political mobilization around public health issues, especially in the nation's capital, with health featuring high on the public agenda. The sanitary reform led by Oswaldo Cruz, at the helm of the General Directorate from 1903 to 1909, transpired within an extremely complex political and social context and was a centerpiece of the major urban reform undertaken in Rio under Mayor Francisco Pereira Passos.[14] While the coalition of forces opposing compulsory smallpox vaccination attracted a very broad and diverse range of interests, subsequent interpretations of the clashes over forced vaccination and the campaign to eradicate yellow fever have accentuated the local population's resistance to arbitrary government or have addressed the controversy as part of a discussion on civil rights.[15] However, I highlight another dimension of the conflict: the concerns about public power versus individual rights (including property rights) in a situation where a social evil presented a menace to all. Law enforcement is a basic attribute of public authority, and at issue here were the coercive actions that could be taken to enforce the law. In this instance, public authority stepped in to keep the negative effects of some people's ill health from endangering others via direct or indirect transmission, thereby protecting all. These actions included draconian regulations to enforce compulsory vaccination and military-style campaigns against yellow fever and plague. These initiatives would succeed only if they were applied across the board, to everyone, without exception and without choice. And the legal mechanisms and other means devised to achieve these ends significantly enhanced state power in the realm of health.

During this first phase, a consciousness of public health interdependence had not yet deeply penetrated society at large but was restricted instead to medical and hygienist circles. And even in these milieus, there were those who clung to a prebacteriological conception of the spread of disease. According to the proponents and observers of these sanitation campaigns, any eventual success in the fight against epidemics and to improve health in the city of Rio would be compromised as long as yellow fever and plague continued to rage in other areas of the country, particularly in the north and northeast. Most jurists and members of the political elite found this threat quite palpable because they realized that only under special circumstances and with prior authorization could the General Directorate act outside the borders of the DF (except for maritime sanitation services).

Despite the success of the campaigns (yellow fever was wiped out in Rio) and despite Cruz's prestige, the political consensus on the constitutional limits of federal action had become so solid that it preempted any widespread action by federal sanitation agencies within the states. The division of responsibility between federal and state governments remained intact, along with the notion that the General Directorate could intervene in the states only under exceptional circumstances. Even the reforms of 1903 and 1904 were considered temporary: no long-lasting organizational structures were created, and no budgetary commitments were made since the reforms were viewed as ad hoc emergency measures that would simply equip state and municipal authorities with the tools needed for battles against specific epidemics. It was understood that once the outbreaks were under control, federal aid could be foregone.[16]

These challenges notwithstanding, the process of state building boosted coercive public power during this period. Health policy made its way firmly onto the national agenda because it directly confronted individual liberties and property rights. The laws and institutional arrangements introduced from 1902 to 1909 (when Cruz left the General Directorate) laid the basis for the public health reforms initiated in the late 1910s. For example, the number of diseases subject to compulsory reporting rose gradually from ten in 1902 to seventeen in 1914. The number of health regulations pertaining to urban real estate also rose. In addition, health authorities received greater power to inspect and oversee housing, food producers and vendors, and medical and pharmaceutical practitioners, while the number of technical and professional staff employed by health agencies also climbed. The outcome was growth in the legal and institutional apparatus and in the human resources that underpinned public health authority.[17]

However, the central government's territorial reach remained limited with regard to legislating and taking action without having to negotiate with local powers. The existence of endemic and epidemic diseases in various corners of the country continued to defy the political configuration of the constitution of 1891 and hamper the success of sanitation campaigns restricted to the DF and São Paulo. Any modification of the 1891 arrangement would depend on reorganizing intellectual and political forces to push for the expansion of the federal scope of action.

The 1910s witnessed a reversal in the process of authority building in the public health arena. States began requesting federal help in the form of technical, financial, and human resources in an attempt to stamp out the breeding grounds for yellow fever and plague vectors; federal commissions such as the Oswaldo Cruz Institute expeditions were also dispatched to survey malaria and health conditions in northern states and areas of the economic frontier in the southeast and south.[18]

In 1910, after an agreement was signed with the government of the northern state of Pará, Cruz led a mission to its capital, Belém, to combat yellow fever, a disease endemic throughout most of the north and northeast.[19] In 1913, the Amazonas state government asked federal authorities to step in to wipe out yellow fever in Manaus and on the border with Peru. This commission was headed by public health doctor Teófilo Torres, a prominent figure and future head of the General Directorate (1918–19). Torres subsequently trumpeted the success of the federal intervention, which was followed by a three-year period in which no suspected cases of the disease were detected.[20] In 1917, Torres led another Federal Sanitation Commission to fight a yellow fever epidemic in Vitória, Espírito Santo, menacingly close to the republic's capital.[21] In 1912 and 1913, some states, among them Rio Grande do Norte, Paraíba, and Rio de Janeiro, requested federal sanitary intervention to beat back outbreaks of plague.[22] And in 1919, the national government, in conjunction with a number of northeastern states, undertook an effort to eradicate the breeding grounds for yellow fever vectors.[23]

In late 1911, the Rio de Janeiro government launched a systematic campaign against hookworm via the state inspectorate of hygiene and public health. Although resources were meager and the campaign was discontinued in 1915, the campaign constituted a pioneering endeavor in Brazil. It also served as a building block for subsequent experiences, such as the 1916 establishment of rural health posts in outlying neighborhoods of the DF (where Belisário Penna had been working as a health inspector for the General Directorate since 1914) and the expansion of federal rural health services starting in 1918.[24]

In 1917 in the state of Rio de Janeiro, the International Health Board of the Rockefeller Foundation began cooperating with state and federal governments to demonstrate the value of hookworm prevention initiatives and establish general health services. The foundation had acquired experience battling hookworm in the southern United States, Caribbean, and Central America.[25] The efforts in Brazil encompassed education, professional training, and research and were soon extended to the DF and the state of São Paulo. These agreements with the International Health Board went nationwide in the 1920s, when a major yellow fever campaign was conducted in the north and northeast. A malaria campaign in the northeast followed in the late 1930s.[26] These experiments in rural health and sanitation gave the government institutional and scientific support and helped legitimize the discourse of the rural sanitation movement.[27]

The earliest and most patent signs that state and federal sanitation services were enjoying greater power emerged basically as a function of the specter of yellow fever in southeastern and southern states, cities, and ports. As the Brazilian "paradigm of territorial interdependence," yellow fever was a wellspring for the formation of social consciousness and the first federal initiatives outside the DF, originally in the form of brief emergency responses and later of longer duration. Bahia and Pernambuco, which were among the states considered the site of prime endemic breeding grounds for the disease, refused federal help or accepted it only in part, though they organized yellow fever services using their own resources. Despite later emphasis on rural health, most of these early efforts at all levels of government and by the Rockefeller Foundation and other international agencies were directed toward stamping out the disease in urban areas.[28] Throughout the First Republic, yellow fever proved an ongoing headache for Brazilian presidents and state leaders as well as for the heads of the country's sanitation services, who saw the disease as one of the bonds of reciprocal dependence that challenged federalism or at least demanded a reinterpretation of the 1891 constitution.

Speaking before Congress in 1912, President Hermes da Fonseca clearly albeit timidly declared that legislators should grant the executive effective tools to obliterate yellow fever across Brazil. The disease's elimination from the DF had practically erased the topic from presidential speeches, but Fonseca reopened the national discussion:

> Considering the tremendous benefits to be derived from eliminating yellow fever throughout the territory of our Republic, the Government has offered its assistance to the states as part of this worthwhile endeavor. Perhaps it would behoove you to arm the Federal Executive with the means of power necessary for rendering greater aid to these states so that a systematic campaign can be conducted and therewith definitively sweep from the territory of our Republic this woe that brings so much dishonor to our country. This would be an extraordinarily notable accomplishment . . . demonstrating that what was achieved in the Capital of the Federal Government can and should be achieved throughout the national territory.[29]

These initial measures by public authority, chiefly targeting epidemic or endemic onslaughts that threatened urban centers, preceded the sanitation campaign that paved the road for a new stage in building public health authority, a process based on the "rediscovery of Brazil" through rural endemic diseases. Discontinuities aside, the undertakings of the General

Directorate in the city of Rio and federal commissions in a number of states were laboratories for training personnel, adopting federal sanitary regulations, organizing local health services, showcasing the potential and successes of public medicine, and educating the public at large about hygiene. These efforts also afforded an opportunity for the various spheres of government to experiment in public health collaboration. Finally, the General Directorate and state agencies slowly but surely built up systems for gathering vital statistics, considered an imperative by analysts of the historical evolution of public health. Collecting these statistics often depended on the government's power to force physicians, hospitals, church parishes, and cemeteries to provide information.[30]

The last major change of the period was the reformulation of the General Directorate of Public Health, which came in the form of Decree 10.821 (March 18, 1914), which contained 357 articles. The new regulations modified some elements of the structure designed by Cruz early in the century and adapted certain measures to keep abreast of advances in medical knowledge and the new, improved scenario of epidemics in Rio. Some observers felt these changes diminished the agency's ability to act in certain areas. For example, responsibility for the inspection of building structures and housing was handed back to the DF, while the special health court was abolished and all judicial matters concerning public health issues were shifted to the regular court system.[31]

Few changes were made to the regime of relations between federal sanitation agencies and the states that had been in place since the inception of the republic. Many health activities remained diffused across various agencies and ministries, particularly the Ministry of Agriculture. Despite appeals by the executive and the preferences of public health doctors, the prevailing interpretation continued to be that the General Directorate should intervene at the state level only in exceptional situations—that is, in cases of "states of disaster" or when a state government requested intervention.

The 1914 reform did, however, bring some notable changes. The first was semantic: the General Directorate now bore responsibility not for rescuing state governments but for coming to the aid of the "populations of the states," relocating the object of intervention. Second, under the new regulation, all local sanitation services would be subordinated to the national agency, while states would be deprived of any decision-making power in the realm of intervention-related initiatives. Finally, since the organization of local sanitation services was considered the duty of the states, they could not allege a lack of resources when requesting federal sanitary intervention.

In fact, the central government was to be reimbursed by state treasuries if called on to control avoidable diseases that had "grown in an exaggerated fashion."[32] States that failed to live up to their obligations would be held accountable and even punished. These changes hint at the relationship between the central government and the states that blossomed in the 1920s.

The new law stiffened measures to prevent infectious diseases, including compulsory reporting, patient isolation, disinfection, and medical surveillance, thereby bolstering the power of health authority.[33] Sanitary defense measures at the ports were substantially strengthened in response both to the peril of epidemic invasions and to international pressure and agreements. The new legislation offered detailed technical and legal instructions for the establishment of nineteen health inspectorates to supervise ports, vessels, and lazarettos. Each inspectorate, now with broader duties, would manage one isolation hospital, one disinfection station, and one attached laboratory. Permanent sanitation programs against infectious disease were confined to cholera, yellow fever, and plague. The structure of health services at the ports, especially regarding the fight against yellow fever, would suffer no major changes under the reforms of the subsequent decade.[34]

The legacy of this first cycle in the formation of public health authority was a state endowed with greater coercive power. Over the first two and a half decades of the republic, the basis was laid for government action in public health and sanitation. Yet the country continued to wrestle with serious sanitation problems because these agencies had no jurisdiction other than the DF and the ports and had but limited legal and technical capacity. The focus remained on urban areas. Furthermore, the reactive approach to impending threats or the actual presence of smallpox, yellow fever, and plague remained a vice. Services were usually shut down when any initiative had attained its goal. Scant attention was paid to the pivotal concern of the political movement shaped during the course of the 1910s—that is, to rural endemic illnesses and maladies that did not present in epidemic form but were nonetheless responsible for a huge number of deaths in Brazilian cities (for example, tuberculosis, diphtheria, leprosy, and venereal disease).

Still, based on the bonds of public health interdependence, some progress was made in two directions: expansion of the government's right to use coercion, and extension of federal services into other parts of the territory, with the former proving more effective and the latter more timid. This federal government presence—or the mere intimation of its presence—then spurred the embryonic organization of public health agencies in some states and their major cities. The municipal-based model put forward in 1891 had in fact been stillborn; at most, it served only until the first decade of the twentieth century for the DF. In São Paulo, considered the vanguard in public health, services were highly centralized at the state level.[35] In short, public health authority in Brazil grew more centralized in nature, rewriting in practice the constitutional clauses that had originally sought to ascribe that authority to the municipal realm.[36]

This centralization did not translate into the unification of all health services within one state or federal agency but instead expressed itself in two ways: as an affirmation of public responsibility for health, principally in the containment of infectious diseases and in protecting the healthy, and as the gradual introduction of a network of institutions, regulations, and personnel armed with coercive prerogatives and enforcement power. This network grew during the 1920s under a new, nationwide public health organization.

In analytical and chronological terms, Brazilian social consciousness found itself engaging with and questioning this institutional and legal legacy. The possibilities and directions of public health reform over subsequent decades depended largely on this interchange of ideas and politics. As Pereira had declared, health reform was the natural solution if Brazil were a hospital but not an insane asylum. Yet the directions and substance of these reforms proved less obvious than the militants in the rural sanitation movement believed. Molding policy to the exigencies of communicable disease was no mean task; on the contrary, making nature conform to political interests would be easier.

Within a little over two decades, public health services had thus evolved away from what had been agreed upon in 1891. Brazil had begun to develop an apparatus with a centralized administration, sectoral autonomy, and the ability to implement policies and enforce laws. In other words, the political dynamics of public health reform now revolved around what was already more salient public power.

Health Reform on the National Agenda: Proposals, Crises, and Decisions

The Public Impact of the Rural Sanitation Campaign

The rural sanitation campaign that built up steam during the 1910s had a substantial impact on Brazilian society. The movement lacked any real organizational format prior to the establishment of the Pro-Sanitation League of Brazil, but after Arthur Neiva and Belisário Penna issued their report and Miguel Pereira's declaration resounded far and wide, sanitation and public health became hot topics in newspapers and medical journals, at professional forums such as the National Academy of Medicine, at schools of medicine, for the National Society of Agriculture and other interest organizations, and eventually for Congress as well. In 1918, both Penna and Monteiro Lobato released compilations of newspaper articles. Both books were designed to spread the word about the campaign for the sanitation of Brazil and in some cases even help finance it. Public health moved front and center in the national political debate, reflecting the preoccupation of certain sectors of the elite with the reigning health picture and the need to achieve consensus about politically viable solutions.

Over time emerged a network of individuals, institutions, and public agencies that shared the belief that understanding Brazil's problems required recognizing the blight of illness, particularly rural endemic diseases. This network included the National Academy of Medicine, the Oswaldo Cruz Institute, schools of medicine, the General Directorate and its services, federal sanitation agencies, state agencies, and other institutions. From the field of medicine alone, the network comprised academics, teachers, professors, researchers, and public leaders and civil servants, many of whom belonged to multiple groups. The members of the Pro-Sanitation League included politicians and other professionals, including engineers, attorneys, journalists, and members of the military, who joined the movement through state branches. All of them had some hand in disseminating the rural sanitation movement's general concepts and proposals within the institutions and organizations to which they belonged. Distinguishing professional, political, and state elites within this network is difficult, and it constituted both a mechanism for and an outcome of greater awareness of interdependence.

Daily newspapers in Rio de Janeiro, among them *O Paiz* and *Correio da Manhã*, gave rural sanitation ample coverage and became forums of debate on the topic. An examination of these papers starting in 1916 indicates that public health made the news every day, not only in articles but also in columns and texts signed by the campaign's most active members and by physicians, jurists, politicians, and others. The papers also featured news on the legislative debate over the reform and executive decisions, thereby influencing public opinion.[37]

The press helped the sanitation campaign by providing evidence of its penetration in various spheres of public life: "The patriotic outcry of alarm sounded by Miguel Pereira, Arthur Neiva, and Belisário Penna, born from the sense of responsibility that the office of medicine demands in defense of public health, has had a salutary effect. . . . Public health matters are spoken of in the halls of Congress. The press has kept the topic in the spotlight, and public opinion is being instilled with the idea launched two years ago by the initiators of this worthy campaign."[38]

Newspapers, specialized journals, and magazines had devoted space to health and sanitation since the dawn of the republic. During the days of urban reform and the campaigns led by Cruz (1903–4), public health marshaled public opinion. But once the initial excitement had died down, the topic made headlines only when an epidemic erupted. At other times, the subject engaged solely physicians and medical institutions and publications. Even the executive branch of the government had little to say about the matter from 1908 to 1918. After officials believed that yellow fever had been wiped out in the DF, presidential messages to Congress included only brief commentaries on the "satisfactory" public health conditions in the nation's capital and said nothing about the rest of the country, an attitude consonant with the checks placed on the central government by the federative order. The rural sanitation campaign and widespread dissemination of its diagnosis of Brazil won a larger audience and new interlocutors for the debate on public health conditions.

Rural health posts began to be established on the periphery of the DF, and states such as Bahia, Pernambuco, and Minas Gerais began to organize public health agencies. São Paulo enacted an unprecedented rural sanitary code in 1917. The press lauded all of these efforts, helping to validate government's role in the field of public health. The focus on rural endemic diseases followed naturally from the declaration that the *sertões* began on the edges of the city of Rio. The government's goal—as the media pounded home—should be to spread prevention services to all corners of the country: "Prevention work has thus been gaining ground and spreading throughout our capital city and is worthy of special note. It remains, however, for this work to move beyond the vast areas of the outskirts of Rio de Janeiro and extend its protective action throughout all regions of the Brazilian *sertões*."[39]

Even yellow fever, a long-standing national problem, acquired new shine in the context of the sanitation campaign. This disease epitomized the dilemma faced by those advocating and implementing public health policy in Brazil. Yellow fever was considered an avoidable ailment, science knew how to combat it, and Brazilian professionals had introduced successful prevention techniques. Furthermore, the Rockefeller Foundation was growing increasingly interested in it.

Newspapers tirelessly denounced the endemic presence of yellow fever in Bahia and other parts of the north and northeast as a constant menace to the ports of the southeast and south and the country's foreign trade. These allegations gained further clout when incorporated into the diagnosis of a diseased Brazil, and institutional solutions would have to take both the yellow fever campaign and the prevention of rural endemic diseases into account. Yellow fever always stimulated the discussion of state government responsibility in the arena of public hygiene. Concurrently, doubts were raised about the federal government's ability to fulfill its task of inspecting ports and barring infected people through the General Directorate.[40]

Proponents of public health measures stressed three general imperatives. First, the government should move beyond the outskirts of the capital and extend public policies throughout the territory. Second, the General Directorate, which was falling far short of the mark in its manifest responsibility to defend Brazilian ports from health threats, needed to be converted into an efficacious agency. By controlling the ports, the agency could keep epidemics from spreading. And third, states should assume greater responsibility for their own public health problems, maintaining or restoring the salubrity of their inhabitants and warding off any threat to the well-being of other states.

Indicative of a heightening consciousness of interdependence is the fact that public concern with the problems condemned by the rural sanitation campaign reverberated throughout the 1910s. At the same time that some Brazilians increasingly demanded stronger public authority, emphasizing the territorial scope of this power, others voiced strong opposition to the idea. Some observers feared that giving federal authorities more power would generate *empreguismo* (job handouts and political appointments) and push up other costs without boosting efficiency. As a result, no consensus arose in favor of any concrete proposal for the reform of federal services and agencies.

Proposals, Debates, and Decisions in Professional Circles

The dispute over which sphere of government should wield public health authority and which organizational model should be adopted dates to the 1891 constitution. The lack of consensus among medical and professional elites about how the February 24, 1891, enactment of the nation's charter would affect public health was evinced by Azevedo Sodré and Nina Rodrigues, distinguished physicians and professors and highly influential figures in Brazilian medical science, who engaged in a controversy published in a series of articles in medical journals during the second half of 1891. Sodré, from the state of Rio de Janeiro, criticized the appointment of

Rodrigues, from Bahia, to the post of inspector general of pub'
for the city of Rio de Janeiro and lamented the fact that the ap
not familiar with the complex reality of public health in Rio, wha.
other qualifications.[41] Rodrigues countered that the position should be oc
cupied by someone who had the best interests of the entire country, not just
the DF, at heart and that he supported "unity of action in sanitary administration," so that states would not be condemned to neglect.[42] Sodré shot
back that an inspector general residing in Rio could not work effectively to
solve problems in other states and distant municipalities. In his opinion,
centralization was useful and in fact indispensable at the Port Health Service, which would be led by the federal government, but for inland public
health, "Each State should have its own autonomous, independent hygiene
agency. . . . Moreover, each municipality should have its own hygiene agent,
with special duties."[43]

Rodrigues's long rebuttal defended the organizational centralization of
public health in the hands of the federal government and rejected Sodré's
call for state-level organization. For Rodrigues, any form of decentralization
would be more vulnerable to political pressure from groups that felt their
interests had been harmed; these local agencies had traditionally grappled
with a paucity of resources and lacked qualified personnel, who were hard
to find in most states and municipalities. If an epidemic were to strike,
Rodrigues believed, a decentralized municipally based system could not
smoothly coordinate the activities of its various components.[44]

Further, according to Rodrigues, "opportunistic exaggeration of decentralization" endangered the goal of public health: the unification of sanitation policy in federal hands. State-level organization, in the terms advocated
by Sodré, was acceptable solely as one stage in a process. However, because
of the "reckless" way autonomy had been granted, there was no guarantee
that all states and territories would actually implement hygiene measures.
Consequently, states with more robust resources could be expected to offer respectable public health services, others would have only problematic
services, and perhaps the majority would offer nothing at all.[45] Since health
and sanitation initiatives often fail to reap immediately tangible or visible
rewards, Rodrigues contended, local authorities might not fund the services. As he saw it, the task of public health doctors was therefore to lay the
groundwork for the future unification of health services and agencies.[46]

The participants in this debate not only were criticizing the newly enacted constitution but also were clearly anticipating future arguments,
criticisms, and proposals. The debate revealed a basic consensus over the

impracticability of organizing health solely at the municipal level as well as exposed the dispute over where exactly these services should be established. Sodré sketched out the arguments underpinning the defense of state-level agencies, while Rodrigues called attention to the structural problems inherent in addressing public health through the federative system adopted in 1891. Rodrigues did not live to see his opponent revise these stances drawn from the 1891 federative pact and instead present a proposal for reforming health services as federal deputy in 1918, then based on centralization at the national level, all with the backing of a good share of the medical elite.

Although doctors and politicians had presented proposals regarding public health since the early days of the republic, the public stir prompted by the rural sanitation campaign propelled these plans out of exclusively medical and scientific circles and imbued them with a markedly political content and intent. Nevertheless, professional and scientific institutions in the realm of medicine still played a major role in formulating proposals and pressuring the federal executive and legislative branches. In 1917, the National Academy of Medicine appointed a commission to draft a plan to serve as a government resource for reorganizing public health services. The commission comprised the foremost members of the medical elite: professors, leaders of institutions and public agencies, and founders and activists from the public health reform campaign.[47]

Also in 1917, the commission submitted its report to President Wenceslau Brás, who met with the group on a number of occasions. The report had a quasi-official status, since it was sent to the Chamber of Deputies as part of a message in which justice and internal affairs minister Carlos Maximiliano requested additional funding. The commission's primary conclusion was that an independent, autonomous federal technical agency would be the most advisable means of truly cleaning up the interior, given the technical nature of the undertaking, the complexities of Brazil, and the fact that the population was scattered across a huge territory and was highly infested with endemic diseases. In the commission's judgment, the answer would be a Ministry of Public Health, created by merging various existing public hygiene and assistance services and headed by a professional of recognized competence.

The commission was not oblivious to the political problems inherent in this idea, which would expand federal powers and strip the Ministry of Justice and Internal Affairs and other ministries of their existing health agencies, unifying them all into one new ministry. To preempt such criticisms, the panel suggested a temporary measure: the creation of a Higher Council of Hygiene to coordinate health and sanitation initiatives throughout the country and encourage states to wage sanitation campaigns.[48]

For the medical elites and their most powerful institution, the National Academy of Medicine, which had close ties to the political elites, the ideal solution would be administrative centralization accompanied by political, technical, and financial autonomy—that is, a health ministry. However, the commission's plan gradually introduced the body, appeasing any fears that conflicts might arise over constitutional jurisdiction in some states and therefore block any change, no matter how small. According to the Academy's president, these fears were "illusory, inconsequential, and offensive" given the critical state of the public health picture.[49]

The Academy's commission also proposed making the Higher Council of Hygiene responsible for overseeing the distribution of quinine, considered vital in fighting and treating malaria. The government would purchase the raw material abroad, process it at an official laboratory such as the Oswaldo Cruz Institute, manage sales, and distribute the drug throughout the country at cost or free to the poor.

According to one member of the Academy commission, the challenges inherent to implementing the plan lay behind Brás's allegation that because he was at the end of his term, he "could not, nor would it behoove him to, bear the onus that would come from adopting" the commission's proposal.[50] However, in a context where public opinion was increasingly troubled by health matters, and given the prestige enjoyed by commission members and the Academy, this proposal became the first step in a far-reaching dispute over public health reform. The escalation of the debate and the emergence of moderate and radical alternatives for reformulating the public health structure indicate that health had become a pervasive public concern and that the efficacy of the constitutional framework defining relations between the federal and state governments had begun to generate debate.

Even though the health ministry was still far from a reality, steps toward reform occurred for several reasons. The sanitation campaign had made a marked impact, professional organizations were presenting proposals, and the nation's president had awoken to the issue after visiting a rural health post. On May 1, 1918, two decrees substantiated these initial steps forward.[51] The first, heavily based on the National Academy of Medicine recommendations, established the Official Drug Service, through which federal officials would buy quinine and the government would manufacture pills and injections for the treatment of malaria and sell or distribute them through the Oswaldo Cruz Institute.

The second decree, the "Wenceslau Brás Administration's Golden Decree," paved the way for the creation of federal rural health services in the states, malaria and hookworm prevention posts in the DF and surrounding areas, and a yellow fever post administered by the Rockefeller Foundation.[52] Under the decree, the federal government and the state administrations of Maranhão, Minas Gerais, and Paraná signed the first cooperation agreements to combat rural endemic diseases, with the states agreeing to finance a portion of the services.[53]

Both decrees relied on funds from the Ministry of Justice's 1918 budget that had been earmarked for public emergency aid and therefore were not subject to legislative approval, decreasing the cost of negotiations with the legislative branch.[54] In a message to Congress setting ministry expenditures for 1919, Brás gave the sanitation movement his relative blessing (although he thought its diagnosis of Brazil somewhat exaggerated) by increasing layouts for incipient rural health agencies and recognizing government responsibility for the public's health: "It may well be that there are reasons to object to the spirited, vigorous protests of some of our professionals in the fields of hygiene and medicine that exaggerate the public danger. . . . Be that as it may, however, the sad truth is that our governments must take all due precautions in the sanitary defense of our people."[55]

Proposals, Debates, and Decisions in the Federal Legislature

These initial changes, which reflected an expansion of public health authority, occurred within the jurisdictional and funding constraints of the federal executive and most state governments. The executive and the public health movement aimed their calls for broad sanitary reform (with its attendant constitutional implications) at the federal legislature, which played a key role here for two reasons. First, it held the power to legislate on federal duties and compliance with the constitution, draw up federal budgets and set expenditures, and amend the constitution, among other exclusive powers granted by Article 34 of the charter. Moreover, every nationwide discussion necessarily echoed through the halls of Congress, exposing the interests, conflicts, and agreements involving the political elites represented in that body.

Second, from a more specific angle, the federal legislature was especially attuned to the question of health and sanitation because a significant number of deputies had medical degrees, and some were even practicing doctors. Around 15 percent of the members of the tenth legislature (1918–20) held such degrees, a much higher percentage than was found in European countries and the United States. Voted in as members and representatives of state oligarchies, some of these physicians cum deputies were not fans of the movement to clean up the hinterlands, and when they were, they had reservations about centralization and the creation of new agencies. Nevertheless, they were responsive to the problem and had played an important part in the legislature and on the Chamber of Deputies's Public Health Committee. They participated in the debates and decisions about the direction of public health that had become a lead item on the legislative agenda starting in 1916.[56]

My analysis of the legislative debate draws inspiration from the interpretation by Renato Lessa and what he calls the Campos Sales model, which construes the legislature as a meeting place for the representatives of state oligarchies, anointed by an electoral process heavily constrained by institutional mechanisms designed to block the entrance of dissidents or any other element that cannot be controlled by each state's reigning elite. These mechanisms endowed the Chamber of Deputies with a striking characteristic: "the political leadership of state bosses."[57] Therefore, in addition to discharging their formal legal duties, federal congressmen were expected to represent the ruling elite of their states, turning the nation's highest legislative body into a key venue for the discussion of a topic dear to the state governors—relations among the states and between the states and the central government.[58]

The diagnosis that Brazil was a diseased country caused a commotion in Congress. For some deputies, the description of a "vast hospital" simply represented a rhetorical overstatement, employed to persuade the country and authorities that living conditions had to be upgraded. Yet many legislators still thought this diagnosis might incite panic and even damage the country's image abroad, jeopardizing trade and immigration. Some congressmen objected to the emphasis on the hinterlands and sought to focus instead on urban areas. Nevertheless, no member of Congress publicly refuted the description of the country's public health situation as reported by movement militants and decried by the press. Even those who shared some reservations about the apocalyptical descriptions of rural Brazil agreed on one crucial point: the absence of public power. Said Dionysio Bentes, a deputy from Pará, "Our hinterlander suffers more from government neglect than from parasitic infections per se."[59] The political elites were divided, however, on proposals to reorganize public health services that implied greater federal power in the realm. According to Bahia deputy Raul Alves,

"Among all peoples, public health issues have always been considered local matters ... and therefore they cannot be ranked among more general issues."[60] Legislative debate erupted after Deputy Azevedo Sodré from the state of Rio de Janeiro submitted the draft law to establish the Ministry of Public Health. Twenty-seven years earlier, Sodré had opposed the creation of a such a ministry, but in 1918, the physician, member and former president of the National Academy of Medicine, professor at the Rio de Janeiro School of Medicine, and member of the Pro-Sanitation League, tried to convince the legislative representatives of the elites that the central government should assume a new, enlarged role in health and sanitation.[61] In August 1918, Sodré proposed the establishment of the health ministry and the reorganization and expansion of the duties and scope of all federal public health structures. In the arguments he used to justify his proposal, he offered an interpretation of relations between disease, society, and public authority, encapsulating them and translating them to the sphere of politics.

Sodré began by questioning the 1891 constitution, which, he maintained, had ignored the matter of sanitary defense. If the federal government were to restrict itself to maritime sanitation services and prevention measures in the DF, in accordance with the prevailing understanding of its duties, then no effective public health could exist. He also criticized the fact that health services were dispersed across a number of agencies, especially in the DF—for example, the Ministries of Justice (to which the entire structure of the General Directorate was subordinated), of Agriculture and of the Treasury (both of which had food inspection laboratories), and of Transportation and Public Works (sewers in the DF), plus the administration of the DF (responsible for issuing occupancy permits; it also had a lab). Public health problems, Sodré contended, stemmed much more from this disorganization than from any shortage of resources.[62] Still, supporters and opponents of the reform consistently agreed on one point: hospital assistance and public aid to the poor and indigent should be the duty of municipalities.

Two arguments found in the proposal to federalize health policy can be traced back to the rural sanitation movement. First, sanitation could not be a local task but had to be national because it demanded time and resources beyond the means of the states (with the exception of São Paulo). Sodré voiced a common perception—the solution to Brazil's public health problems was not complete decentralization, for which the states were financially and technically unequipped. São Paulo, which had voluntarily extended public health care within its jurisdiction, was always protective of its autonomy. Relations between it and the other states, which did little or nothing, would be critical in shaping the political dynamics of public health reform.

The second line of reasoning combined legal and medical arguments in an attempt to reinterpret the constitution in light of public health issues. Because the charter was silent on the topic, observers believed that a statutory law would suffice to redefine the responsibilities of state and federal government. Certitude about the public, national nature of health and sanitation meant the hybrid system adopted in 1891 would have to be abolished and public health services redirected so that they were indivisible. In keeping with this argument, any call for local autonomy in terms of policy was considered inapt, as the nature of the matter was eminently national.

During this debate, physicians became constitutionalists, while jurists looked to the day's medical knowledge for the foundations on which to build demands for the federal unification and centralization of health services and agencies. These allies switched their attention from Articles 5 and 34 of the constitution—the trump cards for those who defended state autonomy and the congressional prerogative to legislate on federal matters—to Article 35, which stated that Congress had the (nonexclusive) responsibility to rule on matters of a federal nature. According to some observers, this provision authorized the central government to oversee matters of hygiene, since communicable disease surpassed the borders of any one state. A number of legal specialists, among them Mário Vianna, backed up these arguments based on the implications of the relations between contagious disease and society: "Considering the nature of the service—for no one would say that the need to maintain the health of a people is a local concern, as it is a matter of national interest—and considering the possible extent of its effects, denying this authority to the federal government would perhaps be tantamount to forcing it to stand passively by as the nation is destroyed by the morbid contagion that the states of the Federation have failed to avert."[63]

Should the elites remain unconvinced that broadening the reach of federal power was not a breach of the constitution but was indeed a necessity, Sodré offered another argument, likewise derived from the sanitation campaign: the ubiquity of endemic diseases and the ever-present threat of epidemics rendered the country's public health status equal to that of a constitutionally recognized state of disaster that would keep Brazil from fulfilling its commitments under various international treaties.[64] The consequences of this state of disaster tended to be embellished so the federal government could intervene in states without having to wait for authorization, by which time intervention might be too late.

Although the judicial framework supported an increase in federal power, thereby helping the movement, Sodré's bill was moderate and realistic, because he knew that opponents would resist any insinuation of intervention in the states. Sodré argued for creating the federal Ministry of Public Health because he was convinced that public health and politics were incompatible. Everyone in the sanitation campaign saw the Ministry of Justice as an eminently political body. The proposed health ministry, in contrast, would not run the risk of seeing its resources "privatized" by interest groups not concerned with "redeeming the *sertões*." Health should be a public good proffered outside of politics, true to technical principles, even if the grievance for it had been lodged via institutionally established political channels.[65]

The ministry would bring together all hygiene services in the DF, all existing maritime and river sanitation services, and all health services handled by other ministries. Rural health and sanitation works within the states, however, would be carried out under prior agreements and through specific funding mechanisms. One of these proposed funding mechanisms established a standard of relationship between the federal government and the states that was something of a sore spot. Preference would be given to public health works in states and municipalities that could bear half the cost. Local governments that lacked these resources could enter into agreements after enacting appreciation taxes on improved land or raising property taxes and after pledging to eventually reimburse the federal government for half of its expenses. The various decrees that regulated the Rural Prophylaxis Service in 1918 and that were proposed under subsequent reform projects offered variations on this formula. One version created a rural sanitation fund that would draw from several sources: a liquor tax, a gambling tax, surplus ministry of health funds, the sale of a sanitation stamp, and earnings from government laboratories. Thus, funds for rural sanitation would always come from outside the budget for the new ministry.[66]

These mechanisms for funding the bilateral agreements to be signed by states and the central government were crucial, since they would define the potential political coalitions that would either veto or ratify the broadening of federal duties in health and sanitation. Representatives of the states that were not central to the oligarchic pact and had meager resources generally felt that the preordained division of resources and responsibilities precluded any agreement. Furthermore, this overwhelming dearth of resources prompted these representatives to take much less orthodox positions when it came to state autonomy vis-à-vis the federal government and to embrace less mainstream interpretations of constitutional provisos on the topic.

Representatives of noncentral states were quicker to adopt a more generous reading of the constitution regarding federal duties in public health and sanitation. The challenge was to convince all political blocs in Parliament to accept the price of this generosity.

Sodré's bill elicited a range of reactions in the Chamber of Deputies. Along with some shows of support came the usual criticisms: the campaign for the sanitation of Brazil was defaming the country, its diagnosis was an exaggeration, the solution was to focus neither on health nor on the hinterlands. The bill made a considerable impact in Congress, the press, and specialized periodicals.

After deliberating on the draft law, both the Finance Committee and the Public Health Committee (on which Sodré served) ruled against it, and there it died. Sodré made no bones about the problem as he saw it: everyone sympathized with his diagnosis regarding Brazil's health but rejected his proposal to improve the country's health conditions.[67]

The chair of the Public Health Committee, Deputy Teixeira Brandão of Rio de Janeiro, was a physician, a professor at the Rio de Janeiro School of Medicine, and a member of the National Academy of Medicine and was the chief architect behind rejection of Sodré's bill. Speaking before a plenary sitting in the lower house, he explained his reasons for voting against a health ministry, quoting from the committee's report: "Assigning this type of task to the federal government would invert the natural order of things and thoroughly undermine the political edifice that was built through the Republican revolution. From this perspective, we unfortunately cannot consent to the proposed reform under the terms in which it has been drafted."[68]

In short, the majority of those on the Public Health Committee believed that the sanitation of Brazil and all health services not directly related to maritime sanitary defense should remain the responsibility of states and municipalities. Furthermore, they and others, including some public health doctors, feared that unifying so many services under one roof would engender a colossal bureaucracy incapable of achieving its ascribed task. While both committees recognized the public value of the bill, they felt that it violated state autonomy and usurped some state and congressional responsibilities. This was one of the habitual arguments of the foes of centralized health. For these adversaries, the matter should be settled on the basis not of substantive arguments but rather of constitutional ones.

Sodré responded to the veto with conciliatory efforts that recognized that the reform envisioned by the public health movement had proven impossible. To answer the criticism about an oversized single body, he stressed that he was not proposing that all services be centralized—some would still be handled at the local level. With regard to state autonomy, he argued, the proposed ministry would amalgamate only those services scattered under the aegis of different authorities in the DF, while federal action within the states would be implemented "through a prior agreement" and solely in the case of rural sanitation. Further according to Sodré, the draft law guaranteed that federal intervention would occur only in those states that proved incapable of responding to the spread of communicable diseases. Finally, taking the direction suggested by the National Academy of Medicine commission, he supported the replacement of the proposed health ministry by a department of hygiene within the Ministry of Justice.[69] The legislature nevertheless remained unpersuaded by the dissemination of the diagnosis of a diseased Brazil, the support of medical bodies, and by attempts to negotiate a less radical reform.

As Brazil's legislators were debating these reforms, a worldwide epidemic of the Spanish flu began, and in the fall of 1918, it struck Brazil, hitting the cities of Rio and São Paulo particularly hard. A few months later, a suspected outbreak of yellow fever victimized states of the northeast, leaving southeastern and southern cities feeling even more insecure.

A Tragic Event and a Constant Peril: Epidemics and the Scope of Public Authority

From September to December 1918, Brazil was attacked by the twentieth century's most devastating pandemic: the Spanish influenza. The city of Rio de Janeiro ground to a halt. Congress lacked a quorum and barely functioned. Estimates suggest that more than half the population of the DF fell ill and between 12,000 and 18,000 residents died between October and November. Food and medicine were in short supply, prices skyrocketed, and public authorities proved utterly incapable of coping with the disease. Brazil had neither gravediggers nor caskets enough for the countless bodies. In the city of São Paulo, 65 percent of the population was infected, and 5,000 people died.[70]

While censored, the press still painted a terrifying picture. The epidemic laid siege to cities, without distinguishing residents by social class, occupation, or region, leading some newspapers to brand the Spanish influenza a "democratic flu."[71] The government was exposed as impotent and unprepared. The epidemic was a unique collective experience for those living in the hardest-hit urban centers, and it had a significant impact on the collective perception of relations between disease and society and on the role of public authority. Fear of the influenza's return hung on so long that the press urged postponement of the 1920 Carnival to discourage the huge crowds of people that might facilitate a new epidemic.[72] The illness even felled the country's newly elected president, Rodrigues Alves, who on March 1, 1918, won 99 percent of the vote for the office he had held more than a decade earlier. Prior to his November 15 inauguration, however, he came down with the flu, and his vice president, Delfim Moreira, from Minas Gerais, took office as interim president, adding to the instability experienced by the country in the wake of World War I.[73] Reaching high into Brazilian officialdom, the epidemic furnished tragic proof that those on both sides of the sanitary reform debate had more than enough reason to mistrust the existing public health system and forged a consensus in favor of changes in public health. The fact that the disease struck the country's elites undoubtedly heightened some parliamentarians' sympathy toward proposals to reorganize public health.[74]

During and after the epidemic, debate raged over the jurisdiction of federal agencies, and many of their heads resigned. Proponents of centralization contended that the existing public structures had demonstrated that they were incapable of solving basic health problems and that a complete overhaul was needed. Opponents, conversely, were unwilling to expand the power of an authority that had already proven itself inept. The chief accusations, arguments, and excuses voiced during parliamentary debate revolved around leader incompetence, the absence of government structures, the dearth of resources for the health sector, and negligence on the part of the government, which was slow to act or had simply resigned itself to what it had deemed inevitable.[75] Thus, the basic consensus about the sanitation service debacle did not equate to agreement on how to solve the problem.[76]

At the same time, national and international concern was growing regarding the endemic nature of yellow fever in the north and northeast, where outbreaks occurred intermittently. The specter of yellow fever exposed serious strife among the region's states over public health policy. Sodré formally requested that the Ministry of Justice provide information on the presence of yellow fever along the coast and on the measures the government had taken to combat the disease.[77] According to news reports, state officials in Bahia denied the existence of yellow fever and refused federal aid. The ministry responded by recognizing the illness's endemic presence and announcing that medical commissions would be sent to some states. On April 25, 1919, the ministry also declared the port of Salvador, Bahia, suspect and prepared to attempt to eradicate yellow fever in various northern and northeastern states. The ministry's response recognized the complex network of interdependence woven by a disease that had historically terrified the country and rendered responsibility for health an increasingly public affair: "It is correct that, pursuant to our written law, responsibility for hygiene services within the states belongs to the latter, but it is no less correct that the current yellow fever issue is such that its unique features give way to more general ones because of how it affects interstate and even international interests. Hence it is no longer purely a local matter but a matter of national interest, in regard to which it falls to the federal government to take action."[78] The fact that local and state authorities could not solve the yellow fever problem because the illness was endemic in effect rewrote the 1891 constitution. Even if federal intervention was couched as episodic, over time it developed a permanent nature. This change benefited not only the fledgling public health bureaucracy but also states that lacked the material and technical resources needed to resolve their public health problems as well as those that possessed such resources but remained under threat from the dreadful health conditions of other states.

The situation was considered so serious that physician and professor Rodrigues Lima and other deputies from Bahia, which prided itself on its medical tradition, declared that "petty superstitions about autonomy [should be] discarded" and support thrown behind federal intervention in the states when it came to health and sanitation.[79] According to Lima, federal sanitation agencies themselves were unequipped and lacked adequate funding.[80] Speaking about the tragic public health panorama in the northern state of Maranhão, his birthplace, Luís Domingues asserted that the problem was nationwide: "There is no 'Maranhão leprosy,' 'Bahian yellow fever,' 'Rio tuberculosis'—their cures interest the whole nation equally."[81]

Representatives of the country's weakest links echoed this argument, contending that the federal government should implement a policy to fight endemic diseases and epidemics, regardless of how much each state could contribute, since the poorest among them would be affected the most.[82] The regions hardest hit by endemic disease were trapped in a vicious cycle of illness and economic hardship. Their representatives believed that this could be overcome through public health initiatives, implemented and financed by the federal government.

Teófilo Torres, head of the General Directorate of Public Health, admitted that the word *intervention* (*intervenção*) had a rather strong taste not easily tolerated by the states. He suggested that they should instead use *aid* (*auxílio*) and asked the legislature to take measures so that the federal government could cooperate with the states.[83] Before the end of 1919, all states in the northeast except for Pernambuco and Piauí had requested federal aid to combat yellow fever. Bahia requested more limited assistance.[84]

The Spanish flu and constant menace of yellow fever lay bare two dimensions of the interdependence issue. The influenza tragedy of late 1918 was a unique but dramatic event that enhanced consciousness of social interdependence and individual vulnerability in the face of an epidemic. The endemic nature of yellow fever made state elites more keenly aware of territorial interdependence and the risk of continuing to leave health matters to the states.

The breakdown of public health services dictated their reform and expansion, along with a broader definition of their jurisdictional scope. Epidemics such as cholera and yellow fever have historically lent strong impetus to public health reform movements in many countries but dictate neither the substance nor the direction of such reforms.[85] Nor do such reforms invariably mean the growth of public power. In Brazil as elsewhere, the details of these reforms were defined principally through politics.[86]

Proposals, Debates, and Decisions after the Epidemic

Moreira served as interim president until July 28, 1919, when Epitácio Pessoa, who had won an April special election for the presidency, assumed office. During Moreira's tenure, federal public health services and agencies saw important changes. Decree 13.358 (April 9, 1919) consolidated the Rural Prophylaxis Service. Originally subordinated to the General Directorate under the decrees passed in 1918, the agency was now attached directly to the Ministry of Justice, and its duties were expanded. In response to a grievance lodged by representatives of the poorest states and territories, states could now receive more aid from the central government through the new agency.[87] While both the National Academy of Medicine and the Pro-Sanitation League of Brazil applauded the move to detach the agency from the General Directorate, some physicians involved with the sanitation services and some professional institutions, among them the Rio de Janeiro Society of Medicine and Surgery, deemed the change an "aberration."[88] Yet this approach was tolerated as a way to expand rural health and sanitation services without the need to wait for a general health reform.[89]

Urbano Santos, justice minister under the Moreira administration, appointed a commission whose members included medical doctors as well as others to study the organization of the Rural Prophylaxis Service.[90] Citing excerpts from the 1917 report by the National Academy commission, the new task force echoed the suggestion that the government create the Ministry of Public Health. The later commission surpassed its predecessor by insisting that the new national services would need to enjoy technical and financial autonomy to efficiently exercise their authority and that such autonomy would be impossible if public health were subordinated to the Ministry of Justice. For the second time the federal executive had ordered a study, and for the second time it had been told that a public health ministry should be instituted.

On the heels of the decree that launched the Rural Prophylaxis Service, the Pro-Sanitation League released a plan for a "national sanitary organization" that was more concrete than the general calls for stronger government heard in earlier years. The League wanted a Ministry of Hygiene and Public Health, or—since it seemed unlikely that this proposal would secure the needed political backing—a "technical and autonomous" National Department of Public Health, with "broad prerogatives and vast means for taking action nationwide."[91] The Rural Prophylaxis Service was seen as the first stage in the process of standardizing and unifying all public health services and agencies that would next move on to the formation of a national department and culminate in a ministry boasting more numerous and greater duties. This national organization would not impede states and municipalities that wanted to set up their own sanitation services, and a federal regulation should define relationships between the various agencies. Now what mattered most was no longer organizational structure but the scope thereof.

The new Brazilian president, Pessoa, was a native of Paraíba, which was not a key member within the oligarchic pact. His election brightened the outlook for demonstrations of support for public health reform and innovations to the country's health services. Pessoa's mandate was stage to the first major public health reform since 1903, ushering in a new cycle in the growth of federal government power.[92]

In September 1919, Pessoa proposed an overall restructuring of health services, drawing inspiration from the ideas that the federal government and Congress had been hearing since 1916 from the chorus formed by the media, pressure groups such as the Pro-Sanitation League, the National Academy of Medicine and its commissions, and representatives of the oligarchies from the states and territories that lacked the technical skills and financial resources to tackle public health problems themselves—including Paraíba. Pessoa was the first president to voice such explicit opinions about public health since Rodrigues Alves. Pessoa's message summarized the arguments that had been laid out since Miguel Pereira had pronounced his diagnosis and the subsequent proposals for reform and testified to their dissemination. Pessoa proclaimed that public health was central to executive branch concerns and aims.[93]

The newly inaugurated president asked Congress to authorize an overall reform of the sanitation services that would include the creation of a Ministry of Instruction and Public Health. More than a simple reorganization, Pessoa's proposal implied standardizing, unifying, and centralizing public health in light of the breakdown of the existing arrangement. However, anticipating the headaches he knew he would face, Pessoa reiterated the urgency of extending federal sanitary powers, whatever the institutional format adopted.[94]

According to the president, creating a new ministry would not burden the federal budget since it would simply unify existing agencies that had previously been spread across multiple ministries. Moreover, a health fund plus financing mechanisms like those Sodré had proposed could be put in place. Pessoa also said that expanding the jurisdiction of public health agencies would require further resources, but they could be generated in partnership with the states or through any other mechanism advanced by Congress.[95]

Pessoa summed up the challenge the country would confront were it to rely on local policies to protect itself from transmissible diseases: "Even when they have the needed technical capabilities in sanitary matters, the states, or at least the vast majority of them, do not have the financial resources commensurate with broad, efficacious measures. Furthermore, unless there is unity of scientific methods and uniformity of action countrywide, only partial, temporary solutions will be found for many of our problems. What would be the reach, for example, of local prevention measures against a contagious disease if the same disease could run free in bordering areas where transmission is easy and no such measures were to block it?"[96]

At the close of his message, the president proposed an arrangement to make the reform viable. Pessoa pointed out that some states had already realized the advantages of entering into agreements with the federal government for the "defense of their sanitary interests," and he was convinced that the leaders of other states would collaborate or at least would not oppose "a rational solution for these serious public health problems throughout the national territory."[97] The reform would have to define the relations between the central government and the states.

Monteiro de Souza of Amazonas was not alone among deputies in his reaction to the president's initiative: "The idea has won out, and thus there is no need to justify it."[98] Pessoa's presidential message became draft bill 576, which proposed the establishment of a Ministry of Instruction and Public Health. The measure's rapporteur, Rodrigues Dória, deputy for the northeast state of Sergipe and a professor at the Bahia School of Medicine, proffered an enthusiastic assessment to the Public Health Committee.[99]

Approved by the Finance Committee, the bill ran into trouble in the Public Health Committee, especially because it posited a single ministry. Teixeira Brandão voted against it because he believed that the myriad arenas involved in public health made them too complex to centralize into a single administrative department. Even the newspaper *O Paiz*, which had come out in support of the sanitation campaign, saw no logic in tying health policy to the "creation of a new bureaucratic center within the federal administrative structure."[100]

Brandão also couched his opposition in terms of respect for the constitution and declared his belief that the coercive nature of hygiene legislation meant that it would best be left inside the Ministry of Justice. In addition, he cautioned the legislature against waiving its prerogative to write law on hygiene and health. Since public health laws implied coercion along with the restriction of individual rights for the sake of the collectivity, even hygiene measures against infectious maladies should be "imposed by Congress, in the imperative form of laws, and overseen by federal authorities."[101]

Other members of the Public Health Committee feared that the reform might allow the central government to use health and sanitation policy to penetrate the strongholds that these men represented in Congress. Such views are palpable in claims that urban sanitation services did not belong in the new ministry when the primary goal was to clean up the interior. These legislators also worried about the creation of a huge bureaucratic organization, with many posts to be filled and substantial power to undertake initiatives both in cities and in the interior but without any requirement to consult with local powers or Congress.[102]

However, Brandão and several other members of the committee who were against the Pessoa-Dória draft law submitted substitute bills to reorganize and expand public health services. Brandão justified his alternate proposal by saying that a compromise was needed to protect state autonomy while expanding federal services and agencies. Rio Grande do Sul's Domingos Mascarenhas and a few other deputies attempted to ensure that no therapeutic or prevention initiatives could be imposed against the will of the people or in contradiction with their beliefs, thereby respecting the individual freedoms guaranteed by the constitution, but these efforts failed.[103] In some senses, Mascarenhas was reiterating a positivist-inspired argument common during early nineteenth-century reforms of public health legislation, but such contentions now had only limited effect. On the one hand, the state had more room to take such coercive measures; on the other, the political elites had absorbed a consciousness of public health interdependence. The pivotal question in public health policy had become not so much how to deal with the compulsory aspects of government power but how to deal with its territorial aspects.

Despite opposition to the creation of a ministry, increased bureaucracy, greater federal jurisdiction, and the loss of congressional power to legislate on health and sanitation, the public health reform had become a nationwide concern that enjoyed growing support in Congress and among the public at large.[104] A rising chorus of voices argued that the government bore responsibility for protecting the health of the people. But exactly how to do so remained contentious because of divergent ideas about how to balance the spheres of government (essentially the executive and legislative branches) and how to balance public authority against society.

The proposed alternatives to the Pessoa-Dória bill did not, however, move in the direction of a reform as envisioned by either the executive branch or by rural sanitation crusaders, in part because those fighting for the health reform and a single ministry soon realized that they should not let their preference for a particular arrangement block the restructuring of federal health services. At the same time, despite opposing the creation of an additional ministry and the inclusion of certain services and activities within it and disagreeing on the degree of autonomy from the legislature and state heads, the substitute bills shared many features with the Pessoa-Dória bill, particularly the funding of rural health and sanitation agencies. In addition, none of the alternative proposals were based on a static institutional arrangement; rather, they absorbed some of the preceding decade's institutional changes and new ways of perceiving the issue.

The deputies who rejected Sodré's and the executive's ideas for a health ministry agreed on the need to establish a new federal agency with much broader powers than the General Directorate of Public Health. They also agreed to reverse the 1914 decision to municipalize hygiene services in the DF. After receiving a green light from the Public Health Committee, a substitute bill to create a National Department of Public Health subordinated to the Ministry of Justice came up for vote on December 24, 1919. The lower house voted 112–0 in favor of the measure. Several requests for fast-track deliberation, some amendments, and a quick Senate vote followed, and the final version of the bill was approved on December 30, 1919. The law went into effect as Decree 3.987 (January 2, 1920). The nascent department heralded a new stage in the development of public health and sanitation policies in Brazil.[105]

Conclusion

The proponents of sanitation expected reform to follow as a natural consequence of the dual "discovery" that the country was one "vast hospital" and that government was missing in action. As they imagined it, the reform would unify and centralize public health, assigning it to the federal sphere and adapting relations between state and federal governments as set out in the constitution to the exigencies of the infectious nature of most of the diseases assailing the country.

An awareness of public health interdependence had penetrated the political elites, who came to recognize that the government should be responsible for a wide gamut of public health problems rather than merely epidemic-driven emergency initiatives. Nevertheless, some of those convinced that reform was needed did not welcome the solutions envisaged by medical practitioners and their institutions—that is, a Ministry of Public Health whose prime virtue would be its power to intervene in all regions of the country.

At the same time, as it became clear that no one could plead ignorance about the national public health picture (any rhetorical exaggeration aside), pressure increased in favor of government action, especially in the realm of rural sanitation. Less orthodox interpretations of the constitution surfaced, particularly a more lenient approach to Article 5, which dealt with the duties of the states and the federal government. The ensuing proposals for change either reinterpreted the constitution or sought ways to get around it, thereby avoiding a need for any outright change to the charter or legislative approbation (for example, the executive decrees that instituted the Official Quinine Service and Rural Prophylaxis Service and the decrees that permitted states and the federal government to enter into bilateral rural sanitation agreements). Though the 1891 charter remained intact on paper, it was rewritten in practice as the country responded to the troubles inherent in interdependence.

Public responsibility for health and sanitation developed over the first two and a half decades of the republic, particularly with regard to the coercive aspects of public power and with public health authority gradually extending its scope of action. In the early twentieth-century, debate centered on the limits of the state's coercive power, while between 1910 and 1920 it focused on how to counter the negative effects of interdependence in light of the prevailing constitutional interpretation, which attributed responsibility for health and sanitation to state and local governments. More radical legal interpretations and demands eventually lost force as reformers sought a national arrangement that would not imperil the federation but would permit action in states incapable of setting up their own health agencies or where such agencies would be so precarious as to preclude any effective containment of epidemic or endemic diseases. Yellow fever and the Spanish flu pandemic gave new life to this perception of mutual dependence and eased the way for a reformist coalition. The expansion of federal sanitary power entered the realm of the possible as a consequence of executive initiative and congressional action—that is, through the institution that brought together representatives of state political elites. The process culminated with the legislative branch authorizing the federal government to promote public health reform.

The reform was the product of a political agreement between stakeholders who gradually relinquished their initial dogmatic stances in the face of constitutional reinterpretations, medical knowledge, or financial concerns. The reformers eventually came to believe that the specific institutional design was irrelevant and devised proposals to establish a national department that did violate the constitution. Various proposals converged into a plan on which there were no dissenting votes. In other words, everyone—the federal executive, state legislatures and governments, the rural sanitation movement, and medical organizations—believed that the arrangement had taken their interests into account. Some participants saw this reform as merely one stage in an inevitable process of unifying and centralizing public health at the federal level; others believed that they had averted an excessive extension of the national government's intervention powers and the loss of legislative prerogatives. Various participants' original stances went through a process of political distillation that resulted in a solution acceptable to all.

Leading figures from the campaign for the sanitation of Brazil received the top posts in the new federal organization. Carlos Chagas, who had been appointed to the old General Directorate of Public Health on October 1, 1919, and had participated in negotiations within Congress, became director of the new National Department of Public Health while continuing to head the Oswaldo Cruz Institute. Belisário Penna, leader of the Pro-Sanitation

League and health delegate with the General Directorate, was named chief of the Directorate of Rural Sanitation and Prophylaxis. Raul de Almeida Magalhães, who had worked with Penna at health posts in the DF, assumed leadership of the Directorate of Inland Sanitation Services. Teófilo Torres and Plácido Barbosa, also prominent in the movement, received appointments to inspectorates within the National Department of Public Health, while others, such as Sebastião Barroso and Souza Araújo, were appointed to head state rural sanitation services. Though the new department did not perfectly fulfill the original hopes of the reformers, they believed they could put their ideas into practice as its leaders. They declared the work of the Pro-Sanitation League completed since its program had been "adopted by the nation."[106]

These debates and conflicts dated to the birth of the republic and intensified over the course of the rural sanitation campaign, and they certainly did not die out with the establishment of the National Department of Public Health. This period constituted but one stage—albeit a significant one—in the crafting of compulsory, nationwide arrangements to address the externalities of communicable diseases. The dispute over federal public health authority took a new turn in 1920, just as the central government's powers were expanded. The initial coalition behind the legislative decision to reform the public health system did not survive its implementation. The development of rural health services across the country yielded new challenges for public power.

In retrospect, the political denouement might seem unexpected, since everyone believed that they had won. Authorship of the new structure was claimed by all. But closer examination reveals a bridge between social consciousness and a coalition of interests that sustained the decision to achieve social protection via public authority.

What specific choices were possible? What decisions were made? And what evaluations underlay them? In short, how did the politics of communicable disease produce this broad coalition in support of a reform that pleased all? How were federal public health services expanded in spite of perceived allegiance to the constitution and the disinterest or even resistance of the legislative forces more concerned with the autonomy of their states? As Miguel Pereira might have asked, why wasn't Brazil to be considered a madhouse? The next two chapters turn to these questions.

CHAPTER 4

Consciousness Converges with Interests

A National Public Health Policy

The readiness with which the states of Amazonas,
Pará, Maranhão, Ceará, Rio Grande do Norte,
Paraíba, Pernambuco, Alagoas, Bahia, Espírito
Santo, Rio de Janeiro, Minas Gerais, Paraná, Santa
Catarina, and Mato Grosso entered into agreements
[under which they will] receive rural health and
sanitation services proves that the ground has been
laid for organizing a single public health agency.

—J. P. Fontenelle, 1922

José Paranhos Fontenelle, a noted physician with Brazil's public health services, took heart from the fact that the states had quickly embraced the rural health and sanitation policy implemented by the newly reformed federal agency. In fact, just two years after the country's health reform had gotten under way, the earlier arguments revolving around state autonomy, bureaucratization, inefficiency, and wastefulness no longer echoed through the halls of the federal legislature; instead, the National Department of Public Health's Directorate of Rural Sanitation and Prophylaxis (the Diretoria de Saneamento e Profilaxia Rural, or DSPR) was working in three-quarters of the states. The champions of sanitary reform saw the country as taking yet another step toward the unification and centralization of public health. How and why did this rapid turnaround transpire?

A tale by Charles Dickens begins to answer this question. Set against the backdrop of what was most likely a cholera epidemic, "Nobody's Story" depicts the relationship between a poor worker and his boss. The third protagonist is the neighboring Bigwig family, whose members speechify about the worker's living conditions but do nothing to change them. The epidemic wipes out part of the worker's family and then takes his boss's young wife and only child. Dickens does a masterful job portraying the conversation of these people in mourning. When the employee extends sympathy to the boss, he blames the employee for the tragedy: the worker's precarious living conditions and questionable morality are at fault. The worker replies that such tragedies and epidemics will always happen unless he receives the means to rise above his ignorance, wretchedness, filth, and other harmful living conditions. Until the Bigwigs finally decide to do something other than just talk, the horrific consequences of the worker's neediness will continue to affect many people in many places, even far away.

From the perspective of the poor, unschooled worker, neighbors notice a nobody like him only when the consequences of his problems impinge on them. With a menacing epidemic raging nearby, the Bigwigs are finally moved by their neighbor's arguments and decide to combat the pestilence. Dickens's tale has a sad ending: after the threat of the epidemic passes, taking fear along with it, all is forgotten, and nothing practical results. The neighboring family goes back to its endless, futile debate until another epidemic descends. Even so, Dickens's narrator tells us, the members of the Bigwig family who succumb to the disease do so believing that they had no bearing on the events. And the worker lives and dies "in the old, old, old way," like a Nobody.[1]

Written in the mid-nineteenth century in the context of one of the many epidemics that struck Europe and the United States, this tale paints a fine picture of a triangular relationship between the destitute, the social elites, and the political elites, whose ties are tightened when thrown together by pestilence. Starting in the 1800s, infectious and epidemic diseases became strong motivators for emergency policies, shows of solidarity, and public action of a more ongoing nature. The privileged realized the personal consequences of the atrocious living conditions endured by others and began calling for prevention and protection initiatives that might eliminate or at least ameliorate the circumstances that had produced these negative effects. An epidemic constituted one such extreme situation, where the more fortunate in society became aware of the unknown wretches who had nothing. However, any sentiments of solidarity fostered by the external effects of an epidemic outbreak did not, in and of themselves, guarantee public action. And even if such action were taken, it might not continue. Social consciousness might or might not spawn policies and institutions. A keen observer of the social evils of his day, Dickens captures the moment when an individual problem is transformed into a collective one. When the civic obligations of the elites coincide with their own material interests, doors are opened for public power.[2]

This shows how, why, and under what circumstances the relevant actors acquiesced to a public health reform they had long fiercely resisted—and did so with the support of the republican constitution. How did the social concerns of the political elites come to align with their private interests? The answer is that a consciousness of social interdependence combined with an awareness of opportunities to prompt Brazilian states to embrace the rural sanitation policy sponsored by the national health authority. This process, in turn, bolstered the central government's power to intervene across the country as a whole. But as chapter 3 suggests, no automatic or mechanical relation exists between consciousness and/or interests on the one hand and public policy on the other. Rather, this relation is highly mediated. How did consciousness converge with opportunity, and how did this union enable the emergence of a public health policy? This chapter explores why certain decisions proved viable and examines the content and impacts of these policies.

The decision-making units in question—that is, the states and their representatives—found themselves wrestling with a series of cooperative dilemmas, resulting in a collective awareness that public evils could not be remedied by individual solutions. The perceived costs of negative externalities fueled a discussion about reliance on exclusively local brands of protection versus the construction of a cooperative arrangement coordinated by the federal government. The latter arrangement won out because it was organized to provide all parties with potential material and political gains. The political viability of this new arrangement can be traced to agreement over the specific rules governing the distribution of benefits—that is, over the costs that the cooperating parties were willing to pay to obtain these benefits through reliance on federal public power and over how the transfer of responsibilities would be accomplished.

For everyone to agree to a public, national mode of protection, the costs of collectivization had to be perceived as lower than the costs of interdependence or lower than the benefits of state intervention. The federal rural health and sanitation policy introduced in the late 1910s and expanded in the 1920s responded to the issues of public health interdependence confronted by the Brazilian federation. One of the most vital consequences of this policy as implemented by the federal government was the creation of a public health authority and the subsequent expansion of its power. Slowly but surely this process thoroughly reshaped the context in which states had agreed to participate and reordered the relations between the federal government and the states and between state and society.

The first part of this chapter offers an interpretive model of the proposed solutions for addressing the problems and impasses of health interdependence and the conditions that had to be met before public activities could be transferred from the local to the national sphere. The second part tests the adequacy of this interpretive model through a discussion of the late 1910s reform and its short-term impacts. Continuing with the model, the third part analyzes the impacts of the reform and indicators of heightened central authority, while the fourth part probes the relations between central power and the states as a consequence of the collectivization of health nationwide. The chapter ends with a general summary of my arguments.

Central Power as a Solution to Public Health Problems

About the Inept and the Negligent; or, Peril Lurks Next Door

In 1918, the General Directorate of Public Health endorsed a policy to prevent the spread of leprosy (Hansen's disease) by isolating and when possible treating sufferers. Succinct and crystal clear, the document highlighted the huge cooperative dilemma occasioned by the pressing need to build leprosaria, or isolation hospitals for patients suffering from this disease. Every state would have to set up its own leprosarium to prevent carriers from moving around the country: if even a few state governments failed to follow through (whether out of incompetence or out of negligence), sufferers residing in those states would move to states that did have facilities, overstretching resources there. More serious, according to the General Directorate's report, "any leprosarium founded in [the DF] would immediately be sought out by lepers from all over the national territory and thus become a hostelry for the lepers of Brazil."[3]

Nearly a decade later, Clementino Fraga, a Bahian physician, professor, and politician and director of the National Department of Public Health from 1926 through 1930, reported that half of leprosy sufferers in the nation's capital came from elsewhere and were pushing up costs as well as risks to the local population. Most of the patients hailed from neighboring states that had failed to comply with the regulation prohibiting carriers from being transferred without the authorization of health officials at the final destination. Complained Fraga, "The states are constantly sending us new patients, not to mention the many who come to the capital of their own volition, although the Inspectorate [for Leprosy and Venereal Disease Prophylaxis, within the National Department of Public Health] has no resources to make them return whence they came."[4]

Leprosy presented the states with a dilemma. For centuries, the disease had stirred prejudice and misunderstanding, and nothing was known about its etiology or transmission. Moreover, no cure existed. The same problem applied to many other communicable diseases, and if even one state shirked its duty or deemed itself exempt from compliance, others would face new costs, and any cooperative arrangement would be undermined, causing damage across the board. It was also common practice to put so-called lunatics or the mentally ill, who were considered "socially contagious," on trains or ships headed toward Rio de Janeiro.[5] From the perspective of an individual state, it would be rational to refuse to collaborate and instead transfer its costs (in this case, its patients) to other states that were providing care, yielding a net benefit for the original state. But if all parties adopted this same rationale, either no public policy would be implemented, or all costs would fall to federal agencies and the nation's capital, aggravating rather than solving the problem. The suggested solution was thus to force states to design policies for leprosy care or transferring the expense and responsibility to the federal government, which was already bearing the bulk of costs in the DF.[6]

A similar issue later arose with food quality control. The food consumed in urban centers, especially the nation's capital, increasingly came from other states and municipalities, and their ability to adequately oversee production within their borders came into question. Since there was no way to guarantee efficacious surveillance everywhere, one state's product could imperil the health of another state's consumers. States could not wield oversight power beyond their borders, and not even federal officials could exercise this power without authorization except in the capital. Worse, even if states and municipalities wanted or were forced to oversee food quality within their jurisdictions, most lacked the technical ability to do so. Oversight was both a municipal duty and the responsibility of various federal agencies, including the Ministry of Agriculture, complicating efforts to coordinate operations. Sanitarians and heads of federal health services believed that Congress should unify federal oversight authority and extend it throughout the country.[7]

Such dilemmas were not exclusive to Hansen's disease or food safety issues. Yellow fever, the Brazilian paradigm of public health interdependence, reveals other facets of this complex problem. Judged crucial to Brazilian public health, the battle against yellow fever ran into hurdles because states needed to lodge formal requests before federal services could do anything about breeding grounds. In addition, some state governments systematically denied the existence of local cases and refused to cooperate. As the head of the General Directorate explained in 1918, "Ask the leaders of our states in the North of the Republic one by one, and from each you shall hear that there are no concentrations of yellow fever whatsoever in his respective territory, yet everyone will tell you that [the malady] resides in nearby states."[8]

The debate among federal legislators from the northeastern states conveys these complex dynamics more sharply. In mid-1918, when an outbreak of yellow fever occurred in Bahia, the press accused state leaders of negligence. Bahian deputies countered that federal authorities were causing Salvador undue embarrassment by labeling it a dirty or contaminated port. According to the Bahians, yellow fever was endemic to some northern states, linked by land and sea, and Bahia should not be treated as if it were the only state exporting the illness to the rest of the country. The Bahian deputies then suggested that at least one case had crept in from Sergipe, sparking protests from that state's congressional bloc. Sergipe's deputies were less protective of their state's autonomy, given the size of its troubles and the dearth of its resources, and it had no medical tradition, so they urged states and the federal government to work jointly to clean up the country's ports and wipe out yellow fever. But the Bahian representatives saw Sergipe's request for and acceptance of federal assistance as tantamount to a confession that the state was the original source of yellow fever.[9]

This perception that the inertia of some was costly to others was not merely interregional in nature, with supposedly more backward regions and states viewed as jeopardizing more developed areas and the nation's capital. Awareness of the problem was also intraregional and often was based on contrasts other than backward versus developed. Gouveia de Barros, the public health director of Pernambuco, one of the most important of the states that initiated local services in the 1910s and a longtime opponent to federal aid, pointed out, "Our state has close ties to other states in the North and South of the country by rail and sea, and when their respective governments have ignored this problem, it has left us in a constant state of alarm about the possibility—oftentimes realized—that our capital might fall prey to reinfection by yellow fever."[10]

Barros's words display a concern over irresponsible governments to the north and south that did nothing to stop the inflow and spread of yellow fever, thereby endangering their neighbors. Intraregional differences thus were seen not only as political, geographic, or economic but also—and chiefly—as differences in the degree of public responsibility toward health issues. In Barros's mind, Pernambuco was not a problem and might not need any help, but others with whom the state maintained relations were a problem and did require assistance. Any efforts by Pernambuco would be fruitless as a consequence of others' negligence.[11]

Much to the chagrin of many sanitarians, state governors or local bosses, not officials with sanitation services, invariably determined whether an epidemic outbreak was occurring. Accordingly, these authorities decided whether to act and/or ask for federal aid. If state and local authorities would not admit to the presence of a disease, they would of course do nothing to prevent its export and would not request federal assistance.[12] States grappling with diseases that doctors believed could be eliminated with enough "will and money" instead took the easy way out politically and blamed their neighbors.[13]

When communicable diseases or other public health menaces surface, a predicament arises: if everyone voluntarily enforces a leprosarium or asylum policy, for example, and trusts everyone else to do the same, one weak link in the chain undermines mutual trust and prompts others to stop enforcing the policy, burdening all parties but especially those who are dutifully investing in the success of the policy. Even if one state honors its commitment and strives to bar the ill being exported by other states, this lone enforcer can never prevent all carriers from entering its territory and taking advantage of its public policy. If individual efforts and voluntary collective arrangements alike are bound to fail, then an outside authority must either coordinate activities and exercise coercive power so all parties are forced to cooperate or intervene directly and implement the needed initiatives.

The control of yellow fever was considered vital not just because it would benefit the north and northeast but also because it would guarantee the definitive tranquillity of the rest of the country, especially the capital, which was obliged to spend enormous resources fighting the disease.[14] Each state could enact its own anti-yellow-fever and antiplague policy, or the states could do so cooperatively, with federal coordination. However, the inertia of some and negligence of others implied that certain states would be home to mosquitoes, rats, and sick people who would roam to other states, which could neither erect impermeable barriers to disease nor constitutionally force the negligent to attend to public health concerns.

Furthermore, imposing barriers and exercising public health control over people, means of transportation, and goods would have negative effects on relations between the parties involved. Hindering the free circulation of people and merchandise would spur serious conflict, much like levying an interstate tax, which was deemed unconstitutional under Article 11 of the constitution. Voluntary, cooperative endeavors of regional or national scope would be doomed to failure by clashes, mutual distrust, and breakdowns in coordination. An interstate sanitary police would be required to deal with the national character of communicable diseases.[15]

These examples underscore the dilemmas and impasses that led to the abandonment of individual solutions and the acceptance of a process that shifted activities to the government and collectivized health care nationwide as Brazil was growing ever more interdependent. Why and how did the federative units ultimately opt to participate in a cooperative arrangement and relinquish their autonomous behavior, free riding, and cost exporting?

Interpreting the Costs and Benefits of Collectivization

If we conceive of the federative body as a figuration and a structured, changeable pattern of interdependence between its units and between them and the central government, then public health problems can be addressed as important bonds of interdependence between the states, because the communicability of disease and public health conditions are externalities. Endemic diseases and epidemic outbreaks tend to spill over the borders of states where conditions are ripe for them to surface, affecting neighboring states, entire regions, and even entire countries via water, vectors, or interpersonal contact as well as via social and economic relations. Public health problems in one locale can thus have negative external effects on other locales, regardless of action or design. These are the constituent elements of interdependence between different but contiguous units within a national territory.

The mere threat of disease transmission is a social evil that no one, by definition, can escape—everyone either consumes it or bears its costs.[16] Similarly, no one can be excluded from benefiting when the problem is finally solved, whether or not he or she has helped solve it. A second feature of a public good/public evil is jointness of consumption—that is, one person's use of this good/ill does not impede others from using or enjoying it to the same extent.[17] These two features—nonexclusion and jointness of consumption—are independent attributes that can vary in degree and that, in different combinations, produce different types of public goods.[18]

In the examples cited here, the most striking feature of a communicable disease is its nonexclusive nature, which can tempt actors to engage in non-cooperative behavior.[19] Jointness of consumption, conversely, can manifest itself to a greater or lesser degree depending on the type of public health matter in question. Vector control (e.g., of mice and mosquitoes) often exemplifies the combination of jointness of consumption and nonexclusion, since an individual has little choice about whether to consume or use this public good.[20] Public health, which combines these two attributes, is usually considered a public good (especially as it affords protection against communicable disease through prevention measures), and it can in large part be provided only by the state, since organizing and funding mass prevention programs on a purely voluntary basis is extremely challenging.[21]

Nonexcludability has a direct bearing on the dilemmas of collective action in the provision of public goods or protection from public evils: when consumers of public evils know they cannot be excluded from the consumption of public solutions or goods, they tend to steer away from voluntarily collaborating in collective arrangements aimed at crafting these solutions and goods. When an individual relies on this approach to diminish costs and maximize benefits, he or she is a free rider. While this behavior is rational, it also greatly compromises the success or efficacy of producing a public good under a cooperative, collective arrangement—for example, organizing and funding a voluntary prevention program.[22] Coercion and side benefits are used to discourage free riding and encourage the parties to the collective problem to buy into the process.[23] The state becomes the option for administrating the negative effects of social interdependence and for solving the problems of collective action, both from the individualist perspective (which views the state as a necessary and tolerable evil that needs to be controlled) and from a historical-structural perspective (which sees the state as an organized actor with distinct attributes). The constitution of public power emerges as the most efficacious solution for coping with these ills and producing collective goods because it affords the elites a way to protect themselves and their economic interests from a distressing situation that has become collective. At the same time, it provides incentives or opportunities for gaining advantages from the regulatory moves of public authority.[24]

These arguments are grounded on a conception where the individual is the unit that decides and makes choices within the framework of the market. In this analysis, the states of the Brazilian federation are these units, following Renato Lessa's Campos Sales model. According to Lessa, under the First Republic, state bosses were recognized as holding monopolies in the representation of their states before the federal executive and legislative branches, and these men had mechanisms for controlling their state's congressional representatives to forestall dissension and its attendant headaches. Interactions among the states and between states and the federal executive and legislative branches transpired through an extraconstitutional "oligarchical condominium" made up of state bosses.[25] With this interpretation in mind, we can view each state as a calculating individual who took part in decisions about the advisability of transforming an activity that was originally his responsibility into a voluntary or compulsory collective activity, much as the market operates in the original formulation of this model. Analytically, ground zero in this process is the federative order established in 1891, based on the autonomy of each of the decision-making units. From this standpoint, there are three hypothetical ways of administrating the negative effects of public health interdependence:

1. A given unit takes individual action to solve its own public health problems and defend itself against the external effects imposed by others. This enterprise is independent from any similar action on the part of others and from any cooperative or coordinated arrangement, although the assumption is that other units will do the same. In other words, each state internalizes the costs of defending against a social evil and producing a good for the people residing within the scope of its territorial authority. This assumes that the units enjoy autonomy from each other.

2. Every state in the federation takes individual action, but they do so simultaneously and in a coordinated fashion in hopes of solving or remedying the effects of their relations of reciprocal dependence. Each unit is responsible for administrating and solving its own public health problems, preventing these problems from reaching other states, and repelling problems originating inside other borders. This solution requires commitment and cooperation between all parties and might also include agreement with a more general normalizing mechanism that regulates relations between the states. This is a fundamentally voluntary arrangement.

3. The administration of public health interdependence is transferred to a supralocal body capable of taking coercive action against any and all parties through the enactment and implementation of compulsory public policies. Under this option, the administration and regulation of both the real and perceived costs inflicted by health conditions in some units are shifted to the federal government, an outside authority

that uniquely combines three expedient attributes: coercive power, territorial reach, and territorial centrality.

In analytical terms, these arrangements for providing a collectivity with a health protection policy are alternative ways of dealing with the problems of collective action that are encountered when producing a collective good or defending against a collective evil. The history of the public nature of health policy is the history of the discovery of the escalating inefficacy of alternatives 1 and 2. Modern society has increasingly limited the autonomy of its parties because it is impossible to internalize all the costs of producing a public good and defending against externalities. Furthermore, there is no way of guaranteeing that all parties to a voluntary cooperative arrangement will keep their part of the bargain over time. Augmenting the duties of supralocal public power is thus perceived as the most efficacious way of coping with the external effects of deprivation, given the predicaments of collective action.

These three alternatives can be considered chronological stages in the emergence of nationwide public health policies because elites' historical solutions to problems stemming from the exponential growth of social interdependence have followed the sequence 1-2-3. The fact that this sequence has repeated itself in different national experiences does not necessarily imply that all worldwide institutional arrangements have been similar or that differing arrangements cannot coexist until one of them gains firm hegemony. Moreover, each stage in the sequence is compatible with the operations of nongovernmental institutions and supranational bodies, which are resources available to the elites.

From the mid-nineteenth through early twentieth centuries, this sequence was the most common path followed by countries that introduced welfare policies. Wherever government-supplied social protection emerged as a response to generalized interdependence, it did so because two simultaneous challenges surfaced: the need to bar or to regulate the imposition of negative externalities, and the need to overcome the quandaries of collective action by establishing supralocal, collective, and mandatory public policies. Industrialized nations tended toward stage 3 after passing from individual, local solutions to voluntary collective arrangements. Given that producing public goods and protecting against public evils tends to encourage free riders and that the negligent and the inept trigger negative externalities, the creation of public power, whether local or national, has been seen as the most efficacious solution, precisely because of enforcement power. Further, solution 3 is associated with territorial centrality, a distinguishing feature of the nation-state.[26]

The passage from one stage of this sequence to another depends on social consciousness as well as on the opportunities derived from collectivizing a good and getting the state to tender it. In other words, the process of collectivization is made possible when a consciousness of interdependence converges with an awareness of opportunities by the units within a federation. When the actors opt for a state solution, it means the sum of the overall benefits to be derived from public health policies plus the specific benefits of the government's collective regulatory action have come to be regarded as positive.

But an awareness of externalities and incentives does not explain why an activity gets shifted to the public sector. First, as Santos has pointed out, it is rational for an individual to pay for the production of a public good, even if doing so benefits free riders, as long as the cost of not producing that good—and thus generating a social evil—is steeper than the cost of producing it.[27] Second, we must consider the hypothesis that some decision-making units might prefer to internalize external costs based on our understanding that externalities are neither a necessary nor a sufficient condition for collectivizing an activity.[28] Sequence 1–2–3—or to use the language of J. M. Buchanan and G. Tullock, shifting an activity from the individual to the voluntary contractual sphere and from there to the public, collective sphere—depends on how each decision-making unit evaluates the external costs, the costs incurred to secure agreement about this transfer, and the expected costs of any adverse decisions by the collective body.[29] Imposition of the last cost might alter the fundamental rights of the decision-making units—in the case of Brazil, curtailing the states' constitutional autonomy.

For a decision-making unit to authorize the transfer of an activity to the central government, either the external costs or the expected benefits must be greater than the perceived cost of government action. Key to this calculus are the rules under which the activity is transferred, since these rules will determine both the decision-making costs and the costs of organizing collective action, which will be borne by participants. It would be rational to choose a set of rules that minimize both the expected costs of participation (and bargaining) and the expected costs of any adverse public decisions.[30]

My analysis posits the "oligarchical condominium" as a mechanism that decreases these bargaining costs or transaction costs and sheds brighter light on the assessments of external costs, adverse decisions, and the formula for organizing collectivization.[31] The 1–2–3 path thus requires each member of the condominium to assess the rationality of migrating from one level and form of government (local and decentralized) to a higher level (state or federal and more centralized).[32]

The federative model of 1891 adopted principles that gave states and municipalities primacy in matters of health and sanitation while leaving the federal government in charge of the sanitary defense of ports and later public hygiene in the DF. The charter's initial design was modified over time as forms of mutual dependence among the parties became apparent, as did the unviability of enforcing individual solutions—that is, as social consciousness took shape. These modifications presented a practical challenge to the initial arrangement.

In this exploration of the emergence of federal, nationwide arrangements in Brazil, we can consider the constitutional framework of 1891 as stage 1. On the one hand, responsibility for hygiene and sanitation fell to states and municipalities; on the other, the federal government was responsible for sea and river ports and had the prerogative of intervening in cases of public health disaster. The first stage thus offered mechanisms for managing interstate relations, which are hard to administrate in cooperative, coordinated fashion.

In light of the problems of interdependence, the obstacle to continued reliance on the first arrangement proved to be the recognized technical and financial frailty of most states and municipalities, generally accustomed to solving their problems through inertia or free riding. But the belief that the costs of losing autonomy through public health intervention would exceed external costs weighed in favor of the status quo, an arrangement that turned everyone into a potential producer and consumer of public evils. A change in the relative calculus of a unit's external costs versus the costs of shifting activities to the state could thus allow a transition to suprastate forms of protection, though the speed of this transition could vary from state to state.

The central government expanded its presence over the opening two decades of the twentieth century, first developing its coercive dimension and then its territoriality. One of the earliest significant advances came between 1900 and 1910, when responsibility for hygiene in the DF was transferred to the federal government with the goal of cleaning up and defending the capital of the republic and fulcrum of political power, whose public health problems were affecting the rest of the country and even foreign relations. Central power continued to make further inroads through federal commissions to fight yellow fever and through the first bilateral agreements between the federal government and the states in the area of rural health and sanitation programs. The federal government claimed responsibility for combating epidemics of yellow fever and bubonic plague in various parts of the country using its own resources—that is, it extended its ability to respond to potentially suprastate or national events, since mosquitoes and mice do not respect borders.

Concomitantly, starting in the mid-1910s, a number of states slowly began to embrace the diagnosis of a diseased Brazil. Thanks to the country's sanitation campaign, the elites increasingly perceived communicable diseases as a bond of interdependence, and this perception played a vital role in reshaping their social consciousness and calculation of the price of this social interdependence. Minas Gerais, Pernambuco, Bahia, Rio de Janeiro, and some other, noncentral states such as Paraná enacted sanitary codes and other pertinent laws and implemented public health and rural sanitation policies, either on their own or in conjunction with the federal government and the Rockefeller Foundation's International Health Board. In other words, some states began to regard the cost of losing autonomy by choosing to rely on the federal government as outweighed by the benefits of receiving technical and financial resources and decreasing externalities.

In São Paulo alone, an individual solution for the problems of collective action prevailed from 1889 to 1930. This alternative took shape during the First Republic as the state set about structuring a substantial network of sanitation services in an effort to internalize external costs and protect state autonomy from federal interference. São Paulo was virtually the only state to formulate a public health strategy and implement permanent policies. The health conditions of its population and territory improved, and the negative impacts on other units decreased, which meant that São Paulo picked up the tab for a collective benefit. The state confronted two challenges: how to sustain its autonomous option despite the heavy external costs imposed by free riding, the inept, and careless neighbors (costs that could not be internalized), and how to minimize the costs of reliance on the federal government.

We can now answer four questions:

1. How was it possible to guarantee that everyone would fulfill their public health responsibilities and not force costs on others? In other words, how could the inept be helped, free riders eliminated, and the negligent dealt with?
2. How could the potential negative effects of interdependence be administrated and everyone protected from a social evil given the failure of voluntary individual or collective arrangements?

3. What were the perceived benefits and costs that explained the calculus behind the decision to nationalize health, and what were the consequences of the institutional design that derived from this decision?

4. How could a party to the 1891 pact collaborate with a compulsory collective arrangement that would reduce external costs without bearing the onus of statism-related costs? In other words, how could a state cooperate with collectivization while safeguarding its political autonomy?

The first two questions were answered by boosting the intervention power of central authority—that is, of the institution whose distinguishing attributes combined coercive action, territorial reach, and territorial centrality. When the nonexclusion clause, the external effects of disease transmission, and the inefficacy of voluntary, individual solutions turned health into a public matter, the nation-state came to the fore as the body that possessed the power to implement health policy nationwide. The answer to the third question, which also applies to the other questions, lies in the incentives and rules that underpinned the emergence of a nationwide policy capable of responding to the wide-ranging external costs of disease and the hardships of managing them. The mechanisms under which the states agreed to shift public health to the federal realm were fundamental, because they kept the process from being perceived as deleterious to the states' interests and did not occasion any costly constitutional changes. The answer to the fourth question was the crafting of a mechanism that permitted the continuation of an autonomous solution, like São Paulo's, that could coexist with a nationwide collective arrangement for all the other states.

Costs, Opportunities, and Rules:
Rural Sanitation as a Nationwide Policy

Benefits, Rules, and Costs of Federal
Provision of Public Health

Once the parties were fully cognizant of the external costs of public health interactions between the states and the dilemmas of cooperation—that is, once an awareness of interdependence had become entrenched—the key issue was weighing the perceived costs and benefits of transferring to federal power part or all of the sanitation and public health tasks originally assigned to states and municipalities. The shift from the status quo of 1891 to a national organization that would draw up and coordinate and/or execute policy countrywide was implicit in the mechanisms of the 1918 and 1919 decrees that established and regulated federal rural health and sanitation initiatives (Decrees 13.000 and 13.001 [May 1, 1918] and Decree 13.538 [April 9, 1919]).[33] The substance of these decrees was cemented and broadened in 1920 with the creation of the National Department of Public Health through Decree 3.987. The decrees themselves shed light on the benefits and costs of relying on the federal government and the rules that governed participation in the public arrangement.

Rural health and sanitation initiatives lend themselves particularly well to an exploration of the model laid out in the first part of this chapter because they are not emergency responses as are initiatives to control epidemics, which, given their immediate, visible, nationwide impact, are readily seen as a federal responsibility. The speed with which the states entered into agreements with the federal agency offers evidence that these states saw allowing federal health authority to operate within their borders as not only advantageous but desirable.

As mentioned in chapter 3, the Rural Prophylaxis Service, which had opened its doors in 1918 under Decree 13.001, was expanded and restructured in 1919 under Decree 13.538, though it maintained its autonomy vis-à-vis the General Directorate. While the battle against endemic diseases and epidemics in the DF and territory of Acre remained in federal hands, Decree 13.358 altered relations between the central government and states. In introducing the new law, Justice Minister Urbano Santos described the Rural Prophylaxis Service as the way to amplify public hygiene services in an efficacious and constitutionally sound manner but did not dispute the predominant discourse in Congress, which remained reluctant to set up a health ministry or any other agency that would be empowered to intervene in the states.[34]

To respect the constitution and take into account the urgent need for rural public health policies, the 1919 decree introduced agreements between the central authority and the states. A similar mechanism, which had first been used in the 1910s during the federal yellow fever campaigns, had been mentioned in Decree 13.001. In a way, the proposed agreements would fall under the constitutional clause that authorized federal intervention at the local level in cases of disaster at the request of interested parties. Above all, the agreements would be voluntary for states and would pull in resources from both parties.

The priority targets under these agreements would be rural endemic diseases (malaria, hookworm, and Chagas's disease), although other endemic or epidemic diseases could be included as well. A special leprosy agency was to be opened, pursuant to specific rules, but "leper colonies" would be established within the states to keep sufferers from circulating around the country.[35] This represented a massive expansion of duties, given that under the 1918 decrees, any programs involving illnesses other than the three endemic diseases were relegated to a secondary level. However, some of the federal services that had targeted rural endemic diseases had already incorporated further duties, such as smallpox vaccination campaigns, while some also offered emergency aid to state agencies when the Spanish flu pandemic hit in late 1918.[36]

The idea of these bilateral agreements between the federal government and states seemed so ripe with potential that one head of the General Directorate soon asked the legislature to extend the mechanisms to enable the waging of a nationwide campaign against yellow fever. He also wanted the federal government to bear all costs, since a number of states were nearly destitute and federal funding constituted the only way to wipe out the disease.[37]

Under Decree 13.538, the terms of the agreements permitted distinct divisions of responsibilities between the two parties. States that set up their own rural health agencies and took charge of them would be obliged to cover two-thirds of total costs, with the remainder falling to federal coffers. But if a state wanted the federal government to organize and carry out the services, the costs would be shared equally. The decree also permitted states to enter into agreements not with the central government but with the Rockefeller Foundation to organize and implement health agencies mandated to target hookworm and malaria and, as possible, other rural endemic diseases. If the state kicked in at least half the costs, it could then ask the federal government to cover another quarter of expenses. Furthermore, federal authorities would continue the work at their laboratories, which made prophylactic drugs such as quinine, and would cover the costs of regional hospitals that cared for and isolated the ill in any state that had established rural health and sanitation agencies.[38]

The presence of federal power also provided other benefits. After personnel had been trained, operational protocols routinized, and government leaders, local bosses, and the public at large educated in public health matters, the state could establish its own health services. After the agreements had run their course and the initial rewards reaped, the federal government would pull out, leaving health initiatives up to the local authorities. From this perspective, which both parties shared, reliance on the federal government would be merely temporary and would serve as a tool for instituting authority within the sphere of the individual states. Similar outcomes were expected under the much more restricted agreements with the Rockefeller Foundation.

The three modalities of agreements were designed to afford states the benefits of receiving federal health services while formally preserving their autonomy. This remedy responded to the tremendous technical and financial hurdles most states would encounter if they tried to combat epidemics and rural endemic diseases without imposing costs on other states. This solution meant that public health policies would be enacted in conjunction with the federal government, benefiting the states while relieving them of some of the costs and responsibilities. The solution also implied tacit recognition of the ineptitude of most states and the infeasibility of a purely autonomous solution. When a state signed a bilateral agreement, it was guaranteeing the federal funding of at least one-third of the state's annual budget for health services, along with an influx of technical, scientific, and organizational resources. Even a more limited agreement with the Rockefeller Foundation could secure a federal contribution of 25 percent of total forecast expenditures. The International Health Board constituted yet another resource available to the states and to the federal government (whatever the foundation's motivations).[39]

Because this formula was grounded on voluntary adherence, the negotiation costs were much lower than they would have been under a more centralizing, interventionist alternative. This approach also saved negotiators from incurring an even bigger cost—that is, the rewriting of the 1891 charter. The 1891 arrangement was modified in 1919 through a new federal decree and approved and broadened late in the year, when Congress voted to establish the National Department of Public Health. A state could therefore choose to address rural endemic diseases and other public health problems by entering into agreements that brought the benefits of federal health authority along with an assortment of other resources. The greater the transfer of state responsibilities to federal agencies (or the less the state's responsibility), the greater the benefits the state would enjoy. This formula encouraged states to voluntarily transfer their responsibilities.

States quickly began such transfers. Paraná, for example, had been setting up its own services since 1916, yet it asked federal officials for rural health assistance on May 1, 1918, just one week after President Wenceslau Brás signed the first two decrees. According to the head of the Federal Sanitation Commission, who was appointed to implement the agreement, Paraná assigned direction of the services to the federal government "so as to enjoy the advantages stipulated" in the decree.[40] Minas Gerais and Maranhão followed suit for the same reasons, also before the close of 1918.

This model of bilateral agreements could be presented as the best possible formula as far as the states were concerned—federal resources for public health policies plus state autonomy—but nevertheless forged power in the federal sphere. First, whatever the modality of the agreement, the federal executive would appoint the state's director of rural health and sanitation, who would be charged with organizing the agency.[41] This individual had to be from the staff of either the General Directorate or the Oswaldo Cruz Institute—in other words, he had to work directly for the federal government.[42] In addition, after entering an agreement, a state would have to decide how much to allocate for the initial year of work and then make this amount available to the federal executive. Once this request had been approved, the Ministry of Justice would ensure that the appropriate state and federal funds were credited to state tax coffers, where they would be available to the agency's director, who would issue instructions for organizing the agency and its staff.[43] Thus, whatever the type of agreement, the central government would control the work to be done as well as the funds disbursed by the state. The legislation therefore promoted a transfer of financial and political resources to federal agencies.

The administrative regulations issued for rural health services provide further information regarding the extent of the power held by the federal authority. The federal government was responsible for issuing general instructions and prescribing administrative measures and prevention methods nationwide (and these instructions were compulsory in the case of the DF and territory of Acre). Since compliance with these instructions represented a precondition for federal aid, the instructions were in effect mandatory for any state interested in signing an agreement.[44] State parties to the agreements also had to create a rural sanitary code that included mandatory measures such as the building of latrines to help prevent hookworm. Further, the Ministry of Justice was empowered to oversee these services throughout Brazil.[45] Federal rural health services were thus the first step in a nationwide process of standardizing federal public health action, boosting the central state's coercive ability and expanding the space where it could wield this power.

Once again, Paraná exemplifies the process. Within two years of adopting these agreements, it had tailored all of its legislation and services to meet federal requirements. By early 1919 it had opened two annual lines of credit at one hundred contos de réis each (the same amount the federal government was required to contribute) and created four rural health posts along with a central post in the state capital. Paraná also entered into a contract with the International Health Board to survey the incidence of verminosis among the rural population and to provide treatment.[46]

The fact that much of the regulatory operationalization of rural health services in Paraná was now defined under administrative directives issued by the Ministry of Justice illustrates the cost of the federal presence. The June 5, 1919, ministerial directive that implemented services in Paraná pursuant to Article 5 of Decree 13.538 clearly signals that power would be concentrated in the hands of the federally appointed chief of service, who would be accountable solely to federal officials. Under his leadership, the rural agency could relocate health posts, propose the establishment and location of hospitals, oversee the marketing of quinine, define eligibility for free receipt of the drug, enter into agreements with planters and rural workers about services to be conducted on their property, require the state to take necessary measures, and control staff, payroll, and accounts, among other powers.[47] Fines for noncompliance with Paraná's rural sanitary regulations could be levied by either the federal or state authority; money from fines, however, would revert to the Rural Prophylaxis Service.[48] Even though the earliest agreements varied from state to state, the immediate costs of reliance on the central government were quite obvious.[49]

The legislation drastically changed relations between local and central powers and thus constituted a crucial stage in the formation of a national public health policy. Because the agreements were voluntary, they did not incur any costs for altering the status quo, yet they enabled the tackling of the public health problems of the states that produced externalities but could not afford to finance their own well-being or protect themselves from the public evils of other states. And the most immediate outcome was the growth of federal services in the states.

The voluntary acceptance of these legal provisions meant the states were willing to tolerate the costs of allocating public health action to the central government—that is, willing to lose their autonomy—given the attendant benefits of rural health and sanitation and the costs of communicable diseases. These new legal mechanisms accelerated the concentration of power in the federal sphere, substantially enhancing the central government's ability to regulate and intervene in matters of health and sanitation, which also affected various other realms of social and economic life. At the moment the decision-making units transferred their responsibilities, they had no way of calculating these long-term consequences.

Public Health Reform: Benefits Come with a Price Tag

The debate over establishing a Ministry of Public Health and reformulating Brazil's sanitation services revealed the challenges encountered in centralizing and unifying public health in federal hands. For some participants in the debate and subsequent decision making, the establishment of the National Department of Public Health represented the defeat of a more centralizing project; for others, it was a compromise between two extremes; and for a third group, it was merely one stage in what they believed to be inevitable sanitary reform.

More important than the institutional label are the substance and direction of the changes that the federal executive and some states began to implement and that the federal legislature incorporated, broadened, and approved for 1920. This round of changes expanded the reform coalition by increasing the benefits of statism relative to its more visible costs—which in actuality differed little from the costs implied under the 1919 decree—and by decreasing bargaining costs.

In August 1918, José Barreto, a deputy from Maranhão, observed that the agreements offered by the Brás administration excluded states that could not raise the obligatory matching funds and thus prevented them from receiving federal aid. According to Barreto, states that already possessed the resources benefited, while "smaller States . . . ravaged by endemic diseases but with paltry budgets that might lack the resources needed to make this contribution[,] would not be rescued by the federal government."[50]

Barreto suggested that work to combat rural endemic diseases be entrusted solely to the federal government, with no financial or administrative contribution asked of the states. Recognizing that the federal treasury had its own resource limitations, he also argued that the services should give preference to the regions hardest hit by endemic disease. In other words, rather than favoring well-off states, Barreto wanted support to go to those that suffered most from these maladies. He submitted a bill to Congress under which the Rural Prophylaxis Service would take care of major rural endemic diseases in the states, with the federal government covering all material and staffing expenditures. Furthermore, the bill proposed that these expenses would be funded by an "insignificant" 10 percent surcharge on alcohol, tobacco, perfume, imported wine, playing cards, and walking canes.[51] The states would in effect match the benefits received from the central government by relinquishing their right to engage in local rural sanitation and related matters. This provision did not appear to present a problem for the majority of states, which lacked the resources to address their grave public health scenarios. Although Barreto's proposal died, the idea of prioritizing the regions hardest hit by endemic diseases was incorporated into the reform of federal services in 1920.

Barreto's plan reflected the wishes of the weakest links in the federation, which wanted a reform that would move toward augmenting central government responsibility. For example, when yellow fever attacked states in the north and northeast in 1919, the region cried out for help: Maranhão, Ceará, Rio Grande do Norte, Paraíba, Alagoas, and Sergipe requested federal aid to fight the disease, and commissions led by federal health inspectors were dispatched to those states. This approach followed the example set in Espírito Santo in 1917 and constituted the first broader endeavor conducted under the control of the national agency. Only the region's two most important states refrained from participation: Pernambuco simply did not ask for assistance, while Bahia, whose public health situation was considered the most serious in the country, had its own service. Under these circumstances, any federal personnel or material sent to Bahia would have been subordinated to the state.[52] Like no other ailment, yellow fever underscored the nonspecific, national character of communicable disease and its effects on interstate and international relations, and the disease thus reinforced and validated the federal government's role in the eyes of those who lacked the resources to aspire to autonomy.[53]

The decrees that founded and implemented the National Department of Public Health and the proposals that preceded it leave no doubt about what was at stake for both state representatives and the federal executive. Everyone involved wanted to relieve states as much as possible of the rural sanitation duties stipulated under the 1918 and 1919 decrees.

The new legislation gave preference to rural health and sanitation work in states or municipalities that could bear at least 50 percent of the financial burden. If a local government could not raise the money, federal services would be available only if the state enacted an appreciation tax on improved land or a property tax surcharge and pledged to reimburse the central government later for half of its outlays.[54] The 1920 decrees thus superseded the earlier, hardly attractive option that had states covering 75 percent of outlays and the federal government, only 25 percent. In practice, the revamped laws meant that any state or municipality was eligible for federal resources without disbursing any matching funds up front. All a state had to do was promise to reimburse federal coffers in the future.

Included in a number of proposals, a special fund to finance sanitation works made its way into this public health service reform. In the reform's final rendition, money for the fund would be drawn from a tax on alcohol, sale of a sanitation stamp, earnings from federal laboratories and research institutes, outstanding balances from various budgets of the Ministry of Justice, and a 15 percent tax on gambling returns.[55] Under mechanisms for funding and operating rural health services, responsibility was transferred to the federal authority and the load lightened for the states. According to the decrees of 1918 and 1919, all agreements had required states to come up with some portion of the resources, but this prerequisite became merely rhetorical following the department's establishment. In practice, all states could receive federal resources for sanitation works by pledging to reimburse the government for half of the expenses. In this way, rural health and sanitation became the department's purview through its newly formed DSPR.

Between 1919 and 1921, in response to independent executive initiative, the legislative branch stretched the scope of rural sanitation initiatives undertaken by federal authorities within the states through a process of regulation and organization. These changes fell under the broader health policies implemented over the 1920s. The contracting parties expected that the federal authority would withdraw after sanitation goals had been met and related works and/or agreements completed, leaving existing state and municipal health authorities to continue their operations. However, the effort to prevent rural endemic diseases required the central government to stay longer and maintain a more well-organized presence in the states because prevention work yielded fewer immediate results than epidemic control. In addition, because work was aimed primarily at rural areas and regions of economic expansion, it was also a more delicate matter politically. Yet at the same time, as the representatives of the central government worked to treat and prevent disease, they of course interacted on a daily basis with the rural population in the interior, state and local governments and their representatives, and local bosses. Public power consequently moved into territories where disease had been diagnosed as a product of the absence of that power.

By sidestepping questions of a constitutional nature and thereby lowering bargaining costs, this approach enabled the federal government to offer financial, organizational, human, technical, and scientific resources, along with incentives for taking advantage of those resources, to those states that wanted to ask for help to cope with the costs inflicted by public health problems. Most states judged the tangible price of losing autonomy by tasking the federal government with these activities to be lower than the price of maintaining this work strictly within the state sphere as well as lower than the benefits envisioned under the agreements. The voluntary nature of the arrangement won the endorsement of those who felt that the cost of a federal presence within their territory was high but nevertheless agreed to that presence in other territories. And for those states that suffered from such monumental public health problems that they could do little on their own, the word *voluntary* really meant *mandatory*.

While the sanitation movement ardently hoped that public health policy would simply adjust itself to the nature of communicable diseases, the politics of these diseases became the object of a bargaining process involving individual choices and collective compromises that reflected one possible pathway to the collectivization of health. This path was blazed through political constraints and economic restrictions. In the context of these calculi, rules, and contingent choices, it was possible to forge a broad coalition and thereby clear the way for the reform of federal services and agencies, ushering in a stage of institutionalization and nationwide collectivization of health and sanitation policies.

Public Health Reform in Motion

Brazil's elites accepted the reform because they realized that no other feasible solution existed for public evils or growing negative externalities and their consequences. For the states, which had virtually no health services until the close of the 1910s, the incentives proffered by the new federal initiatives and the expected benefits well outweighed the expected costs in autonomy.

Congress had authorized the executive branch to implement and organize the new department, which it did in the form of a 1,195-article decree that greatly expanded federal duties (Decree 14.354, July 15, 1920).[56] The central government broadened the original limitations and conditions with the concurrence of the interested parties, which now saw more bonus than onus in expanded federal services, and effectively redefined the boundaries of federal power. The decisions made starting in 1920 had a number of immediate consequences.[57]

States Join and the Federal Government
Acquires New Duties

The dynamics of state participation in rural sanitation agreements illustrate both the success of the arrangement and its somewhat less than voluntary nature. Between the 1918 decrees and the 1920 founding of the National Department of Public Health, Paraná, Minas Gerais, and Maranhão as well as the DF signed rural sanitation agreements. In November 1922, at the end of his mandate, Epitácio Pessoa reported to Congress that the DSPR was active in fifteen states. By 1924, the second year of Arthur Bernardes's administration, the figure had risen to seventeen. The only states that had not signed any agreements with the federal government were Goiás, São Paulo, and far southern Rio Grande do Sul.[58]

As the agency responsible for enforcing federal policies nationwide and with independence from the contracting states, the DSPR saw its duties amplified to accord with the needs of both the central government and the states. The decree that instituted the department had also established the Inspectorate for Leprosy and Venereal Disease Prophylaxis, attached directly to the National Department.[59] This inspectorate operated in the DF and in the territory of Acre, but its health services could be extended via agreements with individual states. The inspectorate would then provide technical guidance and oversight, while the actual work would be carried out by the federal agencies set up in the states.[60] The financial resources for leprosy prevention, including the establishment of leprosaria, hospitals, and dispensaries, were to come from the special rural sanitation fund.[61] Federal control over the services would be exercised in the same fashion as control over rural sanitation.

The new legislation stipulated compulsory vaccination and revaccination against smallpox and imposed penalties and restrictions on those who refused the vaccine.[62] The programs would be conducted under agreements with the states, while the work itself would be performed by state and federal officials, health inspectors at port sanitation services, and physicians with rural agencies.

Once a federal agency had opened its doors in a state, the agency could serve as a tool for implementing policies on top of those to combat rural endemic diseases. Given Brazil's inexhaustible list of public health problems, after an agreement had been signed and the rural health agency had laid down its technical and administrative base, federal responsibility and state benefits could easily be expanded. Moreover, the presence of the central government cleared the way for public authority to engage in further activities, with rural sanitation services being key. From 1920 to 1924, the seventeen states that had signed agreements widened them to encompass the prevention of leprosy, syphilis, and other venereal diseases. Important states such as Bahia and Pernambuco, traditionally reticent about any federal presence even though they incessantly grappled with major health issues, joined in. Rio Grande do Sul entered into a direct agreement with the Inspectorate for Leprosy and Venereal Disease Prophylaxis, and by the mid-1920s, only Goiás and São Paulo lacked a federal health presence.[63]

Now whenever an epidemic outbreak occurred (most often bubonic plague and yellow fever), the rural health agencies in the epidemic zone could assume responsibility for fighting it, though always with state government authorization. In 1922, the DSPR fought yellow fever in Bahia and plague in Maranhão, Ceará, Rio Grande do Norte, Pernambuco, and Alagoas.[64] Moreover, according to National Department of Public Health regulations, if an epidemic outbreak was not contained at its point of origin and thus threatened other regions, the federal government should immediately step in, footing the bill and dispensing with any need for prior state authorization.[65] Anti-yellow-fever and antiplague actions were in fact financed by federal funds. And from 1923 through the end of the decade, this task was shared with the Rockefeller Foundation. The campaign for the sanitation of Brazil had made federal responsibility for handling epidemics a fait accompli.

A number of DF responsibilities were transferred to the department, including a large part of hygiene services and the oversight of foodstuffs and marketing of dairy products and meat. A special health court was also resurrected to assist the public health authority. These actions reversed the trend toward the demunicipalizing of hygiene in the nation's capital that had begun under the 1914 legislation.

Brazilian presidents and public health doctors publicly tended to ascribe ever more concerns and responsibilities to the federal agencies in the states.[66] It was suggested that food safety oversight could be conducted under agreements similar to those involving rural sanitation, especially in the cases of meat and milk, increasingly consumed in large urban centers distant from their sites of production and therefore outside the reach of inspection. The same suggestion applied to child hygiene, an emerging public health problem that had previously been the concern of only a few philanthropic organizations and thus largely off the public agenda. Some ministerial documents suggested controlling not only milk quality but also price to make this essential item in infant nutrition affordable. Public health authorities would in effect have been able to intervene in the market and economic activities to defend and promote collective health.[67] Although price controls were never instituted, the 1920 administrative regulations established the Office of Infant and Child Hygiene and Assistance to operate in the DF. Three years later, new administrative regulations enhanced the office's status by establishing an Inspectorate of Infant and Child Hygiene and permitting agreements under which the DSPR would provide assistance, guidance, and oversight in the area.[68] The department received two other responsibilities under the same 1923 decree: organization of a Sanitary Information and Education Service and an Inspectorate of Industrial and Vocational Hygiene within the DF.[69] Educating the public about health and about industrial labor conditions (a politically more sensitive matter) represented novel challenges on the health agenda.[70]

Five years after enactment of the first rural health and sanitation decrees, the majority of the states had entered into bilateral agreements, and federal authority had acquired new duties at a great remove from the rural endemic diseases and epidemics that had originally inflamed public and professional opinion. Public power was extending its territory, responsibilities, and capacity to implement health policy.

Covering the Map of Brazil: Public Power Grows

By 1922, a total of eighty-eight rural health posts were operating in fifteen states and the DF, including some traveling posts in Amazonas and Pará that served riverside populations. Another sixteen main posts existed in state capitals, plus thirty-three subposts. Excluding main posts, the central-west state of Mato Grosso had the fewest posts (two), while twelve of the fifteen states had from three or four (AM, PA, MA, CE, RN, PB, PE, AL, BA, ES, RJ, SC; see appendix 2 for the names of states). Almost half of the posts were located in Minas Gerais (eighteen), Paraná (eight), and the DF (seventeen). The last figure was likely so high because the DF, which was unequivocally under federal responsibility and thus had no need for negotiations or agreements, had been a pioneer in this arena. Minas Gerais and Paraná had been the first to sign rural health and sanitation agreements, doing so even before the creation of the National Department of Public Health, and consequently had fairly well-organized services by 1922. Outside the DF, seven regional hospitals attached to federal services had been founded (one each in PA, MA, and PB and four in MG), along with twenty-seven dispensaries for the treatment of syphilis and other venereal diseases, with at least one in each of the capitals of the fourteen states that had entered into agreements for leprosy and venereal disease prevention (AM, PA, MA, CE, RN, PB, PE, AL, BA, MT, RJ, MG, PR, SC). Leprosaria were under construction in Pará and Maranhão as well.[71]

In addition to federal health posts, fifty-eight posts to treat hookworm and other parasitic worm diseases were run in cooperation with the Rockefeller Foundation in fifty-six municipalities spread across eleven states and the DF: MA (two), PE (six), AL (two), BA (three), MG (six), ES (two), RJ (ten), PR (three), SC (four), RS (five), SP (twelve), and the DF (three).[72] Rio Grande do Sul and São Paulo signed agreements with the Rockefeller Foundation rather than with the DSPR.[73] The International Health Board's Brazilian arm maintained four anti-malaria posts in the state of Rio de Janeiro and also helped set up permanent municipal hygiene services in Minas Gerais and São Paulo.[74] Although the Rockefeller Foundation initially limited its activities to hookworm prevention in states possessing heftier resources, it expanded into northern and northeastern states and into the spheres of teaching, research, and malaria and yellow fever prevention, keeping pace with the diversification and spread into the interior of public authority in the realm of public health.[75]

While the states differed in when they began participating in these arrangements, the available resources, and the modality of agreements, public health authority had soon been established throughout the nation, mainly in the form of initiatives to prevent rural endemic diseases, leprosy, and venereal diseases and to prevent and combat epidemics. A national public health infrastructure was gradually creeping in through the doors pushed open by the rural sanitation agreements, filling in spaces devoid of public power but rife with disease.

Benefits Have Costs; Costs Have Benefits

The nonfinancial terms of these agreements reveal the scope of federal public health power in the states. For example, Pará, a state accustomed to receiving federal sanitation commissions, like the one on yellow fever, and whose key public health problem was the ubiquity of malaria, signed a December 1920 agreement centered on the DSPR's war against rural endemic diseases stipulating that the state would accept "all sanitary laws, provisos, and instructions" issued by the federal authority and "foster" the same acceptance among the state's municipalities. The agreement also provided that the state's health agencies be organized "exclusively at the criterion" of the department and "preferentially" set up in the regions that were hardest hit by endemic disease, most densely populated, and most important economically. The services encompassed under this type of agreement would be carried out by commissions established by the national agency "without the interference of any state or municipal authority," although they should render "moral support" and aid and facilitate the work of the federal services. The federal government agreed to pay for and build a leprosarium, which would give preferential admission to sufferers residing in Pará and would charge them a fee for treatment.[76]

The general terms of the agreement with the city of Belém, signed two years later, on January 11, 1922, resembled those of the state agreement, especially regarding the independence and power of the federal authority. However, while the municipality would be responsible for food safety oversight, it would have to comply with pertinent federal legislation. In addition, services related to sanitary policing and household hygiene services, where public power could exercise greater coercive action, would be undertaken jointly by rural and municipal agencies, with fines and penalties dictated by federal legislation. One financial clause specified that part of the municipality's contribution go toward the purchase of quinine salts to be used by traveling services to treat malaria along a railway track that cut through the municipality.[77]

Under a revision of the administrative regulation of the National Department of Public Health (Decree 15.003, September 15, 1921), a specific 1922 agreement was signed with the Pará state sanitation agency that set out federal responsibilities within the state and stipulated that the amended administrative regulations pertained to all of Pará. In addition to its basic duties, the federal Rural Sanitation and Prophylaxis Service would be responsible for oversight of the practice of medicine, pharmacy, dentistry, and obstetrics as well as of pharmaceutical products, serums, vaccines, and other biological products throughout the state; the sanitary police, general prevention of communicable diseases, and specific prevention of reportable diseases and venereal diseases in outlying and rural areas; and when necessary oversight of the isolation of patients other than tuberculosis sufferers. Within the urban perimeter, this work would fall to the state agency except for leprosy and venereal diseases, which were the exclusive purview of the federal authority. The state authority would also be responsible for school hygiene services and public and hospital assistance. Sanitary police and household hygiene were assigned to the federal services, although the state could reserve the right to inspect private residences, except for brothels and the homes of suspected carriers of venereal disease.[78]

Pursuant to the administrative regulations for the National Department of Public Health as revised in 1923 (which remained in effect through the end of the decade) and to other public health laws, public authorities had the right to intervene directly in many aspects of social life and in countless economic pursuits. Thus, it is clear that with state governments' approval, the duties of federal rural sanitation agencies had expanded and grown more complex since the first experiments in the DF and the decrees of 1918 and 1919.

The formulas for financing the rural health agreements offer some insight into the dynamics of participation. Two kinds of financing existed, with both derived from Article 9 of Decree 3.987, which created the National Department of Public Health. The state left half of its promised share on deposit for the duration of the period of the services, an amount matched by the federal government. If the state lacked the required resources to do so, it could still receive federal services, but it would have to make annual installment payments for a stipulated period, thus indebting itself to the federal treasury. The state also had to agree to levy a tax on improved land or a property tax surcharge. The timelines for the agreements varied from two to four years, and states had about ten years to make good on their debts. Pará's 1920 agreement, for example, covered three years of work at a value of 900 contos de réis, and the state's half would be amortized through ten annual installments of equal value starting in 1922.[79]

According to the federal director of rural sanitation and prophylaxis, five of the fifteen states that entered into agreements opted for the first formula (MA, MG, PE, RJ, RN), while the remainder (AM, PA, CE, PB, AL, BA, ES, PR, SC, MT) chose long-term reimbursement, meaning that most agreements required the federal government to have 100 percent of the funds at its ready. Except for Minas Gerais, all of the states that chose the ten-year reimbursement plan entered into agreements that entailed annual expenditures higher than those of the states that chose to pay their share up front.[80]

That the states sought to squeeze as much as possible from the federal government is confirmed by the fact that services had just barely begun when seven of the fifteen states asked to increase the value of their agreements, thus putting further pressure on the federal budget. Of those seven, four (MA, RN, PE, MG) went with the first formula, while three (PA, AL, PR) chose the second, with all but Minas Gerais requesting additional funds equal to 70–100 percent of the initial commitments.[81] Federal resources were expected to come from a special fund created to help finance sanitation works. Initial, optimistic predictions held that the fund would collect one million dollars during the first year alone.[82]

Everyone wanted to enjoy maximum benefits immediately while postponing debt settlement. Although no precise information is available on actual debt repayment, the wretched finances of the 1920s likely meant that most states and municipalities had no way to collect the mandated taxes. Moreover, the tax on improved land and the property tax would impact rural lands, which presented a sticky political problem. Even the federal government had to struggle to enact an income tax in 1922.[83] The states and municipalities probably never collected the taxes and would have had limited funds with which to reimburse the central government; therefore, they would have delayed debt payment if they could renegotiate and still count on federal resources. Under the terms of a 1925 agreement between Bahia and the federal government to extend rural health and leprosy prevention services for another three years, the state could settle its earlier debts through ten annual installment payments, starting in 1926.[84] As long as the states could renegotiate their debts, and the federal budget allowed it, rural sanitation policy and other public health initiatives were implemented and financed by the central state.

Health reform thus inaugurated a new cycle in the expansion of public power. The participation of the majority of the states indicates that the perceived benefits of a federal presence were calculated as outweighing perceived costs. A good share of these costs and benefits were defined not by the legislature or even by political dynamics during 1918–19 but rather by the actions of federal authority itself as it reached agreements with states and implemented health services. In this regard, rural health and sanitation policy constituted an instrument for transforming health into an ever more public and national endeavor through voluntary agreements, federal regulations and action, and local expediencies. Through a bumpy yet steady process of public policy implementation, health authority gradually gained shape and took on new and greater duties, endowing Brazil with public buildings and institutions and the country's people with access to medical exams, physicians, vermifuge, personnel, educational lectures and leaflets, residential records, statistics, vaccines, and regulations.

In the States or *of* the States?
The Construction of Public Health Authority

While federal rural health and sanitation expanded swiftly, two opposing viewpoints battled over the ultimate role of the federal government and its action at state and municipal levels. The political coalition that emerged when consciousness coincided with opportunity and everyone felt they had received their fair share did not persist for long after public policy was implemented.

From one perspective held chiefly by the executive branch, a portion of the new federal activities within the states would only be temporary, focused on more pressing public health problems and meant to assist and often organize local services. States and municipalities should create their own health sanitation agencies and increase their financial contributions until they eventually assumed full responsibility for routine initiatives. In this view, bolstering the power of the central state was seen as a necessary but temporary detour from the original distribution of power.

This line of argument was often repeated by Presidents Epitácio Pessoa and Arthur Bernardes in their addresses to Congress from 1920 to 1926, in which the topic of public health occupied a much more pivotal spot than had previously been the case. In 1923, Bernardes stated that the decision to centralize services constituted a response to the "widespread nature and intensity" of endemic diseases and to the "inadequate technical or financial capacities" of some states. The goal was to eventually replace this temporary scheme with a more stable, permanent one under the responsibility of state and municipal administrations.[85] From this angle, rural sanitation agencies in the states would be transformed into agencies of the states, diminishing pressure on the federal budget and safeguarding the central government from any political fallout as a result of its daily dealings, which often entailed the use of coercion, the selection of appointees whom local bosses might find hard to accept, and so on. In 1924, the president told Congress, "The current administrative modality of these agencies . . . is a temporary regime that shall soon be replaced with another, definitive one, when the achievements of these agencies and an awareness of their unique usefulness compels municipalities to take them upon themselves, rightfully bearing the costs. State administrations must aim at this goal, for only the regular, effective organization of municipal hygiene will bring about the generalized, ongoing sanitation of our vast interior."[86]

Looked at from this angle, the response to the *sertão*-hospital (or neglect-disease) conundrum discussed in chapter 2 was the introduction of public health services. However, given the size of the country and magnitude of the problem, the three branches of government needed to coordinate their efforts. The federal sphere had an initial role to play in setting up and organizing sanitation and health initiatives in response to the impasses of interdependence in emergency situations. However, after these problems had been vanquished and services organized, the states would have to take over the regular, ongoing work, while the central government would coordinate and normalize services, regulate interstate and international issues, and conduct emergency initiatives.

But from the initial implementation of federal rural agencies in the states, a number of other leading voices had called for the central government to permanently bear the onus of all health-related expenditures without asking states for a matching quota, much less requiring reimbursement. This stance was espoused by those who still believed rural sanitation to be a national issue and the 1920 reform yet another step toward definitive state responsibility for the health of the Brazilian population. This viewpoint was widely shared among public health doctors holding key posts in federal rural sanitation agencies and linked to the DSPR and among the heads of federal commissions in the states, who were generally civil servants or activists from the previous decade's sanitation campaign.[87]

In the opinion of those who did the actual work and were very often the first or the primary representatives of public power on the ground, voluntary actions alone would never come even close to solving the challenges of public health interdependence. To the contrary, as a temporary policy, these agreements merely drove home the need to shift health services to the federal sphere and collectivize them nationwide. Belisário Penna, head of the DSPR, described a few possibilities:

> Let us imagine that State A is bordered to its north by State B and to its south by State C. A and C contract health services from the federal government, but B refuses to do so, although verminosis, malaria, bubonic plague, and yellow fever rage through its territory in endemic and epidemic forms. Either A and C maintain costly, permanent surveillance at their borders with B to avoid the invasion of these communicable diseases, or after their agreements are up and they simply cannot afford to renew them, they abandon surveillance and allow the diseases to invade, sacrificing all effort and money invested to that point. . . . Let us, on the other

hand, imagine the case where the three contiguous states set up sanitation services under two-year agreements with the federal government, which are not renewed for one reason or another at the end of their validity. . . . Once the agreements expire, are the hospitals, dispensaries, and Health Posts closed? Are their patients left uncured in the middle of treatment?[88]

Viewed in these terms, demanding that the states continue to make financial contributions toward the services carried out by the central government would be tantamount to denying the nationwide nature of the problem, guaranteeing the discontinuity of this public policy and condemning the states to the same past conundrums as soon as a financial or other crisis kept them from renewing their agreements. To guarantee the solidity of federal mechanisms for financing ongoing health and sanitation work in the states, money would have to be directed from the federal budget as well as from the special fund stipulated in the National Department of Public Health decrees—a fund that did not, according to all indications, ever exist.[89]

The activities of the central state made inroads for public authority throughout Brazil, whether or not these activities were viewed as temporary. The federal government was not politically, technically, or financially capable of taking on public health across the country, but a return to the original status quo was equally untenable—precisely because the status quo had been altered by the work of public power. Calculi made against the backdrop of the 1891 order yielded policies that altered this order. The need for regular, ongoing public health initiatives and the challenge of endless new problems also bred the need for new relations between federal authority and the states. At the same time, public health had modified the balance between the central government and the states, to the detriment of the latter.

Many states lacked the political ability to conduct certain activities that would interfere with local power. In Bahia and other locales where state bosses had trouble controlling and coercing the various local factions in the 1920s, public health agencies met with resistance outside capital cities. Sebastião Barroso, head of rural sanitation services in Bahia at the dawn of the decade, reported on the major roadblocks that municipal potentates erected to federal services, especially in terms of oversight and punitive measures and the policing of vector breeding grounds, which required health officers to enter private homes and other property.[90] One crucial difference existed between state and federal agencies, however: when excessive resistance was met, federal personnel could summon troops or threaten government intervention.[91] According to Barroso, "Politics is a very tense thing in Northern States, and a political friend is supported or an adversary combated through every means possible. Laws usually carry no weight and local governments usually cannot enforce them. There is only one element that commands respect and that works: federal action."[92]

So in addition to its other benefits, a federal presence brought to the table the real, effective presence of public power in its prime sense: law enforcement. Federal services proved much more efficacious because they could rely on the coercive power of the central government and help establish public authority in areas outside the reach of state governments.

Over time and at varying paces, the states increased their public health responsibilities by organizing their own agencies and enacting legislation, boosting their budget allocations, and partially replacing the federal presence in a range of activities. In some states, such as Bahia, the leadership of federal and state agencies began to overlap, reflecting both the endeavor to rationalize public health work and the growth of state responsibility. Over the 1920s, other states simply did not renew their rural health and sanitation agreements or leprosy and venereal disease prevention agreements as a consequence of financial constraints, political strife, or the belief that these agreements were no longer needed.[93] Contemporary observers noted that almost all states raised their annual expenditures on public health and assistance, irrespective of any investments under these bilateral agreements. As a result, in some cases these activities came to receive a more significant slice of the state budgetary pie.[94]

Nevertheless, federal services retained responsibility for various programs in the states, which were still grappling with financial problems. Federal responsibility remained particularly strong in the case of the prevention of rural endemic diseases, leprosy, and venereal diseases; smallpox vaccination; and responses to epidemic outbreaks.[95] Budget expenditures for the department climbed significantly in the 1920s as new initiatives were added, more staff were hired, and the agency's structure grew more complex.[96]

The department added the goal of training doctors, nurses, and public health workers in newly established medical courses and schools and responsibility for overseeing professional practice and organizing statistical services for all of Brazil. At the same time, public health agencies maintained the tradition of countrywide sanitation campaigns, educating the public in hygiene practices and raising the awareness of the elites in the nation's capital. Innovative methods such as hygiene courses for the public at large and educational radio programs supplemented the conventional tools of lectures and leaflets in an attempt to reach broader swaths of people.[97]

With funding by the Rockefeller Foundation, the Ana Nery School of Nursing, attached to the department's Superintendence of Nursing Services, was founded in Rio de Janeiro in 1923. States would send students there for training, after which they returned to their local agencies. Other students took advantage of opportunities for scholarships to the United States.[98] In 1926, the Rio de Janeiro School of Medicine, in partnership with the Oswaldo Cruz Institute, added a specialization course in hygiene and public health. In the words of President Bernardes, the goal was to form "a corps of career hygienists dedicated exclusively to sanitation tasks."[99]

One significant outgrowth of this process was the shaping of professional identities among the technical personnel groomed to serve at and head public health facilities. Gradually but perceptibly, clinical practitioners became differentiated from public health doctors, for example. While being a physician was initially considered the appropriate qualification for holding these posts, by 1929 they were restricted to doctors trained in the specialty of public health. The growing state presence in health strengthened the emergence of new and distinct professional identities, a trend that dated to the end of the nineteenth century.[100]

The mid-1920s saw a push to produce, normalize, and publish demographic and health information, but this effort was stymied by the absence of statistical services in most states and municipalities. Moreover, in many cases, this kind of information simply was not collected or published on a regular basis. Port health inspectors and the heads of rural sanitation agencies in the states began to receive this information at their workplaces and then forward it to the department's Inspectorate of Sanitary Demography. When this was not the case, federal employees would contact justices of the peace and notary publics to obtain information on deaths, births, infant mortality, and other vital statistics. The overall idea was to assemble a nationwide database not restricted solely to the DF and states boasting more organized sanitation services (for example, São Paulo, Minas Gerais, Rio de Janeiro, Bahia, and Pernambuco). State governments signed agreements with the heads of federal agencies in the states to adopt the death certificate model employed by the National Department of Public Health in the nation's capital.[101] In short, these were the first steps toward compiling nationwide vital statistics that could be used in policymaking, resource allocation, and the planning of public health initiatives.[102]

With health authority becoming entrenched, new issues were added to the public health agenda and old ones were reintroduced, ultimately broadening the concerns, responsibilities, and initiatives of public authority at all levels and throughout the country. From an analytical perspective, the expansion of public power did not depend on its locus. The transfer of responsibilities to the federal sphere depended on agreements whose bases shifted during implementation. At any given moment, the work of public health authority could have caused the perceived external costs to have dropped below the perceived costs of a federal presence.

Health and sanitation initiatives thus provided valuable tools for building public power under the First Republic. The slow and steady transformation of agencies *in the states* to agencies *of the states* did not come about because the central government retreated or lessened its commitment or because the champions of autonomy were victorious and transported Brazil back to the world of 1891. Rather, this transformation signified the successful construction of public authority. Central power, which thanks to its unique institutional features had no competitors, achieved a tremendous ability to define and implement sweeping policies. Consciousness in tandem with interests gave rise to political decisions that, when implemented, altered the original calculus and even changed the decision-making units themselves.

Conclusion

Designing and enforcing a nationwide policy of rural health and sanitation, approved by the legislative branch and carried out by the executive, became feasible because the policy incorporated rules and mechanisms that kept the costs of relying on central power lower than both the external costs and the benefits of the arrangement. The implementation of the policy upped the consequent benefits and costs of nationalization, and nearly all decision-making parties to the agreements with the federal government deemed the results positive. Cooperation was born not only from public health consciousness but primarily from material incentives. The federal government's activities equipped the states with financial, human, and organizational resources and allowed the central authority to cut off free riders, act against those who did nothing, and aid the inept.

The viability of a nationwide rural sanitation policy was contingent on the specific conditions under which reliance on central power would reap benefits. Once the external costs were known, each state could decide whether to acquiesce to the presence of federal authority or bear the onus of not doing so, and allowing this choice circumvented any objections of a constitutional nature. A reformist coalition was possible as long as the policy was voluntary, subject to each party's individual assessment of costs and benefits. The coalition thus depended on the rules by which the responsibilities of the states were transferred to the federal realm. Based on their initial calculi, eighteen states concluded that the external costs outweighed the costs of federal intervention and that these costs were in turn lower than ensuing benefits. The transfer of health to federal hands can be expressed as sanitary reform = external costs > costs of transferring to the state < benefits from the state.

The implementation of public health policy acquired its own dynamics, and its earliest results indicated that the parties were interested in furthering the benefits of the presence of central power and therefore were willing to grant the federal government more responsibility and greater independence. Over time, these changes reshaped the calculus that had informed the initial accord. Public power moved into unoccupied spaces and opened up new ones, backed by the public health consciousness and interests of the state elites. The construction of public health authority was so successful that many activities could be taken over by other spheres of government. In the 1920s, the reform led to the creation of a network of nationwide institutions, regulations, laws, bureaucrats, and public services that may not have actualized the sanitation movement's more radical centralizing proposals but nevertheless impeded any attempt to backtrack to a prereform world.

The establishment of public health authority was one aspect of the process of concentrating and centralizing authority, extending its territorial reach, and normalizing social life.[103] Federal health agencies promoted public power through their work—that is, through sanitation (drainage and sewerage works); public health education (leaflets and lectures); vaccination; medical procedures (diagnoses, exams, drugs, hospitalization, and the like); the compilation and publication of demographic and health statistics; the enactment and enforcement of public health legislation (building inspections, sanitary policing to control breeding grounds for mosquitoes and rats, isolation and compulsory treatment of the ill, oversight of household and commercial activities, and so on); and the building of public facilities that symbolized the institutions behind them (permanent and traveling health posts, dispensaries, leprosaria, and regional and isolation hospitals). The execution of these activities, which were increasingly detailed, ongoing, and specialized, required the permanent presence of a group of professionals and bureaucrats who represented public power and could therefore interfere in property rights and individual freedom.

As public health authority went about shaping and implementing policies, it steadily enhanced its autonomy from the political and economic interests that had supported its creation. The implementation of a nationwide public policy had important effects on the politics that had framed it.[104] The First Republic witnessed the growth of the state and its infrastructural power, unequally distributed between the central government and state and municipal governments.

The calculus of the costs and benefits of shifting activities to the state along with the evaluation of the terms of participation had engendered an arrangement where social consciousness converged with tangible interests. The implementation of this arrangement influenced federalism itself as well as its state members and their relations. A national public policy was not a straightforward outcome of the impositions of communicable disease but a product of political agreements and decisions whose mechanisms would benefit many and affect all. Yet at the same time, this covenant was also deft enough to accommodate São Paulo, a state that many—itself included—considered an exception on the national public health scene.

CHAPTER 5

São Paulo Exceptionalism?

Political Autonomy and Public Health Interdependence

While the idea of sanitation inhabits the realm of lip service in Rio de Janeiro, in São Paulo it occupies the hard ground of facts.

—Monteiro Lobato, *Problema Vital* (1918)

Monteiro Lobato, an activist and something of an informal press agent for the rural sanitation campaign, encapsulated the singular, exceptional nature and early development of the public health experience in São Paulo. In Lobato's mind, Paulista reality stood in stark contrast to Rio rhetoric. Moreover, in his view, the achievements of São Paulo's public health services should encourage the development of health policies in other parts of Brazil. São Paulo could not stop because, if it did, according to one director of state public health, "the little that's being done elsewhere around Brazil will come to a halt."[1] Some later scholarship has also recognized São Paulo's role as a trailblazer in public health and has ranked its experience as unparalleled in Latin America and even something of a rarity among the more advanced nations of Europe and North America.[2]

Such outstanding success with public health policy at the state level cannot be examined without acknowledging São Paulo's privileged, autonomous, and differentiated position within national politics. The state's public health and sanitation policies were an integral part of this discourse as well as an inspiration for the quintessential image of the relation between the state and the federation: São Paulo as the locomotive of Brazil.[3]

A good share of the analyses of health policies under the First Republic fall in line with this perspective, holding São Paulo up as the paramount success story in state public health and confining their discussions to São Paulo as an exception, failing to tie this position to the national dilemmas that made it possible. These studies often embrace the contemporary evaluations that separated the São Paulo locomotive from the twenty heavy train cars it was supposedly hauling.

But São Paulo was not unique because it voluntarily omitted itself from national public health; rather, São Paulo was unique because it represented an answer to the problems of public health interdependence faced by Brazil's elites. The Paulista case was the exception that confirms and reinforces the conclusions reached in the last chapter.

Under the public health reforms that commenced in 1918–20 and expanded in the early 1920s, São Paulo acquiesced to a nationwide arrangement in which the federal government played the dominant role. Central power consequently augmented its presence in other states, but São Paulo had begun implementing its own reform in 1917 and continued along this path, saving itself from federal public health intervention. The victory of a more national solution over a purely autonomous alternative, like São Paulo's, evinced the growing unviability of trusting public health interdependence to individual solutions. Yet this solution was feasible only because it rested firmly on the assumption that states could freely opt out of bilateral agreements with the central government. In reality, however, São Paulo was the only state that possessed this freedom of choice. The notion of Paulista uniqueness was embedded in the formula that eventually drew a bridge between political autonomy and public health interdependence.

My interpretation coincides with analyses that suggest no contradiction between regionalism and the process of national integration and that hold that the functions of government grew in various spheres during the last two decades of the First Republic—well before the post-1930 period considered a milestone in centralization and integration.[4] As Joseph Love contends, national integration was a product of two processes: social, political, and economic interpenetration and the transfer of decisions and resources to the central government.[5] In the realm of economic policy, especially regarding coffee, the São Paulo elites resorted to the federal government, relying on and even occupying the executive to ensure their own supply of labor power, bolster coffee prices through immigration and foreign exchange policies, and receive endorsements for foreign financing. The same did not hold true, however, for public works, especially in health and sanitation.

Minas Gerais, which shared control of national politics with São Paulo, had a greater penchant for turning to the federal government for public works aid and federal posts.[6] In fact, the Paulistas were alone in viewing reliance on central power as purely optional and as depending on priorities, reciprocity requirements, and costs.[7]

In the opinion of E. P. Reis, the decision to let central authority rather than the market regulate the economy laid the groundwork for centralization and characteristically authoritarian government interventionism.[8] I maintain that São Paulo went along with the existence of federal health agencies in other states out of self-interest and that the unforeseen outcome was a marked increase in federal capacity to intervene throughout the national territory and society. Though Love and Reis travel different routes, their works reach the same destination: shedding light on Paulista exceptionalism, undoing the false dichotomy between autonomy and interdependence that is intimated in certain public health studies, and clarifying the more general consequences of autonomy combined with interdependence.

This chapter explores Paulista exceptionalism. The first part presents an overview of the development of public health policy in São Paulo and highlights its main features.[9] The second part shows how Paulista exceptionalism was identified both by leading figures in the Old Republic and by more recent analyses that hammer home the uniqueness of the São Paulo experience. The third part offers my interpretation based on the arguments laid out in the previous chapters. The conclusion summarizes the chapter and frames it within the central themes of the book.

A Brief Overview of Public
Health Policy in São Paulo

According to most scholars, one of the driving forces behind the development of São Paulo's health services was the state policy of importing foreign workers to meet the labor needs of the coffee economy, a policy that began in the last two decades of the nineteenth century.[10] With rural São Paulo's coffee frontier pushing westward, planters needed to secure a steady influx of immigrants. Because the port of Santos and the state capital were mandatory stops for any immigrant on his way to the large estates and plantations of the interior, these sites hosted the first sanitation and sanitary control initiatives. Diseases that might trigger epidemics or take up endemic residence in São Paulo had to be barred at these points. Behind this effort to avert any threat to domestic or foreign labor and improve the salubrity of Brazilian cities lay the worry that the countries then supplying these workers—primarily Italy—might discourage or even prohibit emigration or that epidemics might disrupt the backbone of the state economy.[11] The prime targets of sanitation measures were bubonic plague and yellow fever, along with smallpox and malaria. Public health in São Paulo was thus tightly bound up with the interests of the coffee elite.

In addition to playing a key role in the influx of labor power, Santos was the hub of the foreign coffee trade, while the city of São Paulo was emerging as the political and economic power center of the agricultural export economy. The level of insalubrity in both places imperiled the infrastructural foundations of the São Paulo economy and its foreign relations.[12] Over the course of the First Republic, the state's health agenda also came to incorporate the issues of popular housing, maternal and child care, tuberculosis, and venereal diseases. In reforming its services, São Paulo also had to address the growing complexity of the coffee sector in its westward march and attend to troubles in regions of decay and to the new social problems spawned by urbanization and industrialization. In a number of cases, São Paulo was a step ahead of the pack, enforcing measures such as compulsory smallpox vaccination that were later enacted by the federal government.

The expansion of the coffee economy, in conjunction with the push to industrialize, produced a figuration that demanded ongoing public action, capable of promoting wide-ranging coercive policies to protect the health of Paulista citizens. As far back as the 1890s, the development of state-level services had begun convincing the coffee barons and their state legislative representatives that they stood to benefit from public health expenditures as long as they included defined constraints on interference with private property.[13] In other words, the elites defended their political and economic interests in pragmatic ways.[14] Problems of mutual dependence on the national level were mirrored in relations between state governments on the one hand and municipal powers and local oligarchies on the other. The same held true for government versus individual freedom. The institution of state-level public authority in São Paulo provided a means for taking coercive action against the population and intruding on the local elites while maintaining independence from the federal government. The uneasy coexistence of municipal autonomy alongside financial and therefore political dependence provided an early sign of how public health authority would eventually end up in the hands of the state bosses.[15]

J. A. Blount makes special note of political clashes over the boundaries of public authority and of municipal and state jurisdictions in health and sanitation from 1889 through 1896. Criticisms about municipal autonomy in these realms focused increasingly on the lack and inefficiency of local policies, which fueled more calls for broader state responsibility in public health agencies, which were engaged in hygiene campaigns and a war on the epidemics assailing the state.[16] There is something of a consensus that state services advanced while opposition to their expansion gradually weakened. However, nothing in the record indicates that state-level public authority extended its reach to large estates or plantations. Until the late 1910s, no legal regulations in health and sanitation affected these properties in any significant or enduring way.[17] Since the law was basically concerned with urban areas, public agents possessed restricted jurisdictional authority. Even so, the idea of regulating labor conditions inside factories, as some state deputies advocated, received serious attention only when the 1917 labor movements erupted.[18]

The reforms to São Paulo state services between 1896 and 1917 bolstered the power of public authority to regulate a wide array of health-related facets of social life and stretched the territorial scope of these initiatives. The 1896 reform reflected both the drive to boost the power of state agencies vis-à-vis municipal authorities and greater acceptance of the government role in health.[19] Facing technical and financial challenges in promoting public health policies, municipalities increasingly saw a legitimate need for state authorities to act, since the state government could keep precarious sanitary conditions in one location from generating problems that might spread into other municipalities and could coordinate action statewide if proliferation occurred.[20] From 1898 to 1911, São Paulo's agencies battled plague and yellow fever, with particular success at the port of Santos and state borders. Collaboration between state and federal authorities in fighting epidemics was always a source of tension, with relations characterized at times by cooperation but at other times by outright state rejection of federal interference. In 1899 and 1901, for example, São Paulo refused to go along with prevention measures against plague.[21] In the opinion of Blount and Nancy Stepan, these tensions reflected rivalry and competition between the two spheres of government in the realm of health, São Paulo's protection of its political autonomy and the autonomy of its agencies (even if federal officials were responsible for the sanitary defense of ports), and internal political clashes among state elites over the policies of the federal government, then led by Manuel Ferraz de Campos Sales, a Paulista who was in office from 1898 to 1902.[22]

Throughout the First Republic, São Paulo attempted to organize its research and production infrastructure so that it could furnish the serums, vaccines, and drugs needed for local health initiatives without having to depend on federal agencies. The Bacteriological Institute was founded in 1892 and was joined by the Butantan Institute (1901) and the Pasteur Institute of São Paulo (1903), both of which researched and produced drugs. In the late 1910s, the Rockefeller Foundation sponsored the establishment of a chair in hygiene at the São Paulo School of Medicine and Surgery, which had been founded in 1912. Developed by the São Paulo government, this network of public health research and production hubs began collaborating with federal agencies, laying the scientific foundations that would guarantee the effective independence of the state's services.[23]

Another factor that contributed to the prestige and political consolidation of public health policy in São Paulo was the early twentieth-century campaign against yellow fever in the interior. The endeavor was based on state-of-the-art knowledge and techniques that developed out of the work of the U.S. Army Yellow Fever Commission to Cuba, especially regarding the role of the mosquito as causal agent. The success in Cuba offered further proof of São Paulo's place as a Brazilian pioneer in public health and scientific research and foreshadowed the sanitation campaign model adopted in the Federal District when Oswaldo Cruz was at the helm of the General Directorate.[24]

The 1906 reform in São Paulo removed from the municipal sphere duties that had been left untouched under the reform of 1896, thereby concentrating power in the hands of state agencies. It also installed a commission for the prevention and treatment of trachoma, an eye infection that had gained epidemic proportions in the interior, especially among immigrants and foreign workers. This commission, which lasted only two years, offers evidence of the trials and tribulations encountered when blazing inroads for sanitation services in rural areas. The early 1910s brought failed attempts to revive it. According to Castro Santos, the 1911 reform signaled a retreat in state-level services and a corresponding advance at the municipal level, which took over responsibility for vaccination, isolation hospitals, and the generation of statistics for the state agency. Municipalities also accrued greater responsibility in the construction of public health facilities, provision of public assistance, and regulation and inspection of construction

projects and factories.[25] In short, municipal authorities saw their responsibilities—and their expenses—grow. At the same time, the 1911 reform
introduced a general sanitary code that covered nearly all aspects of urban
life and for precisely this reason proved hard to enforce.[26] Still, the code
legally amplified the coercive power of public authority, intensifying regulation of the social and economic life of São Paulo's citizens. From 1911 to
1917, state agencies undertook campaigns against smallpox, typhoid fever,
and leprosy.[27] Some of the literature has called attention to what it regards
as favorable performance in the development of public health initiatives in
urban areas during this period.

The last of this series of major reforms to São Paulo state services occurred in 1917, under the leadership of Arthur Neiva, a leading figure in
the rural sanitation campaign. This reform brought two vital changes: the
introduction of hygiene services targeting rural areas and a rural sanitary
code. The innovations entailed intense political negotiations, with stiff opposition from the state Chamber of Deputies. The reform occurred on the
eve of the inauguration of the federal rural health and sanitation services.
Once again, São Paulo was one step ahead of national policy.

The introduction of a rural sanitary code and establishment of a state
Inspectorate of General Prophylaxis Services (though less comprehensive
than its urban counterpart) stretched public power into rural areas. The
agency began implementing policies to fight malaria and hookworm as well
as trachoma, a problem that had caught the attention of the representatives
of the state oligarchies because of its severe impact on immigrant workers
and consequently on the coffee economy. After heated political debate, coffee planters somewhat relaxed their resistance to government intervention.[28]
In 1917, São Paulo's public health agency agreed to Rockefeller Foundation
collaboration, at first only in the area of hookworm prevention but later in
medical education and research as well.[29]

The Paulista elites and their representatives came to accept government
authority in rural São Paulo as a result of the prior agreements that limited
government interference, as is demonstrated by the stipulation that state
agencies would have authority only over large estates established after the
1917 law went into effect.[30] These restrictions notwithstanding, the instal-
lation of rural health posts and the enactment of sanitation policies applicable to large estates, rural worker health, and urban areas solidified the
power of state-level health and sanitation services vis-à-vis local bosses and
reinforced the state's singular position within the nation.[31] Castro Santos
points out that as time went by, private interests realized the advantages of

public action and planters themselves began requesting rural sanitation works, thereby further legitimizing and strengthening state authority.[32]

According to estimates, by 1920 more than half of São Paulo's municipalities had sewer systems, and the vast majority had public water supplies.[33] Some authors suggest that Paulista public health boasted enough resources to sustain its activities on its own and that per capita health expenditures were comparable to those of U.S. cities.[34]

According to Castro Santos, the entrenchment of state government power in the field of health and sanitation enabled a certain degree of decentralization during São Paulo's 1925 reform. After three decades of mounting success in the control of communicable diseases, this reform targeted new public health issues stemming from urban development, population growth, and economic advances. Questions such as milk and food safety, maternal and child assistance, and venereal diseases had slowly drawn the attention of public power, as had the problems spurred by industrial labor conditions. This reform also constituted an attempt to find new answers to tuberculosis and some of the country's other unsolved problems. This organizational reform was based on the creation of regional health centers that would reach a broader public, formerly served solely by rural posts.[35] This restructuring of São Paulo's services—the last major reform of the First Republican period—heralded the transition to a format that revolved more around permanent health initiatives and less around emergency action to combat specific diseases.

Thus, São Paulo's state public health network developed along much the same route as did federal services, beginning with public health legislation and coercive actions of limited geographic reach but ultimately penetrating the whole state. Public authority gained an ever stronger foothold as it multiplied its responsibilities and built more enduring structures to address health issues over a wider expanse of the state, gradually abandoning localized, sporadic initiatives. By the time the federal government saw the scope of its power grow in the 1920s, public health authorities in São Paulo had already attained firm geographical footing and wielded ever greater policymaking power. This lag between the two spheres resulted from a rational strategy.

São Paulo Exceptionalism: A Misleading Notion

The notion of Paulista exceptionalism that permeates many recent analyses dates to the São Paulo public health reforms under the First Republic. In the 1910s and 1920s, "except for São Paulo" was perhaps the most oft-heard phrase in debates on public health and sanitation. Every public statement, presidential address, legislative debate, or publication that spoke to the relations between central power and the states underscored this distinction. The idea was repeated to the point where it became an unquestionable truth.

At the dawn of the republic, the relations between autonomy, centralization, and the strengthening of public health services inspired discussions and debates. Analyzing the 1890 regulation of São Paulo state services, Bahian physician Nina Rodrigues affirmed that the Paulista trend to assume public health responsibility set a good example for other members of the federation: "The powerful centralization to which the administration of public hygiene is subject and the autonomy of sanitation authorities . . . are clearly evident. [These are] highly apt provisions, worthy of imitation." São Paulo, the state that was the most "jealous of its autonomy and the ultimate champion of the federal republican regime," had quickly discarded the notion that public health should fall to municipalities.[36]

Three decades later, at the twilight of the First Republic, São Paulo still felt the need to assert its public health independence. When yellow fever paid an unexpected return visit to the nation's capital in 1928, panicking the rest of the country, São Paulo's public health director lauded his state's successful programs, which had kept the disease at bay despite heavy trade and other forms of communication with the DF. He cited with pride the success of São Paulo's public health agency, "which is wholly autonomous in relation to the National Department of Public Health."[37]

The São Paulo success in public health and sanitation led to the assumption that any new federal health and sanitation arrangements should not encroach on the state. Such involvement was not necessary because the state had demonstrated its technical and financial capability to implement public health policy on its own.

Belisário Penna, the most ardent advocate of the sanitation of Brazil and administrative and technical centralization in public health, recognized that São Paulo's work in health and education made the state "a people apart within the national community."[38] In a text addressed to President Francisco de Paula Rodrigues Alves, Neiva, director of São Paulo public health from 1917 to 1920, proudly declared that "with the exception of São Paulo, where great progress has been made in hygiene services, Brazil lies forsaken, for little or nothing has been done about hygiene in the remainder of the states."[39]

With São Paulo immune to accusations of public health irresponsibility or incompetence and the federal government presided over by Paulista bosses for much of this period, reformists had difficulty pushing through any remedies that implied a restructuring of federative relations that would arm the central government with further intervention powers. And since any nationwide arrangement would need São Paulo's stamp of approval, the state had to be transformed from a recognized exception into a constituent element of the national community. The foundation for this transformation would be the specter of communicable diseases.

For the most part, recognizing São Paulo as unique simply meant recognizing that the state had provided an efficacious local solution to public health problems, independent of the federal government and other states. But this apparently commendable status quo camouflaged a larger issue: no matter how efficient Paulista agencies, they ultimately could not keep communicable diseases generated elsewhere from violating state borders or force other states to undertake health initiatives. The idea of viewing São Paulo primarily as an exception stands on shaky ground in that it isolates the state from the rest of the country. I see the notion of São Paulo exceptionalism as one of the possible approaches to the nationwide problem of public health interdependence.

Studies of São Paulo's public health policies have generally analyzed them within the context of oligarchic politics, restricting the matter to state-level dynamics while failing to explore the relations between Paulista policy and the public health problems faced by the central government and other states within this same context.[40] Some authors justify their focus on the São Paulo reforms by arguing that the state hosted the most rapid development of the capitalist mode of production.[41] In this sense, health policy was a São Paulo matter because it was bound up with labor and production. In addition, many scholars see São Paulo's approach as a response to the demands of international capitalism.[42] From this perspective, analyzing São Paulo becomes much like explaining public health in Brazil largely by reference to the dynamics of capitalism, with the state and oligarchic politics seen as manifestations of bourgeois rule.[43]

These same studies shed little light on the relations between São Paulo policy, the movement for the sanitation of Brazil, and decisions on the reform of federal services. Scholars have devoted little space to these relations, perhaps based on the same assuredness felt by Lobato, who believed that the sanitation of Brazil was effectively occurring in and from the state of São Paulo.

The in-depth work of Blount documents a shift in how Brazilians and foreigners saw public health conditions in São Paulo during the First Republic. While the state's sanitation troubles contributed to an initial perception that it was not a good place to live or even visit, it gradually reshaped itself into Latin America's model of public health organization.[44] Contemporary observers are cited to affirm the progressive nature of public health in São Paulo and the state's unique situation within Brazil, whereas scant heed is paid to relations between Paulista and federal policy.

At the same time, some studies on the public health movement during the First Republic do not include the São Paulo experience as a vital, constitutive, albeit singular element in the formation of a national health and sanitation policy. Such research has fallen prey to a different error, approaching public health in Brazil primarily from the angle of federal initiatives in the nation's capital.[45]

Since both avenues of research overlook these relations even at a secondary level, they tacitly assume that no exchange or communication took place between the Paulista and federal experiences. And when this relation does get attention, it merely underscores a dispute or conflict between individuals (Neiva versus Carlos Chagas, for example) or between scientific institutions and projects (the Butantan Institute versus the Oswaldo Cruz Institute), in an allusion to the traditional São Paulo–Rio de Janeiro rivalry.[46]

The literature also presents varying assessments of São Paulo's success in public health. Some authors argue that state health reforms failed over the First Republic, an assessment based chiefly on the fact that certain health issues persisted even after the reforms.[47] The same can be said about some assessments of the work of the National Department of Public Health from 1920 on.[48] Blount argues that the Paulista experience succeeded, using as his criteria the establishment of agencies and services, the improvement of public health conditions, and falling mortality rates for communicable diseases. Still, he acknowledges that countless public health problems did not go away and that some even worsened.[49]

Castro Santos places the São Paulo reforms within the context of the national sanitation movement and contrasts the success of the Paulista experience in state-level policymaking with that of Bahia and Bahian "backwardness." Unlike other authors, he centers his analysis on the process of forging institutions and public authority and thus concludes that the São Paulo experience was positive in both the short and long runs. Taking chronological and geographical divisions into account, he breaks the sanitation movement and health policies under the First Republican period into distinct stages that urge more specific, complex interpretations. He moves beyond the limits of determinist analyses that draw direct, unmediated relations between class interests and international pressure in shaping government health policy or that address policy in a wholly undifferentiated manner. According to this author, the strength of São Paulo's public health movement can be measured by the construction of bureaucratic apparatuses, the fashioning of a set of sanitary laws, the making and implementation of public health policy, and scientific advances in public health.[50]

Castro Santos further attributes the success of these endeavors to a particular conjugation of political, economic, and ideological forces not found in other states: the cohesion of São Paulo elites, their demand for Brazilian and immigrant labor power for the coffee economy, the absence of an established medical tradition and a consequent openness to medical and scientific innovation, an intellectual environment concerned with national issues, and an understanding of progress that favored action by public authority.[51] Both Castro Santos and Blount (though less explicitly) suggest that São Paulo cannot be explained merely as a response to the exigencies of an agricultural export economy, which most studies construe as an independent variable.

In a later article on the pioneering nature of public health in São Paulo, Castro Santos posits sanitary reform there as a concrete instance of conservative modernization (modernization from above) and as an instrument for "controlled change." São Paulo's reforms of its public health system are thus seen as part of a process of modernization led by the state's ruling elites in response to state demands and interests. In this view, the reforms contributed to controlled structural changes such as state building, alterations to the demographic profile, and urban and agricultural development.[52] Castro Santos shifts this general analytical frame of reference from the nation-state level, where it was conceived, to the level of state within a federation, thereby reinforcing the idea of São Paulo as an exception. This conceptual shift casts São Paulo more as an isolated case than as an integral part of the national experience.

I offer a more integrated analysis of reforms by São Paulo and the federal government, grounded on chapter 4's interpretation of the legal and institutional arrangements that emerged during the 1910s and 1920s. The analytical frame that explains the rest of the country also explains São Paulo, just as the national solution can only be understood as it relates to the Paulista experience. São Paulo's singular approach to public policymaking constituted an attempt to solve the negative effects of public health interdependence within the Brazilian federation. The relationship between São Paulo and the other states influenced the specific content and extent of the state's sanitation policies and national public health policies in the 1920s.

Reframing São Paulo Exceptionalism

The creation of state-level public power in São Paulo did not occur independently of events elsewhere in Brazil. As the state became aware that the individualist approach was proving ever more inefficacious in coping with the apparently skyrocketing costs of reciprocal public health dependence, São Paulo decided to collaborate with a solution that would minimize these costs within an arrangement that would also guarantee its autonomy. São Paulo's much-touted exceptionalism would in fact become part of a collective solution.

I now explore this interpretation from three vantage points, each representing a major component of the São Paulo transition from autonomy to cooperation within the nationwide public arrangement. In analytical terms, these stages correspond to the 1–2–3 sequence discussed in chapter 4.

Everyone Looks Out for Himself:
A Paulista Health Proposal

The proposed reform of federal agencies put forward by Neiva during Rodrigues Alves's 1918 presidential campaign provides insights into relations between São Paulo's public health project and national public demands for centralized policies derived from the sanitation movement. Alves's January 1919 death preempted Neiva's appointment to head the federal public health services and brought the demise of Neiva's project, which the president-elect had approved.[53] Delfim Moreira's inauguration as interim president, Epitácio Pessoa's election to the office, and the 1919 selection of Carlos Chagas, director of the Oswaldo Cruz Institute, to run federal services did not bode well for Neiva's proposal. But even though his program was defeated, it expressed the Paulista concept of federal public health policy.

Neiva's reform proposal suggested only timid changes to the structure of the General Directorate of Public Health, São Paulo's own services, and federal policies. Under its terms, the General Directorate would continue to restrict its sphere of operations to the nation's capital and the ports. Improvements to hospitals, lazarettos, sewerage, garbage collection, and so on would focus on the city of Rio de Janeiro and devote scarce attention to the rest of the country. However, the fight against yellow fever and the overhauling of port health services were not limited to the DF.

Yellow fever remained endemic along the coast from Bahia to Ceará and thus continued to threaten Rio and the rest of Brazil. Under Rodrigues Alves, the federal government would have sought "to eliminate throughout the country the malady that was wiped out in Rio de Janeiro" during his 1902–6 tenure in the nation's highest office. Neiva understood the challenges of convincing Bahia that financial aid for this purpose should be accompanied by federal technical intervention. Bahia's state agency had proven incapable of doing away with yellow fever; there were misgivings that the local government might misuse federal funds: "On several occasions, the General Directorate of Public Health offered to eliminate the malady, but while local powers accepted the offer, they wanted to transform it into currency to be used in specific prophylaxis, something they never managed to obtain, since it was apparent beforehand that these resources would be deviated from their true purposes."[54]

According to Neiva, yellow fever remained such a menace to Brazil that tougher federal action was warranted in intractable states. In addition, he argued, if Brazil did not eliminate the disease, the Americans would—an allusion to the sanitary campaigns in Cuba and Panama.[55]

Neiva's proposal was particularly concerned with improved health supervision at the ports where immigrants embarked for Brazil, especially in Japan and Italy.[56] This consideration related to the health of immigrant laborers, especially those headed to São Paulo, and also represented a way to keep immigrants rejected by other countries for health reasons from easily entering Brazil. In addition, Neiva's proposal would have revamped sanitation services at ports and lazarettos. Neiva also stressed the need to help inspectors tackle two problems hampering the supervision of ships and passengers at Brazilian ports: low wages and a lack of equipment. To complement this effort, he wanted lazarettos to be remodeled to shelter ailing travelers or those suspected of harboring disease. Abandoned control and quarantine stations could be resurrected to act as barriers to disease and prevent ships that had been refused entry at one port from sailing on to another or from dropping anchor offshore.[57]

In short, the Paulista program was cautious, placing greater emphasis on the prime issues on São Paulo's agenda and suggesting no major changes to the federal responsibilities that had been traced out by the legislation or organization of the General Directorate during the 1910s. The state sought to cope more efficiently with the bonds between Brazilian ports and between

Brazilian and foreign ports, protect the flow of foreign labor, and address a disease that still threatened to disrupt domestic and foreign trade.

Neiva, who had begun implementing São Paulo's rural sanitary code in 1917, devoted a mere paragraph of his proposal to the possibility of enacting a similar code for Brazil as a whole and instead concentrated on the DF. His suggestions for the reform of the General Directorate's health and sanitation division were even more evocative of the Paulista project for a nationwide public health policy. From the outset, Neiva connected the sanitary reforms in São Paulo to the needs of the rest of Brazil: "The work that must be done is to expand what has been achieved in the state of São Paulo during my administration, that is, the prophylaxis of malaria, ancylostomiasis, and syphilis—three endeavors that are well under way—along with trachoma, where [work is] about to commence."[58]

For Neiva, the main target of public action and available funds should be urban areas. He believed the *sertões* were less a sharply bounded geographic area than a realm as yet unreached by public authority. His proposal concerned "the sanitation of the cities in nearly all states, where almost everything remains to be done; we need only bear in mind that in the country's most advanced locality, on the edge of our nation's most cosmopolitan city, we had to set up a post to combat hookworm, in Santo Amaro, linked to the capital city of São Paulo by an electric trolley."[59]

Echoing Afrânio Peixoto's shrewd insight that the Brazilian *sertões* began right at the fringes of the majestic heart of the nation's capital, Neiva saw their frontier as fixed at the fringes of the country's fastest-growing city, São Paulo. Urban areas are spaces of human interdependence, where public health conditions play a vital social and economic role. According to Neiva, an enormous disparity existed between the number of São Paulo cities equipped with sewers and water supplies (sixty) and the number of cities in other states that boasted such facilities—for example, in Rio Grande do Sul, a state he considered more "advanced," just two towns had sewer systems. São Paulo alone had more cities with water and sewer than did all the other states combined. Since these utilities were deemed the responsibility of local power, what role fell to the federal government? Neiva's answer: to "induce, advise, request, and entreat state governments to work to supply water and build sewers for the cities in their states."[60]

Neiva's project was extremely judicious about autonomy and the most clear-cut state and municipal prerogatives. Central power should be responsible for nothing other than what had been set out in the legislation on the General Directorate, emphasizing the control of ports and immigration (matters of concern to the Paulista elites) and assistance to northeastern states in the fight against yellow fever. Such assistance had been ongoing since 1910, particularly because Bahia and other states resisted such aid and thus presented a hazard not only to São Paulo but to the rest of the country. Neiva was reticent almost to the point of silence on the subject of the rural health services created under agreements between the federal government and some states beginning in 1918. Thus, his plan called for São Paulo's accomplishments to be copied by the other states, with the aid of the federal government, while preserving the principle of state autonomy and the independence of public health agencies.

Perhaps the finest expression of the Paulista project for the sanitation of Brazil is found in the sequence of events imagined by Lobato, a fervent champion of the cause: "The areas that have been cleaned up will become a purified oasis, and the number of oases will grow as the endeavor perseveres; and after some years have gone by, all São Paulo will be an oasis. And one day, all Brazil."[61]

São Paulo Looks Out for Itself and Others: *Internalizing Costs*

The development of São Paulo's public health services was part of a twofold response. First, the coffee economy needed healthy labor power, both foreign and national, and needed to protect its international coffee trade. The crop's westward expansion within São Paulo and the process of urbanization heightened the magnitude of these problems. Second, the looming threat posed by the dire public health conditions in other states compelled São Paulo to build and enlarge its agencies to protect its territory, population, and economy. In both cases, calls for action were accompanied by calls for continued autonomy and independence from federal agencies.

São Paulo insisted that the General Directorate fulfill its duty to control ports and the DF and that it help the states when epidemics struck; in other words, the state wanted the federal agency to concern itself above all with interstate communication. In this view, other states and the territory of Acre should set up or improve their own agencies. As envisioned by São Paulo, the national community should be a cooperative arrangement where each state looked out for itself while central power took care of national sanitary defense. Neiva's project reflected this approach.

But the development of São Paulo's services also required a policy for internalizing the costs imposed by other states—that is, the cost of protecting the state's citizens and its lands, especially from epidemics. São Paulo would need to develop agencies and sanitation campaigns inside its borders while on some occasions conducting and financing sanitation campaigns in neighboring states. When São Paulo funded these services, it was replacing not just the governments of other states—often at their invitation—but also federal authorities.[62]

Governor Altino Arantes described this policy to the São Paulo legislature in 1918:

> The Sanitation Service was concerned with the campaign against communicable diseases and took special measures against smallpox, which was assailing the federal capital and a number of other states that enjoy communication with São Paulo; at the height of the outbreak, some of the ailing entered [the state] from Rio Grande do Sul, disembarking in Santos, while others came from Rio de Janeiro or were infected there, and one from Uberaba, who fell ill in Ribeirão Preto the day after his arrival.
>
> The Sanitation Service was consequently forced to step up vaccination across the state and administered 82,688 vaccinations and 111,759 revaccinations. To keep the contagion from spreading in from the northwest[ern part of the state], where large numbers of people were heading, the agency had to ask the federal intervenor from the state of Mato Grosso for permission to perform vaccinations in Três Lagoas and Campo Grande to forestall an outbreak of smallpox in [those two cities of Mato Grosso], which were in constant contact with the state of São Paulo. The initiative was most well received by the municipalities of Mato Grosso . . . while analogous services were provided in neighboring places in the states of Rio de Janeiro and Minas Gerais.[63]

São Paulo also assisted sanitation campaigns in neighboring areas.[64] To protect São Paulo, therefore, state government leaders preferred bearing the onus of providing injections in other states over paying the price of doing nothing.

Given certain specific circumstances, one state thus decided to act alone to produce a collective good even though, by definition, doing so might very well benefit those who contributed nothing toward the production of that good. In other words, the costs of consuming a social evil bred by collective inaction were perceived as exceeding the costs of crafting a solution or taking prevention measures independently, whether or not this good would benefit those who did not help foot the bill. The political and financial costs of conducting a sanitation campaign in other states in the place of local government were perceived as lower than the economic and human costs that might be incurred by failing to stop an epidemic at the borders. For São Paulo, the potential costs of opting to forgo campaigns in other states were perceived as outweighing the costs of assuming the task.[65]

Another factor important to São Paulo dynamics were the agreements with the Rockefeller Foundation involving rural health services. Through the International Health Board (IHB), the foundation began working in Brazil in the 1910s, and the states undoubtedly viewed it a potential source of technical and financial assistance in beating back rural endemic diseases.[66] The 1919–20 legislation had rendered these relations more institutional and fostered them by including federal resources in the partnerships between states and the foundation.[67] The new laws also required that the programs target malaria in addition to hookworm.[68] These agreements thus offered the states another form of political, technical, and financial support in rural health and sanitation while relieving a bit of the federal government's burden. The Rockefeller Foundation consequently represented yet another instrument available to state and federal officials in the realm of public health initiatives.

Some authors have argued that both the federal and state governments saw cooperation with the IHB as another way of strengthening reliance on public health and sanitation as an expedient for establishing public authority in regions not yet reached by the state or where local oligarchies had raised obstacles.[69] In the case of São Paulo, the logic behind collaboration with the foundation differed. The U.S. agency not only provided technical and financial support for state-level rural health and sanitation initiatives but also helped train public health doctors by offering fellowships abroad and establishing the chair in hygiene at the São Paulo School of Medicine and Surgery.[70] Starting in 1917, São Paulo's agreement with the Rockefeller Foundation served as yet another element in the autonomous development of state services, especially in the field of rural health and sanitation. In fact, the agreement that Neiva negotiated with the Rockefeller Foundation explicitly excluded the federal government.[71] Here again, São Paulo stood apart from other states, seeking support and resources without federal interference. As a result, by 1922, the state had rural health posts in a dozen municipalities under an agreement with the foundation and had obtained the agency's assistance in organizing permanent municipal services.[72]

By framing the agreements with the Rockefeller Foundation within Paulista logic, we can account for what some analysts see as a peculiar contradiction: Neiva sought aid from an agency that represented U.S. interests even though he was actively aligned with the nationalist campaign for the sanitation of Brazil.[73] The agreements with the Rockefeller Foundation afforded São Paulo another way to internalize public health costs without resorting to federal aid and while preserving state autonomy—a rational strategy that superseded Paulista leaders' ideological stances. Moreover, São Paulo retained room to negotiate the technical and financial terms of the agreements with the IHB, whereas other states who wanted to work with the office were forced to establish relations with the federal government.

The São Paulo solution meant that the state would undertake public health initiatives on its own, go after outside resources independently, and internalize the costs of interdependence. But the state could not forever endure all attendant costs. The realization that the price of transmissible diseases was rising prompted São Paulo to negotiate a broader arrangement.

São Paulo Looks Out for Itself, While the Federal Government Takes Care of the Rest of the States: A Viable Public Health Policy

As the figuration of 1891 became increasingly complex, it demanded new responses. The vast majority of the states obviously lacked the financial and technical wherewithal to implement health and sanitation policies. The federal government itself had broadened its scope of activities in the DF and ports and had increased aid to states and cities hit by yellow fever and bubonic plague. There were limits to how much São Paulo (and the DF) could internalize the costs of protecting health, since the state could not simply close its doors against every outside sanitation problem. São Paulo had organized skilled public health agencies and laid a foundation for research, teaching, and production that allowed it to respond to issues while maintaining political autonomy. Yet it could not wage battle against every public health peril, force other states to do so, or replace federal officials in other states (even though it had done so on an emergency basis). As the bonds of dependence within the federation grew more complex, the costs internalized by São Paulo rose.

The response to this dilemma was a proposal to create a nationwide public structure that could manage the effects of health interdependence. The crucial calculus was how the costs of interdependence internalized by São Paulo could be balanced against the costs of creating and running a national government agency.

The establishment of rural health agencies and the National Department of Public Health ultimately shaped administrative and financial mechanisms that helped São Paulo address the conundrum of how to give federal authorities greater power to intervene in other states, thereby reducing its costs without jeopardizing its autonomy. These mechanisms would also respond to a problem confronted by all states: How could the federal government assist in combating any serious public health problems that São Paulo could not resolve within its own borders and that consequently threatened other states without imposing on all parties afflicted by the problems of public health interdependence? How could a São Paulo veto be avoided?

The solution lay in the specific rules of the agreements on rural health and sanitation policies. The institutional design adopted in 1919, which was maintained and expanded with the January 1920 opening of the National Department of Public Health, offered a viable remedy for both São Paulo and the other states because these agreements would be optional. Furthermore, any project, like the creation of a health ministry or the establishment of the National Department, had to be approved by the Chamber of Deputies Finance Committee—packed with Paulistas—and by a plenary session of the federal legislature, where the state did not constitute the biggest bloc but still carried much weight. Moreover, São Paulo wielded great power within the federal executive. For the vast majority of the states, which could not make or keep their territories healthy, what was on paper a voluntary choice was in practice a mandatory imposition. For São Paulo, however, any agreement was indeed voluntary. The nature of communicable diseases had revealed the price of social interdependence but did not in and of itself ensure any reform or determine the content thereof. The political coalition that enabled the shifting of responsibilities to the federal government was born from a calculus regarding not just the costs and benefits of this move but also the rules governing it.

All parties to the problems of interdependence were encouraged to participate for a variety of reasons. The states envisioned opportunities to benefit from technical and financial resources that would improve public health conditions. The intimation contained in the São Paulo project of 1918 had now been replaced by a veritable obligation since most states had few alternatives. São Paulo's awareness of interdependence brought an accompanying realization that the state could not continue internalizing costs and that an individual solution to the ills of communicable disease was increasingly inefficient. But once São Paulo had the option of voluntarily excluding itself from an arrangement that boosted the power of federal health authorities, it felt comfortable yielding to a broader national organization and thus could truly choose to participate.

Under this formula, the costs São Paulo would bear as government expanded (costs fundamentally sustained by the other states) and the perceived costs of organizing collective action (borne by the federal government and all interested states) were lower than the perceived costs of health interdependence imposed on São Paulo by other states. At the same time, other states saw the costs of augmented central power as lower than the costs of its absence—that is, than the presence of disease. Above all, as they saw it, the benefits of federal action outweighed the benefits of preserving state autonomy.

São Paulo—without a federal presence inside its borders but with the benefits of this presence in other states—came to throw its support behind a nationwide arrangement and to benefit from public health agreements with the central power precisely because the state was allowed to opt out. And so it went until the close of the First Republic.

Conclusion

São Paulo exceptionalism should be appreciated from a more nuanced interpretive angle. Under the First Republic, the Paulista elites developed and administered prodigious sanitation services, avoiding any interference or intervention by federal authorities while taking advantage of their singular form of agreements with the Rockefeller Foundation. When federal agencies began broadening their scope of work in the 1910s, they found São Paulo's agency advanced and firmly rooted statewide. Yet São Paulo could not continue internalizing all the costs imposed by its public health interdependence with other states while addressing its own internal troubles. With a burgeoning awareness that transmissible diseases were becoming very pricey, the Paulista political elites realized that the relations between signatories to the pact of 1891 were more intense and complex than previously thought.

To reduce the negative effects imposed by other states, São Paulo therefore decided to collaborate in establishing a nationwide public arrangement that would create public health policies, especially to fight rural endemic diseases and epidemics of yellow fever and plague. The precondition to the state's participation was the nonmandatory nature of the scheme, and in this regard, the formula adopted in 1918 and expanded starting in 1920 was the key to the emergence of a national health and sanitation policy. When São Paulo decided to collaborate so that other states could receive federal rural health services, the state was agreeing to take part in an arrangement that was compulsory for other states but voluntary for itself, thereby guaranteeing São Paulo greater autonomy. With São Paulo's approbation came its right to remain unique. This model let São Paulo's elites maximize their political and administrative autonomy while minimizing the costs inflicted on them by the public health ordeals of other states.

Other states could not afford grand visions of autonomy, but this arrangement provided them with federal technical and financial resources to fix public health problems and featured the self-interested approval of the locomotive of the federation. The immediate upshot was that São Paulo would minimize the costs of its interdependence while averting the onus of a federal presence inside its territory, whereas other interested parties could enjoy the benefits of central power, though they had to pay the price of its presence.

Throughout the First Republic, public health policy was the product of choices grounded in tense, singular interactions involving São Paulo, other states, and central power. The country's national health policy arose from a specific combination of state autonomy and health interdependence, not from the mere isolation or uniqueness of São Paulo, as a reading that contrasts state autonomy with central power would suggest. As Love suggests, "regionalism was not the antithesis of interpenetration and integration."[74]

My argument complements the interpretation presented by Reis—that is, that the São Paulo elites chose to rely on federal regulation of economic activities rather than on the market when doing so was in the state's interest, and that this decision had unforeseen consequences.[75] São Paulo took advantage of central power in the economic realm, rejected it in sanitation and health, and agreed that it could be offered to other states. Welcoming a federal presence in other states to cope with the effects of public health interdependence was much like turning to the federal executive to regulate the coffee economy, an option that reaped short- and medium-term net benefits for São Paulo. The Paulista elites selectively availed themselves of central power, both in dealing with public health interdependence between São Paulo and the other states and in regulating the coffee economy.

In the long run, an initially voluntary arrangement became mandatory for nearly everyone. In addition, the arrangement substantially enhanced the federal ability to implement public policy, increasingly with no need for the consent of the political elites, including those who imagined they had minimized the costs of the presence of the central power. This approach laid the groundwork for a concentration and centralization of power and for government activism not foreseen by the elites when they drew up their calculus and decided to shift activities to the federal government. Many historians see the period beginning in 1930 as a break with the past in the shaping and institutionalization of both social policy and government centralization, but the construction of public power had been moving along apace over the previous two decades. This is one of the legacies of the movement for the sanitation of Brazil.

CHAPTER 6

Final Thoughts

"I want to see him, doctor."
There was a pregnant pause.
"Have you been vaccinated?"
"I have."
"Have you ever seen anyone with smallpox?"
"No."
"Do you like this young man?"
"He's my friend."
The director [of São Sebastião Hospital]
thought it over. Then he said, "It's better if you
don't see him. Take my advice. He wants for noth-
ing. You, sir, seem so upset. Have hope, and go
rest. At a time like this, emotions are bad for us."

—João do Rio, "A Peste" (1910)

It is hard to adopt a strictly neutral scholarly perspective on Brazilian public health policy, a topic that has us staring hard in the face of human suffering and misery. Throughout this study, I have tried to follow the hospital director's advice (though the young man in the story did not). Keeping an analytical distance from my object of study meant eschewing any inclination to pass judgment on the concrete results of rising government responsibility for the health of the Brazilian people, the decisions that were eventually made, and the main actors and institutions involved. It also meant holding my tongue about more contemporary issues. So now, at the close of this book, I am visiting my sick friend.

This book shows why, when, and how public health policy in Brazil was transferred to the federal government and collectivized nationwide, calling attention to the often-overlooked signs that this process began during the

First Republic. Describing the historical foundations of Brazilian public health policy and elucidating how health was collectivized there helps in providing an understanding of how it came to be the right of the citizen and a duty of the state, as set out in the 1988 constitution.

Yet—and here I come to "my sick friend"—while compiling this study, I often found myself captivated by the ideas, politics, and personalities that inhabited my narrative. Ultimately, considering the onslaught of criticisms currently being hurled at Brazil's public health system, I find it quite tempting to pass favorable judgment both on the drive to restore and preserve the health of the population during the First Republic and on the accompanying proposals, policy formulations, and initiatives. Even when these intellectual and political efforts proved unviable, somewhat feeble, or even contradictory, they signaled the emergence of a public consciousness as Brazil discovered the atrocious living conditions and neglect to which the vast majority of its citizens had been relegated. At the same time, these efforts ushered in public policies that eventually extended across the entire country. Through the republican experience, public health rarely received so much attention from the government or from the public at large.

Special interests won out when Brazil forged its public health policy, and by the end of my research, I found myself nourishing a tremendous personal empathy for the civic and heroic dimensions of many of the ideas put forward, irrespective of the ideological convictions or political stances of the personalities behind them: most of these people were of authoritarian bent or at best liberal. These actors wanted to use social policy to make rural populations an integral part of the nation, in a protective albeit hierarchical way. What drew me the most, without a doubt, was the generosity and social concern that echoes through their discourses and actions, framed within a forceful world of interests and tangible opportunities.

The research that underlies this book has been challenged by critical formulations about active government and by some people's desire to contain that government, a matter that was on Brazil's national agenda when I originally wrote this book in the 1990s and that remains relevant in the second decade of the twenty-first century, when the country's universal health care system (Sistema Único de Saúde) is constantly called into question. I refer especially to the public discussion over which duties should be considered inherent to the state and which should have nothing to do with its purpose. Some have depicted this distinction as a so-called natural one that should guide decisions about what to leave in federal hands, what to privatize, and what to shift to other spheres of government. Those who adhere to this perspective feel that the challenges of the contemporary state should be met by a reform that returns to society activities that have been "unnaturally" and "unduly" placed in the care of the state and would operate more efficiently under market logic.

From this perspective, I realized I had been studying a process of collectivization at precisely the time in the 1990s when an apparent international consensus had been reached about the need to move in the opposite direction. During a time of privatization, deregulation, and return to the market, with history unfolding in a political and institutional climate unfavorable to state activism, I was exploring the formation of the state and its social policies. Not coincidentally, the reform of Brazilian public health during the 1980s and 1990s, as many have pressed home, ran counter to the neoliberal reforms of the state then in fashion elsewhere in Latin America and in Eastern Europe.

Yet far from going against history, my subject should be understood as a two-sided coin: heads, constitution of the state; tails, reform of the state. Furthermore, this analysis can help us gauge the supposedly inherent nature of the state's legitimate duties. After all, the first three decades of the twentieth century were first and foremost a period of political experimentation and reform.

An awareness of the communicable nature of disease, the attendant dilemmas, and the calculus of the costs and benefits of related government expansion underpinned the decision to extend this authority. While the problem of social interdependence may be an inevitable facet of modern urban-industrial societies, the consequent institutional arrangements do not necessarily have to be similar across different experiences or historical moments. Shaped by the public health movement, a consciousness of the supralocal, national character of the threat of communicable diseases does not necessarily lead to a transfer of activities to the federal sphere. Even if that road is taken, the same dilemmas can produce different public policies. The political responses that prove feasible within given institutional contexts drive the convergence of consciousness and interests.

Based on calculations made under specific conditions, the political choices and decisions of this period engendered laws, regulations, institutions, public action, and government actors that launched the development of a nationwide governmental infrastructure in public health and rural sanitation. These dynamics then molded subsequent decisions and policies whose outcomes had not been anticipated by the parties to the initial agreement. The factors underlying the original calculus about external costs versus the benefits and costs of more government were profoundly altered, as were the context and constraints that informed these decisions. Shifting responsibilities to the central power and establishing federal health authority throughout the country eventually reshaped the universe of the pertinent decision-making units and forums—along with the questions that were demanding answers. As attention turned to the main targets of public concern in the 1910s and 1920s—that is, rural endemic and epidemic diseases—the public health agenda itself began focusing on different sets of issues, both old and new.

The legal and institutional arrangements that hastened the growth of public authority were in large part proposed, approved, and implemented by those who would at first glance be harmed by these measures: state bosses and political elites. Less resistance arose to government expansion per se than to the specific formulas for transferring activities to the sphere of central power. Awareness of interdependence conjoined to incentives offered through government activism eased the way out of an impasse and toward a politically viable arrangement for all parties involved. The elites concluded not only that they could not compete with federal authority in solving the ills generated by ubiquitous disease but also that they could benefit from that authority.

Some of the public health activities added to the basket of government goods were the object of conflict and political negotiation, while others were incorporated more gradually as the state implemented public health. The transfer of duties to the government, especially to the central power, was a product of choices and bargaining among the units initially tasked with these activities under an earlier political pact, the constitution of 1891. The long-term results of this transfer were not foreseeable when the decisions were made.

The growth of government intervention was not a process determined by the fact that these activities naturally belonged in the public sphere. Given the complexity of the process by which government is formed, it is a thorny task to debate and analyze the reform of the state based on any "natural" criteria that would legitimize its duties. My analysis has focused on politics as one of the mechanisms that has defined the scope of the public sphere over time. Historically speaking, the foundations of public care for health in Brazil were the object of negotiations in which ideas, consciousness, and interests came together. In any era of reform, what will ultimately remain in the care of the state may well depend on just how this encounter transpires.

As I put the final touches on this English translation of *A Era do Saneamento*, I bear witness to contemporary negative discourses on the role of the state that are just as fundamentalist as the discourses of the public health movement explored in these chapters. And while substantively quite divergent, the discourses of yesterday and today manifest a need for sanitation—that is, a need to clean up the country and its people. But it would also be wise to note that during the era explored here, the word *saneamento* not only referred to the act of making something healthy or curing ills, whatever their nature, but also carried another, more positive, and perhaps now archaic connotation applicable to an imagined Brazil: change, reconciliation, and inclusion.

APPENDIX 1

Institutions, Agencies, and Departments

English Long Form	Portuguese	Notes
Ana Nery School of Nursing	Escola de Enfermagem Ana Nery	Established in 1922 as part of the National Department of Public Health
Bacteriological Institute	Instituto Bacteriológico	Established in 1892 in São Paulo
Bahia School of Medicine	Faculdade de Medicina da Bahia	Established in 1808 in Salvador
Butantan Institute	Instituto Butantan	Established in 1901 in São Paulo
Directorate of Inland Sanitation Services	Diretoria de Serviços Sanitários Terrestres	Established in 1920 as part of the National Department of Public Health
Directorate of Rural Sanitation and Prophylaxis	Diretoria de Saneamento e Profilaxia Rural (DSPR)	Established in 1920 as part of the National Department of Public Health
Federal Sanitation Commission	Comissão Sanitária Federal	
Federal Serum Therapy Institute	Instituto Soroterápico Federal	Established in 1900; renamed the Oswaldo Cruz Institute in 1908
Finance Committee	Comissão de Finanças	

General Directorate of Public Health	Diretoria Geral de Saúde Pública	Established in 1896 and attached to the Ministry of Justice and Internal Affairs; reformulated in 1914 under Decree 10.821; abolished with the 1920 creation of the National Department of Public Health
General Inspectorate of Hygiene	Inspetoria Geral de Higiene	Established in 1886 under the Higher Council of Public Health as part of the Barão de Mamoré Reform
General Inspectorate of Port Health	Inspetoria Geral de Saúde dos Portos	Established in 1886 under the Higher Council of Public Health as part of the Barão de Mamoré Reform
Higher Council of Hygiene	Conselho Superior de Higiene	Proposed by the National Academy of Medicine commission in 1917 but never formed
Higher Council of Public Health	Conselho Superior de Saúde Pública	Established in 1886 as part of the Barão de Mamoré Reform
Inspectorate for Leprosy and Venereal Disease Prophylaxis	Inspetoria de Profilaxia da Lepra e das Doenças Venéreas	Established in 1920 under the same decree that created the National Department of Public Health
Inspectorate of General Prophylaxis Services	Inspetoria dos Serviços de Profilaxia Geral	São Paulo state agency established in 1917
Inspectorate of Industrial and Vocational Hygiene	Inspetoria de Higiene Industrial e Profissional	Established by the National Department of Public Health pursuant to 1923 administrative regulations
Inspectorate of Infant and Child Hygiene	Inspetoria de Higiene Infantil	Established by the National Department of Public Health pursuant to 1923 administrative regulations
Inspectorate of Sanitary Demography	Inspetoria de Demografia Sanitária	Established by the National Department of Public Health pursuant to 1923 administrative regulations
Ministry of Hygiene and Public Health	Ministério de Higiene e Saúde Pública	Ministry proposed by the Pro-Sanitation League of Brazil but never created

Ministry of Justice and Internal Affairs	Ministério da Justiça e Negócios Interiores	Created in 1822 as the Ministry of Justice; known as the Ministry of Justice and Internal Affairs from 1891 through 1967, when it was again named the Ministry of Justice
Ministry of Public Health	Ministério de Saúde Pública	Ministry proposed by the Brazilian public health movement but never created under the First Republic
Ministry of Transportation and Public Works	Ministério de Viação e Obras Públicas	
National Academy of Medicine	Academia Nacional de Medicina	Founded in 1829
National Defense League	Liga de Defesa Nacional	Founded in 1916
National Department of Public Health	Departamento Nacional de Saúde Pública	Created under Decree 3.987 (January 2, 1920)
National Library	Biblioteca Nacional	
National Museum	Museu Nacional	
National Society of Agriculture	Sociedade Nacional de Agricultura	Founded in 1897 in Rio de Janeiro
Nationalist League	Liga Nacionalista	Founded in 1916 in São Paulo
Office of Infant and Child Hygiene and Assistance	Seção de Higiene Infantil e Assistência à Infância	
Official Drug Service	Serviço de Medicamentos Oficiais	Established in 1918
Official Quinine Service	Serviço de Quinina Oficial	Established in 1918
Oswaldo Cruz Institute	Instituto Oswaldo Cruz	Established in 1900 in Rio de Janeiro
Pasteur Institute	Instituto Pasteur	Established in 1903 in São Paulo
Port Health Service	Serviço de Saúde dos Portos	
Procedural Regulation of the Sanitary Justice	Regulamento Processual da Justiça Sanitária	

Pro-Sanitation League of Brazil	Liga Pró-Saneamento do Brasil	A movement that championed public health action in the interior of Brazil; founded in 1918
Public Health Committee	Comissão de Saúde Pública	
Rio de Janeiro School of Medicine	Faculdade de Medicina do Rio de Janeiro	Established in 1808
Rio de Janeiro Society of Medicine and Surgery	Sociedade de Medicina e Cirurgia do Rio de Janeiro	Founded in 1886
Rural Prophylaxis Service	Serviço de Profilaxia Rural	
Rural Sanitation and Prophylaxis Service	Serviço de Saneamento e Profilaxia Rural	
Sanitary Information and Education Service	Serviço de Propaganda e Educação Sanitária	Established by the National Department of Public Health pursuant to 1923 administrative regulations
Sanitation Service	Serviço Sanitário	
São Paulo Eugenics Society	Sociedade de Eugenia de São Paulo	Founded in 1918
São Paulo School of Medicine and Surgery	Faculdade de Medicina e Cirurgia de São Paulo	Established in 1912
Specific Yellow Fever Prophylaxis Service	Serviço de Profilaxia Específica da Febre Amarela	
Superintendence of Nursing Services	Superintendência de Serviços de Enfermagem	

States and Territories of Brazil under the First Republic (1889–1930)

AC	Acre (annexed as a Federal Territory in 1903)
AL	Alagoas
AM	Amazonas
BA	Bahia
CE	Ceará
DF	Federal District
ES	Espírito Santo
GO	Goiás
MA	Maranhão
MG	Minas Gerais
MT	Mato Grosso
PA	Pará
PB	Paraíba
PE	Pernambuco
PI	Piauí
PR	Paraná
RJ	Rio de Janeiro
RN	Rio Grande do Norte
RS	Rio Grande do Sul
SC	Santa Catarina
SE	Sergipe
SP	São Paulo

Notes

Chapter 1. When Health Becomes Public: State Formation and Health Policies in Brazil

1. See also Reis, "Agrarian Roots"; Reis, "Elites Agrárias"; Reis, "Poder Privado."
2. Reis, "Poder Privado," 43–44.
3. Reis, "Agrarian Roots"; Reis, "Poder Privado."
4. Castro Santos, "Pensamento Sanitarista"; Castro Santos, "Power, Ideology and Public Health."
5. De Swaan, *In Care of the State.*
6. Elias, *Processo Civilizador*; Elias, *State Formation and Civilization.*
7. Elias, *Introdução à Sociologia*; Elias, *What Is Sociology?*; Elias, *Processo Civilizador*; Elias, *State Formation and Civilization.*
8. Elias, *Introdução à Sociologia*, 73, 78.
9. Ibid., 103; Elias, *Processo Civilizador*, 194.
10. Elias, *Introdução à Sociologia*, 143.
11. De Swaan, *In Care of the State.*
12. Ibid., 2.
13. Ibid., 2–4.
14. Olson, *Logic of Collective Action.*
15. De Swaan, *In Care of the State*, 10.
16. Elias, *Introdução à Sociologia*, 33.
17. De Swaan, *In the Care of the State*, 7.
18. Ibid.

19. Fraser, *Evolution*, ch. 3.

20. Santos, *Razões da Desordem*, 52.

21. Baldwin, *Contagion and the State*; Briggs, *Cholera and Society*; Duffy, "Social Impact of Disease"; Fraser, *Evolution*; Hamlin, *Public Health and Social Justice*; Rosenberg, *Cholera Years*.

22. This argument points to a tendency for different countries to display similar behavior in the areas of public spending, public policy, and institutional arrangements. See also Mishra, *Society and Social Policy*, 39–49.

23. Nettl, "State as Conceptual Variable."

24. See also Olson, *Logic of Collective Action*.

25. Buchanan and Tullock, *Calculus of Consent*, 61.

26. Ibid., 45–46.

27. See also Santos, *Razões da Desordem*, 51–59.

28. Peter A. Hall and Taylor, "Political Science"; Immergut, *Health Politics*, 18–33; Thelen and Steinmo, "Historical Institutionalism."

29. Ashford, *History and Context*.

30. Mann, "Autonomous Power."

31. Mann, *Sources of Social Power*, 55.

32. Mann, "Autonomous Power," 201.

33. J. A. Hall and Ikenberry, *O Estado*, 12–14; Hintze, "Calvinism"; Rokkan, "Dimensions of State Formation"; Tilly, "Reflections," 70–71; Weber, *Economía y Sociedad*, 1047–59.

34. Mann, "Autonomous Power," 188; Mann, *Sources of Social Power*, 59.

35. Mann, "Autonomous Power," 189; Mann, *Sources of Social Power*, 59.

36. Mann, "Autonomous Power," 201–2.

37. De Swaan, *In Care of the State*, 13–51.

38. See Buchanan and Tullock, *Calculus of Consent*.

39. Mann, *Sources of Social Power*, 84–85.

40. See Skocpol and Amenta, "State and Social Policies"; Skocpol, *Protecting Soldiers*.

41. Skocpol, *Protecting Soldiers*, 41.

42. Ibid., 58–59.

43. Pierson, "When Effect Becomes Cause."

44. All references to states of Brazil also include the Federal Territory of Acre, annexed in 1903.

45. Nettl, "State as Conceptual Variable," 579, uses the term *saliency of the state* (stateness).

46. Reis, "Elites Agrárias"; Reis, "Poder Privado."

47. This paucity of data was recognized by public health leaders in the 1930s. In 1930, the director of the National Department of Public Health, Brazil's highest federal health agency, complained that "the history of the recent development of our sanitation services is destined to present huge gaps because neither our ar-

chives nor the archives of the former Ministry of Justice and Internal Affairs hold any vestiges whatsoever of the annual reports of the director of the [National] Department of Public Health from 1920 on, except for the 1927 report" (Arquivo Belisário Penna). Similar remarks concerning the absence of organized information on the period were made by J. P. Fontenelle, an important physician, federal public health staff member in the 1920s and 1930s, and author of countless works on public health (*Saúde Pública*, 1).

Chapter 2. The Microbe of Disease and Public Power: The Public Health Movement and a Growing Consciousness of Interdependence

1. Edson, "Microbe as a Social Leveler," 424, 422.
2. Ibid., 425.
3. Ibid.
4. Pelling, "Contagion/Germ Theory."
5. See De Swaan, *In Care of the State*.
6. Elias, *Introdução à Sociologia*, 143.
7. Baldwin, *Contagion and the State*; Pelling, "Contagion/Germ Theory"; Temkin, "Historical Analysis."
8. Dwork, "Contagion," 75–77; McGrew, "Contagion," 77–79.
9. *Mosby's Medical Dictionary*, 921.
10. Pelling, "Contagion/Germ Theory," 314–15.
11. Ibid., 309–10.
12. Barroso, *Doenças que Pegam*, 14.
13. Temkin, "Historical Analysis," 144.
14. Hannaway, "Environment and Miasmata"; Pelling, "Contagion/Germ Theory."
15. On yellow fever, see Duffy, "Social Impact of Disease." On cholera, see De Swaan, *In Care of the State*, 124–28; Fraser, *Evolution*, 59–60. On the Spanish flu, see Crosby, *America's Forgotten Pandemic*. Some historians of medicine consider "collective fear" the strongest social force behind the emergence of public initiatives to combat disease. In the opinion of Richard H. Shryock, this fear springs from the sudden violence of an epidemic, ignorance about its causes or means of transmission, and the lesions that may be left behind, visible to all (*Medicine in America*, 141). However, in these interpretations, social forces are not central but rather complement the medical and scientific prerequisites for fighting a disease.
16. Rosen, *History of Public Health*.
17. De Swaan, *In Care of the State*, 131–37.
18. Ackerknecht, "Anticontagionism." Although I have presented simplified versions of both the germ and miasmatic theories, I am well aware of the tremendous complexity and long historical evolution of the noncontagionist and contagionist

theories. Ackerknecht, "Anticontagionism," offers a classic text on the clashes between these two interpretations in Europe through the nineteenth century and on
the origin of diseases and their means of transmission. Pernick, "Politics, Parties,
and Pestilence," is an important source on these debates and their ramifications
in the United States, especially regarding yellow fever epidemics. On national and
regional quarantines in the context of U.S. federalism, see the writings on yellow
fever in the southern United States by Humphreys, *Yellow Fever*; J. H. Ellis, *Yellow
Fever*. For critiques of Ackerknecht's perspective, see Baldwin, *Contagion and the
State*; Hamlin, "Commentary"; Stern and Markel, "Commentary."

19. Murard and Zylberman, "Raison de l'Éxpert."

20. De Swaan, *In Care of the State*, 134.

21. Schwartz, *Public Health*, 128.

22. Kramer, "Germ Theory," 245–47; Kunitz, "Explanations and Ideologies";
Kunitz, "Hookworm and Pellagra."

23. Schwartz, *Public Health*.

24. Murard and Zylberman, "Raison de l'Éxpert," 60–61.

25. Pelling, "Contagion/Germ Theory," 309.

26. Temkin, "Historical Analysis," 146–47.

27. Ibid., 147.

28. Kramer, "Germ Theory"; McClary, "Germs Are Everywhere"; Richmond,
"American Attitudes"; Tomes, "Private Side."

29. McClary, "Germs Are Everywhere"; Barroso, *Doenças que Pegam*, 53.

30. Marcus, "Disease Prevention."

31. Castro Santos, "Estado e Saúde Pública"; Castro Santos, "Pensamento Sanitarista"; Castro Santos, "Power, Ideology, and Public Health."

32. Albuquerque et al., *Ciência Vai à Roça*; Britto, *Oswaldo Cruz*; Lima and
Britto, "Salud y Nación"; Lima and Hochman, "Condenado pela Raça"; Lima,
Sertão Chamado Brasil.

33. Costa, *Lutas Urbanas*; Labra, "Movimento Sanitarista"; Iyda, *Cem Anos*;
Merhy, *Capitalismo e a Saúde Pública*; Ribeiro, *História Sem Fim*.

34. Castro Santos, "Power, Ideology, and Public Health."

35. For a brief biography of Oswaldo Cruz (1872–1917), physician and director of the Oswaldo Cruz Institute from 1902 to 1917, see Hochman and Azevedo,
"Oswaldo Cruz."

36. Benchimol, *Pereira Passos*; Castro Santos, "Power, Ideology, and Public
Health," chs. 2, 3; Costa, *Lutas Urbanas*, ch. 2.

37. Blount, "Public Health Movement"; Blount, "Administração da Saúde
Pública"; Castro Santos, "Reforma Sanitária 'Pelo Alto'"; Ribeiro, *História Sem
Fim*; Telarolli, *Poder e Saúde*.

38. Castro Santos, "Pensamento Sanitarista"; Castro Santos, "Power, Ideology,
and Public Health," ch. 3. For a broader discussion on race and health in Brazil,
see Hochman, Lima, and Maio, "Path of Eugenics," 493–510.

39. Castro Santos, "Power, Ideology, and Public Health," ch. 6.

40. Joll, *Europa desde 1870*, ch. 8; Hobsbawm, *Nations and Nationalism*.

41. One of the most oft cited international examples of how war has stirred debate on determinism and so-called racial improvement is the mobilization of the British troops in the Boer Wars and the impact of the humiliation of those troops on Edwardian England's heated discussions of the "physical conditions of race," which culminated with the National Health Insurance Act of 1911. See Porter, "Enemies of the Race," 161, 172–74; Porter, "Public Health," 1256.

42. Fontenelle, "Higiene e Saúde Pública"; Patterson and Pyle, "Geography and Mortality."

43. Skidmore, *Black into White*; Skidmore, "Racial Ideas and Social Policy"; Lúcia Lippi de Oliveira, *Questão Nacional*.

44. Castro Santos, "Pensamento Sanitarista"; Castro Santos, "Power, Ideology, and Public Health"; Lúcia Lippi de Oliveira, *Questão Nacional*.

45. Neiva and Penna, "Viagem Científica," 74–224. The Oswaldo Cruz Institute incorporated and replaced the Federal Serum Therapy Institute, which had been established in 1900 during the bubonic plague epidemic in Rio de Janeiro. Under the direction of Oswaldo Cruz (1902–17), it became a major research and training center for public health professionals. From 1917 to 1934, its director was Carlos Chagas. On the institute's role in Brazilian science, see Benchimol, *Manguinhos*; Benchimol and Teixeira, *Cobras, Lagartos*; Chagas Filho, *Carlos Chagas*; Luz, *Medicina e Ordem*; Schwartzman, *Formação da Comunidade Científica*; Stepan, *Beginnings of Brazilian Science*.

46. Pereira, "Brasil É Ainda," 7.

47. On the debate about the armed forces and compulsory military service in Brazil during World War I, see Lúcia Lippi de Oliveira, *Questão Nacional*, 119–22; Carvalho, "Forças Armadas," 193–95; Skidmore, *Black into White*, 146–72.

48. Pereira, "Brasil É Ainda," 7. On the history of Chagas's disease, see Kropf, *Doença de Chagas*.

49. Ibid. The next day, at a dinner in honor of Chagas, Pereira reaffirmed and expounded on his arguments, now sounding a tad more optimistic about the country's future (cited in *Jornal do Comércio*, October 22, 1916, Arquivo Carlos Chagas). The second speech also received a great deal of press (Britto, *Oswaldo Cruz*, 21–23).

50. Dominichi Miranda de Sá, "Interpretação do Brasil"; Dominichi Miranda de Sá, "Voz do Brasil."

51. During the first two decades of the twentieth century, researchers from the Oswaldo Cruz Institute traveled the Brazilian *sertões* on scientific expeditions, producing an abundance of information on the incidence and spread of disease and thus nourishing the debate on national problems. These expeditions were driven by railway construction, hydrographic surveys to gauge the economic potential of the São Francisco and other river systems, and civil engineering projects by water-resource authorities such as the Inspectorate for Works against Droughts

(Inspetoria de Obras contra as Secas) (Albuquerque et al., *Ciência Vai à Roça*; Lima, *Sertão Chamado Brasil*; Schweickardt and Lima, "Inferno Florido").

52. Albuquerque et al., *Ciência Vai à Roça*; Lima, *Sertão Chamado Brasil*.

53. Albuquerque et al., *Ciência Vai à Roça*; Schweickardt and Lima, "Inferno Florido"; Lima, *Sertão Chamado Brasil*.

54. Neiva and Penna, "Viagem Científica," 121. The romantic version of the rural dweller came from Euclides da Cunha's highly influential *Os Sertões* (1902; tr. *Rebellion in the Backlands*, 1944), which was a major textual reference for the movement. It colored the hinterlander as strong but uncultured and uncivilized. *Rebellion in the Backlands* also drives home the importance of getting to know Brazil empirically, an essential notion in texts and commentary by the public health movement. See Lima and Hochman, "Condenado pela Raça"; Lima, "Public Health and Social Ideas; Lima, "Doctors, Social Scientists"; Lima, *Sertão Chamado Brasil*.

55. Neiva and Penna, "Viagem Científica," 199.

56. One example of this negative image grounded in the individual (or perhaps in race) can be found in writer Monteiro Lobato's first version of his character Jeca Tatu, painted as a naturally lazy *caipira*, a term generally applied to someone from the Brazilian interior who is of mixed European, indigenous, and/or African ethnicity. In essays published in the news daily *O Estado de S. Paulo* in 1914, Lobato argued that the hinterlander was Brazil's foremost national plague, describing him as a "sinister parasite of the land . . . a barren man who is incapable of adapting to civilization" (*Urupês*, 271). But then, under the influence of the rural sanitation campaign, Lobato jettisoned his fatalism. In 1918, he wrote, "Jeca wasn't made the way he is; he was made into the way he is [Jeca não é assim, está assim]." Health played a central role in Lobato's subsequent "resurrection of Jeca": a hinterlander rendered lazy, poor, and backward by illness learns to believe in medicine and follow its precepts, ridding himself of hookworm and consequently snapping out of his permanent state of despondency. Restored to health, he becomes a prosperous planter, entrepreneurial and modern (Lobato, *Mr. Slang*, 329–40). See Campos, *República do Picapau Amarelo*; Castro Santos, "Pensamento Sanitarista"; Lima and Hochman, "Condenado pela Raça"; Lima "Brasiliana Médica"; Lima, *Sertão Chamado Brasil*; Ribeiro, *História Sem Fim*.

57. Neiva, *Discursos-Pronunciados*, 23.

58. Lúcia Lippi de Oliveira, *Questão Nacional*, 95–109; Castro Santos, "Pensamento Sanitarista"; Castro Santos, "Power, Ideology, and Public Health"; Skidmore, *Black into White*.

59. Neiva and Penna, "Viagem Científica," 198.

60. Writing in 1918, Lobato captured how medical science had soothed the anguish of a generation of intellectuals: "Today we breathe easier. The laboratory has given us the argument we so eagerly sought. Grounded in it, we shall counter Le Bon's sociological condemnation with the higher voice of biology" (Lobato,

Mr. Slang, 298). For a discussion of this topic in greater detail, see Lima and Hochman, "Condenado pela Raça."

61. Souza Araújo, *Impaludismo no Norte*, 75.

62. Acácio Pires, head of the Rural Sanitation and Prophylaxis Service in Paraíba, to Belisário Penna, director of federal Rural Sanitation and Prophylaxis, July 7, 1921, BRRJCOC BP 02-02, Arquivo Belisário Penna.

63. Although Janaína Amado makes no specific mention of the relations between the hinterlands and public health in the 1910s, I have relied on her review of the differences within the category of *sertões* ("Região, Sertão, Nação").

64. "While a scant few do escape the disease, many have two or three infestations. . . . We are quite often distressed and alarmed to see public schoolchildren whose teeth are chattering away from the chills of the ague. . . . And this is not in the backwaters of Brazil but here in the Federal District, in Guaratiba, Jacarepaguá, Tijuca. . . . For let us have no illusions, 'our *sertões*' begin somewhere at the end of Avenida Central" (Peixoto, "Discurso Pronunciado," 31–32). This quotation comes from a May 19, 1918, speech that Peixoto gave to honor Miguel Pereira and was heard throughout Brazil. Lobato, a major proponent of the campaign, also believed that the periphery of urban centers should be the key target of a sanitation campaign (*Mr. Slang*, 313–14).

65. Bello, "Problema Nacional," iii–iv.

66. *O Saneamento do Brasil* is a collection of articles that first appeared in the news daily *Correio da Manhã* from November 1916 through January 1917. In addition to presenting the program of the Pro-Sanitation League of Brazil, the book was also a campaign fund-raiser.

67. Penna, *Saneamento do Brasil*, 122.

68. Ibid., 157, 158.

69. Ibid., 149.

70. Ibid., 150.

71. Cavalcanti, "Canaan Sertaneja"; Lobato, *Mr. Slang*. Jeca's resurrection appears in the last chapter of Lobato's collection of essays denouncing Brazil's abysmal health conditions, published in book form in 1918. This argument appears in Lima and Britto, "Salud y Nación"; Lima and Hochman, "Condenado pela Raça"; Lima, *Sertão Chamado Brasil*. The view that agriculture played a central role in the Brazilian economy accounts for relations between the movement and the National Society of Agriculture, which hosted the Pro-Sanitation League's head offices and many of its meetings. More than simple rural sanitation, Penna advocated an "Agrosanitation Policy for National Salvation [Política Agrossanitária de Salvação Nacional]" (*Saneamento do Brasil*, 329). For the agrarian elites and the work of the National Society of Agriculture, see Mendonça, *Ruralismo Brasileiro*.

72. Penna, *Saneamento do Brasil*, 149–50.

73. Ibid., 158.

74. Ibid., 137.

75. While the fight against hookworm did play a symbolic role, Penna also underscored the fact that "incalculable is the damage done to our nation by ancylostomiasis, a malady that does not frighten the masses as do smallpox, plague, or yellow fever, because its march is chronic, its effects slow and progressive. . . . In short, it lacks the violent face of acute illnesses, although it injures and victimizes many more people than the others" (*Saneamento do Brasil*, 218). Governments, however, were only willing to take action against epidemics, which cause "alarm, because they strike many people all at once and kill within a few days" (19).

76. Ibid., 165–66.

77. The emphasis on rural endemic diseases, especially hookworm, was in no way unique to the Brazilian public health movement. The Rockefeller Foundation mounted a very active campaign against hookworm worldwide, including Brazil, and later undertook efforts against yellow fever between 1915 and 1930 and malaria during the 1930s in the northeastern part of the country (Benchimol, *Febre Amarela*; Cueto, *Missionaries of Science*; Cueto, "Ciclos de la Erradicación"; Faria, "Fase Pioneira"; Hochman, Mello, and Elian Santos, "Malária em Foto"). In characterizing local populations, analyses of Rockefeller Foundation activities in the southern United States reveal striking similarities with the findings of Brazilian public health reports. In both instances, the physical frailty and unproductive nature of these populations were often linked to the parasitic diseases caused by the "germ of laziness" (Ettling, *Germ of Laziness*). The literature on the southern United States draws attention to the challenges of constructing an American national identity given the huge numbers of supposedly indolent and unproductive citizens. To some extent, the controversies and discomfort kindled by urban America's encounter with its unfamiliar compatriots—veritable foreigners—in the rural South during the Progressive Era predate and foreshadow the perplexity felt by the Brazilian elites when introduced to the inhabitants of the *sertões*. The distinguishing feature for both the southern United States and the Brazilian hinterlands was disease. These suggestions for comparison are based on Boccaccio, "Ground Itch"; Breeden, "Disease as a Factor"; Cassedy, "Germ of Laziness"; Ettling, *Germ of Laziness*; Link, "Privies, Progressivism"; Marcus, "South's Native Foreigners"; Marcus, "Physicians Open"; Sullivan, *Our Times*, 290–332.

78. Penna, *Saneamento do Brasil*, 71–72.

79. Ibid., 55.

80. During this period, many statistics supposedly captured the unproductivity caused by disease in Brazil. For example, Afrânio Peixoto calculated that an Italian was worth 2,100 contos de réis; an American, 10,500; a Frenchman, 3,600; and a Brit, 2,400. Judging the supply of labor power to fall short of demand in Brazil, Peixoto set a Brazilian's worth at 9,600 contos de réis, meaning that it would be cheaper and more profitable to rehabilitate a diseased, unproductive Brazilian than to import an immigrant laborer (*Higiene*, 12–13).

81. Lobato, *Urupês*.

82. In another book, Penna also used the differential effect of health on development to explain why Minas Gerais had become "the most unfortunate of states" despite its fertile land, mineral riches, sizable population and territory, and political weight. Rio Grande do Sul, boasting nothing of the potential of Minas, was much more prosperous. In Penna's view, "health was, is, and will be the main economic wellspring, the main reason for wealth and progress" (*Minas e Rio Grande*, 22).

83. *Saúde* 4–6 (1918): 247.

84. For an analysis of the content of this journal, see Labra, "Movimento Sanitarista"; Lima and Britto, "Salud y Nación."

85. Penna, "Discurso Pronunciado," 223.

86. Penna, *Defesa Sanitária*, 10–11.

87. Fraga, "Saneamento Urbano e Rural," 528; Fontenelle, "Higiene e Saúde Pública," 52; Britto, *Oswaldo Cruz*; Castro Santos, "Power, Ideology, and Public Health"; Labra, "Movimento Sanitarista"; Lima and Britto, "Salud y Nación"; Lima and Hochman, "Condenado pela Raça." These early experiences in the outlying neighborhoods of the country's capital should not be overestimated. Both the health posts themselves and the services they offered were quite precarious, as Penna described in a 1931 letter: "One sanitary guard and I set up the first rural health post, in Vigário Geral, in a house lent to us at no cost; [the post] was later transferred to Parada de Lucas and then to Penha, always and solely in buildings ceded free of charge, as were the necessary furniture and materials" (Belisário Penna to Getúlio Vargas, June 2, 1931, BRRJCOC BP 02-02, Arquivo Belisário Penna).

88. My reading of secondary sources on the U.S. public health movement grounds my contention that this was an innovative phenomenon. Although the public health debate in the United States likewise grappled with the problematic relations between state autonomy and the external effects of sanitary interdependence, the movement never proposed anything close to what the Brazilian movement did in the 1910s and 1920s. This was true even during the height of U.S. mobilization, which stretched from 1878 (when a major yellow fever epidemic struck southern states) to 1912 (when the Public Health Service was established). This rough comparison is drawn from Duffy, *Sanitarians*; J. H. Ellis, *Yellow Fever*; Kagan, "Federal Public Health"; Marcus, "Disease Prevention"; Tobey, *National Government*; Warner, "Local Control"; Waserman, "Quest."

89. Seidl, "Função Governmental," 67.

90. Penna, *Saneamento do Brasil*, 111.

91. Penna, "Discurso Pronunciado," 101–2; Penna, *Saneamento do Brasil*, 293–351.

92. Penna, "Discurso Pronunciado," 101.

93. Penna, *Saneamento do Brasil*, 293–94.

94. Ibid., 295.

95. Ibid.

96. Barroso, *Pela Saúde Pública*; Article 5 of the 1891 constitution reads, "It falls to each State to provide for the needs of its Government and administration, at its own expense; however, the federal government shall render aid to that State which so requests it in the case of a public disaster." Article 6 stipulates the conditions under which the federal government could intervene in the states: to fend off foreign invasion or invasion by another state; to preserve the federative republic; or to reestablish peace and order at the request of the state government. A July 3, 1926, constitutional amendment greatly expanded federal power to intervene and significantly modified Article 6. The amendment was a response to general turmoil under the administration of President Arthur Bernardes (1922–26).

97. Barroso, *Pela Saúde Pública*, 24. Article 65: "States are hereby granted: . . . §2. In general, any and all power or right that is not denied them through any clause expressly or implicitly contained in the clauses laid out in the Constitution." Article 68: "The states shall be organized so as to guarantee the autonomy of municipalities regarding all that is of their exclusive interest." Another argument was that the federal government had the exclusive right to sign treaties and agreements with other countries (Article 48). How could the federal government sign international public health agreements on yellow fever, plague, and Chagas's disease, the reasoning went, if it were not responsible for enforcing the initiatives that would ensure compliance with the agreements (Barroso, *Pela Saúde Pública*, 34–35)?

98. Penna, *Saneamento do Brasil*, 293.

99. Shapiro, "Private Rights"; Berge, *Mission and Method*; Hamlin, *Public Health and Social Justice*.

100. Barroso, *Pela Saúde Pública*, 14–15. Numerous accounts detail physical and legal constraints on the work of sanitation services in the name of the inviolability of residence, both in state capitals and in cities of the north and northeast interior. The most notorious of these incidents was a November 1904 revolt against compulsory smallpox vaccination in the city of Rio. Such matters became less likely to reach the judicial system as the Supreme Court gradually established the government's legal mandate to curtail individual liberties based on public health concerns as long as they were ordained by law and not by regulation (see Diniz, *Estado*, 9, 16). In 1926, the press made much of the fact that a federal judge from Maranhão granted habeas corpus relief from the compulsory smallpox vaccine to a group of individuals who alleged that they were under the duress of the director of rural sanitation, since the law that would enforce the compulsory vaccine (no. 1.261, October 3, 1904) had yet to be enacted. The Federal Supreme Court overturned the decision (*A Noite*, January 21, 1926, Arquivo Carlos Chagas). There are reports that habeas corpus was granted in the case of mosquito brigades working to protect against yellow fever in Bahia in 1921; these writs were likewise overturned by the Supreme Court (Sebastião Barroso to Belisário Penna, Bahia, July 31, 1921, BRRJCOC BP 02-02, Arquivo Belisário Penna).

101. Seidl, "Função Governmental," 54–55.

102. Chagas, *Discurso*, 17.

103. William Shakespeare, cited in *A Profilaxia Rural* 1, no. 1 (1922): 16; Shakespeare, *William Shakespeare*, 994–95.

Chapter 3. Public Health Reform; or,
Who Should Be Responsible for Communicable Diseases?

1. "During this time, we witnessed the full realization of two conflicting endeavors: grounded on the despotically centralizing organization created by prince Dom João, all sanitation actions were municipalized; later, in a steady move in the opposite direction, the administration of public hygiene was uniformly and wholly returned to the hands of the Central Government, the only separation being as regards inland and maritime services" (Fontenelle, "Higiene e Saúde Pública," 27).

2. Barbosa and Rezende, *Serviços de Saúde Pública*; Fontenelle, "Higiene e Saúde Pública," 1–27, 77–78.

3. Fontenelle, "Higiene e Saúde Pública," 28–29.

4. *Gazeta Médica da Bahia* 10 (April 1892): 423–25.

5. Brazil, *Coleção das Leis . . . 1904*, 1:3–11; Fundação Casa de Rui Barbosa, *Governo Presidencial*, 183–84.

6. For historical overviews of epidemic diseases in Brazil, especially yellow fever, including the initiatives undertaken to combat them, see Cooper, "Oswaldo Cruz"; Cooper, "Brazil's Long Fight"; Barbosa, "Pequena História"; Benchimol, *Micróbios aos Mosquitos*; Benchimol, *Febre Amarela*.

7. The state of São Paulo had been organizing its own public health agency and conducting successful yellow fever and bubonic plague campaigns since the late 1890s. During this period, Rodrigues Alves served as governor of the state of São Paulo (Blount, "Public Health Movement"; Blount, "Administração da Saúde Pública"; Stepan, *Beginnings of Brazilian Science*).

8. For the public health reforms of this period, see Benchimol, *Pereira Passos*, 294–305; Benchimol, *Manguinhos*, 22–26; Benchimol, "Reforma Urbana"; Castro Santos, "Power, Ideology, and Public Health," 100–121; Costa, *Lutas Urbanas*, 57–79; Fontenelle, "Higiene e Saúde Pública," 35–42; Meade, *"Civilizing" Rio*, ch. 3.

9. For South American treaties in the late nineteenth century, see Chaves, "Políticas Internacionais"; Chaves, "Poder e Saúde." For the role of the Pan-American Sanitary Bureau, see Cueto, *Value of Health*. For a more general perspective, see Hannaway, "Environment and Miasmata"; Harrison, "Disease, Diplomacy"; Stern and Markel, "Commentary."

10. Rosen, *History of Public Health*.

11. During the same period, the federal government assumed international commitments with South American countries (chiefly Argentina, Uruguay, and Paraguay) designed to protect against influxes of plague, cholera, yellow fever, and other diseases. The International Sanitary Convention of 1904 granted each country the

right to implement prevention measures on vessels that were suspected of transporting contaminated people or goods or originated in ports with high incidences of such diseases. The agreement discarded measures like quarantines and benefited Brazil, whose foreign trade had suffered under the restrictive policies adopted by other countries (Fontenelle, "Higiene e Saúde Pública," 40). Many ships preferred to make harbor in Argentina or Uruguay rather than at Brazilian ports, considered unsafe from a public health perspective (Castro Santos, "Power, Ideology, and Public Health," 107). Brazil signed two other international sanitary conventions (Montevideo, 1914, and Paris, 1912) in which it agreed to maintain well-equipped sanitation services at its ports.

12. Fontenelle, "Higiene e Saúde Pública," 34–35.

13. Brazil, *Coleção das Leis . . . 1904*, 1:3–11.

14. Benchimol, *Pereira Passos*; Costa, *Lutas Urbanas*; Meade, "Civilizing Rio de Janeiro"; Meade, *"Civilizing" Rio*.

15. Castro Santos, "Power, Ideology, and Public Health," 108–17; Meade, "Civilizing Rio de Janeiro"; Benchimol, *Pereira Passos*; Benchimol, "Reforma Urbana"; Chalhoub, *Cidade Febril*; Costa, *Lutas Urbanas*; Sevcenko, *Revolta da Vacina*; Carvalho, *Bestializados*.

16. Barbosa and Rezende, *Serviços de Saúde Pública*; Fontenelle, "Higiene e Saúde Pública," 41–45. The compulsory vaccine bill that stirred up so much controversy never actually became law. For a long time, consequently, citizens could appeal to the federal courts for an override of the required vaccine certificate. In his 1916 report as head of the General Directorate, submitted to the Ministry of Justice and Internal Affairs, Carlos Seidl delineated the problem created by the lack of regulation (*Relatório*, 3–10). Castro Santos, "Power, Ideology, and Public Health," 118, speaks to the challenges encountered throughout the 1910s in implementing the compulsory vaccine in the DF and rest of the country; he also addresses the smallpox outbreaks in the DF, São Paulo, and Bahia. For a more in-depth history of smallpox vaccination in Brazil, see Fernandes, *Vacina Antivariólica*; Hochman, "Priority, Invisibility, and Eradication."

17. The basic duties of the General Directorate of Public Health in 1897–1904 included studying the nature, etiology, treatment, and prevention of communicable diseases throughout the country; providing medical and hygienic assistance to local populations at the request of the relevant governments in cases of states of disaster; producing antitoxic and curative cultures and serums; overseeing medical and pharmaceutical practices; organizing demographic and health statistics; managing sanitation services at sea and river ports; drafting a Brazilian Pharmaceutical Code (Código Farmacêutico Brasileiro); and implementing a bacteriology laboratory. Between 1902 and 1904, other duties were added: providing defensive hygiene services and residential hygiene initiatives in the DF; providing for sanitary policing of households and public places and streets; and conducting initiatives

in the general and specific prevention of communicable disease. The Specific Yellow Fever Prophylaxis Service and the Health Court (Justiça Sanitária) were also established in the nation's capital (Fundação Casa de Rui Barbosa, *Governo Presidencial*, 183–84).

18. Albuquerque et al., *Ciência Vai à Roça*; Benchimol, *Manguinhos*, 46–57; Fontenelle, "Higiene e Saúde Pública," 45–49; Lima, *Sertão Chamado Brasil*.

19. This commission was dispatched shortly after Cruz's journey to the region that is now the state of Rondônia, where the Madeira-Mamoré Railroad was being built. There, he studied health conditions and the work being done to prevent malaria, which afflicted around 80 percent of the project's laborers (Benchimol, *Manguinhos*, 51; Costa, *Lutas Urbanas*, 73).

20. T. Torres, "Serviço Sanitário Federal em Manaus," 219.

21. T. Torres, "Relatório dos Serviços Efetuados."

22. Fontenelle, "Higiene e Saúde Pública."

23. Ibid.

24. Ibid., 49–52; Penna, *Defesa Sanitária*, 175.

25. See Ettling, *Germ of Laziness*; Farley, *Cast Out Disease*; Palmer, *Launching Global Health*.

26. Castro Santos, "Power, Ideology, and Public Health"; Cueto, "Ciclos de la Erradicación"; Faria, "Fase Pioneira"; Faria, *Saúde e Política*; Labra, "Movimento Sanitarista."

27. Sanitary inspections by an International Health Board commission in the states of Rio de Janeiro and São Paulo are cited as the source of the information that roughly 90 percent of the population in the visited areas had hookworm (Fontenelle, "Higiene e Saúde Pública," 51; Penna, "Discurso Pronunciado," 219–22). This datum translated into the estimate that 70–80 percent of the Brazilian population suffered from the malady. Coming as it did from a prestigious, experienced foreign philanthropic foundation, this information lent credence to the outcry about the wretched health of the rural population. Monteiro Lobato warned government leaders that there were "seventeen million sufferers of hookworm!" among a population of twenty-five million (*Mr. Slang*, 232–37). For the work of the Rockefeller Foundation in Brazil from 1915 through 1930, see Faria, "Fase Pioneira"; Faria, *Saúde e Política*.

28. An International Health Board commission headed by Gen. William Crawford Gorgas, who boasted experience in the early twentieth-century extinction of yellow fever in Havana, arrived in Brazil in October 1916 to study the possibility of undertaking joint efforts with national authorities to eradicate yellow fever on the Brazilian coast (Benchimol, *Febre Amarela*; Faria, "Fase Pioneira"; Fontenelle, "Higiene e Saúde Pública," 54–55). Only in the 1930s did scientists corroborate the existence of the sylvan (or jungle) variety of yellow fever, where primates host the virus after being bitten by *Aedes aegypti* (the only vector of urban yellow fever) or

other mosquito species. From 1900 through 1930, anti-yellow-fever strategies had centered on urban hubs and been based on the notion that only humans could serve as hosts (Cooper and Kiple, "Yellow Fever"; McGrew, "Yellow Fever," 356–57).

29. Brazil, Presidente, *Mensagem Apresentada*, 31. The years 1910–14—which corresponded to the election, administration, and succession of President Fonseca—were marked by troubled relations between the federal government, Congress, and state executives (see Bello, *História da República*, 278–304).

30. Rosen, *History of Public Health*, 148–52, 235–39; Schwartz, *Public Health*.

31. Brazil, *Coleção das Leis . . . 1914*, 1:934. Observations made at that time and those found in later analyses all fall prey to the same interpretive problem—that is, they deem any setback in the process of state centralization as negative, even if associated initiatives endured in the public, albeit local, sphere. This brand of analysis, which views centralization as a natural, triumphant march forward, ignores the possibility that decentralization may in some cases lead to a more efficient rearrangement of government duties in light of experience (see, for example, Fontenelle, "Higiene e Saúde Pública," 48–49). For the full text of the regulation, see Brazil, *Coleção das Leis . . . 1914*, vol. 1, pt. 2, 860–944.

32. Brazil, *Coleção das Leis . . . 1914*, vol. 1.

33. Ibid., 905–25.

34. When public health reforms were regulated into law in the 1920s (under Decree 14.354 [1920] and Decree 16.300 [1923]), the articles on ports directly referenced the 1914 decree.

35. Blount, "Public Health Movement"; Blount, "Administração da Saúde Pública"; Mota, *Tropeços da Medicina Bandeirante*; Ribeiro, *História Sem Fim*; Telarolli, *Poder e Saúde*.

36. Physician Sebastião Barroso, who analyzed how state constitutions addressed municipal and state executive and legislative jurisdictions in the realm of public health, found that some sharp differences notwithstanding, only the constitutions of Rio Grande do Sul and Pernambuco failed explicitly to recognize the federal government's right to intervene in this arena. The majority of the state charters—with the exceptions of Espírito Santo, Mato Grosso, and Santa Catarina—tended to consider hygiene "more general than local, belonging more to the center than to the periphery" (Barroso, *Pela Saúde Pública*, 26–30).

37. Lima and Britto, "Salud y Nación."

38. *O Paiz*, July 28, 1918, 4.

39. *Correio da Manhã*, May 31, 1918, 2.

40. *Correio da Manhã*, April–June 1919. Fontenelle discusses this matter in "Higiene e Saúde Pública," 49–57.

41. Sodré, *Brasil-Médico*, June 8, 1891, 152.

42. N. Rodrigues, "Inspetoria Geral de Higiene," 46–47.

43. Sodré, *Brasil-Médico*, August 22, 1891, 252.

44. N. Rodrigues, "Higiene Pública: A Organização do Serviço Sanitário," 331–32.

45. Ibid., 337.

46. In 1892, Rodrigues voiced harsh criticism of the affidavit handed down by Brazil's Higher Council of Public Health in support of a decentralized, municipally based public health model wherein the federal government would be responsible solely for maritime services. Rodrigues believed that "autonomous, wholly independent organization at the municipal level has proven a poor choice everywhere; here, among us, it would be an utter disaster" ("Higiene Pública: A Classe Médica," 421).

47. Commission members were Miguel Pereira, Carlos Chagas (director, Oswaldo Cruz Institute), Miguel Couto (president, National Academy of Medicine), Afrânio Peixoto (professor, Rio de Janeiro School of Medicine), Carlos Seidl (director, General Directorate of Public Health), and Aloysio de Castro (director, Rio de Janeiro School of Medicine). Information on the commission can be found in Couto, "Criação do Ministério," 383–84. Its report was reproduced as part of the July 4, 1917, message from justice and internal affairs minister Carlos Maximiliano to the chamber's Finance Committee published in Brazil, Câmara dos Deputados, *Anais da Câmara dos Deputados* (hereafter cited as *ACD*), September 10, 1917, 364–67.

48. The Higher Council of Hygiene would comprise five physicians and would have power and autonomy in the areas of human resources, oversight, and the budgeting and authorization of expenditures, including postal, customs, and transportation charges related to products, publications, and personnel. The council would coordinate services in areas plagued by endemic disease and negotiate a general public health plan with states and municipalities. It would receive responsibility for malaria, hookworm, leishmaniasis, Chagas's disease, yellow fever, and syphilis, ranked as the most debilitating of the maladies afflicting the rural population. The new agency would also conduct and release studies and educate the public in matters of hygiene (*ACD*, September 10, 1917, 364–67).

49. Couto, "Ministério da Saúde Pública," 37.

50. Couto, "Criação do Ministério," 383.

51. These were Decrees 13.000 and 13.001, both found in Brazil, *Coleção das Leis . . . 1918*, 2:533–35.

52. Souza Araújo, *Profilaxia Rural . . . Paraná*, 15. It was modified by Decree 13.055 (June 6, 1918).

53. Legislation on the production of medications was tied directly to the activities of rural sanitation agencies. Laws concerning the official quinine and rural health agencies grew much broader under Decree 13.139 (August 16, 1918) and Decree 13.159 (August 28, 1918) (Brazil, *Coleção das Leis . . . 1918*, vol. 3). Rural health and sanitation decrees are discussed in greater depth in ch. 4.

54. Brazil, *Coleção das Leis . . . 1918*; Fontenelle, "Higiene e Saúde Pública," 52–53; Fraga, "Saneamento Urbano e Rural," 528.

55. *ACD*, July 12, 1918.

56. Of the 200 deputies whose occupations I could determine, 32 were physicians. Another 122 held bachelor's degrees, and 20 had graduated as engineers. Nine of the 63 senators were physicians (see *ACD*, 1917–20; Abranches, *Governos e Congressos*; Castro and Castagnino, *Senado Federal*; Leite Neto, *Catálogo Biográfico*). Between 1889 and 1914, France's lower house averaged 11.2 percent physicians. According to J. D. Ellis, during this era, France had Europe's highest ratio of physicians in the legislature and topped the United States as well (*Physician-Legislators*, 3–6).

57. Lessa, *Invenção Republicana*, 107. On oligarchical politics during the First Republic, see also Viscardi, *O Teatro das Oligarquias*, and Holanda, *Modos da Representação Política*.

58. Some studies addressing the topic of sanitary reform in the 1910s and 1920s overemphasize the arguments and proposals of physicians and their institutions while paying scant attention to the fundamental locus of decision making, which was Congress. The research that does pay heed to this aspect sticks so closely to the sanitary movement's discourse that its evaluations of the performance of any given proposal are contaminated by the rhetoric of the era, losing sight of the political interactions that produced outcomes distinct from what was initially intended. See, for example, Labra, "Movimento Sanitarista," 88–172; Castro Santos, "Power, Ideology, and Public Health."

59. *ACD*, August 27, 1918.

60. Ibid., August 19, 1918.

61. Sodré's key speeches and proposals appear in Sodré, *Saneamento do Brasil*; Sodré, *Trabalhos Parlamentares*.

62. *ACD*, August 21, 1918.

63. Cited in Penna, *Saneamento do Brasil*, 311. Arguments by jurists such as Vianna, Prudente de Morais Filho, and Silva Marques and by ministers of the Federal Supreme Court such as Pedro Lessa and Pires de Albuquerque, appear in Penna, *Saneamento do Brasil*, 309–12, with commentaries in Penna, *Defesa Sanitária*, 8–11. These legal specialists drew from the arguments developed by Sebastião Barroso regarding the jurisdictional authority of the federal government and the states. In Barroso's opinion, the federal government should not wait for the states to request assistance before moving in to fight an epidemic: to do so "would be to deny that a communicable illness is of interest to everyone wherever transmission can occur" (*Pela Saúde Pública*, 35).

64. *ACD*, August 21, 1918.

65. For Sodré, the new ministry need not necessarily be managed by a physician, but it should have a technical advisory board. Proposals from the National Academy of Medicine and physicians with ties to public health agencies, conversely, placed the post of minister in the hands of a physician who enjoyed peer recognition.

66. The project also included provisions for the funding of special works projects through a 2 percent surcharge on the import taxes collected in states that would benefit from the works. Under the constitution, such a tax should be transferred to the National Treasury even when collected by the state (Article 7 and Article 9, Paragraph 3). The 1919 and 1920 sanitation service reforms did not adopt the idea. The complete project appears in Sodré, *Saneamento do Brasil*.

67. *ACD*, November 11, 1918.

68. Ibid., November 18, 1918. In addition to Brandão and Sodré, committee members were Palmeira Ripper (SP), Rodrigues Lima (BA), Zoroastro Alvarenga (MG), Otacílio Camará (DF), Domingos Mascarenhas (RS), Alexandrino Rocha (PE), and Afonso Barata (RN). All were medical doctors.

69. Ibid., November 29, 1918.

70. Fontenelle, "Higiene e Saúde Pública," 59; T. Torres, "Saúde Pública em 1918," 37–48; Bertolli Filho, "Gripe Espanhola," 31. Some authors put the number of deaths from September to October 1918 at 550,000 in the United States and 2,300,000 in Europe. Estimates of deaths in Brazil range from 30,000 (Fontenelle, "Higiene e Saúde Pública," 22) to 180,000 (Patterson and Pyle, "Geography and Mortality," 14). Worldwide, fatalities have been estimated anywhere between 15,000,000 and 50,000,000, though Patterson and Pyle suggest 30,000,000 as a more accurate number ("Geography and Mortality," 14). We now know that it would have been impossible to prevent or cure a disease that spread aggressively by air and was resistant to the disinfection and isolation measures available at the time (Tomkins, "Failure of Expertise").

71. Britto, "Dansarina," 11–30.

72. *O Paiz*, February 12, 1920. The report by Teófilo Torres, head of the General Directorate, appears in T. Torres, "Saúde Pública em 1918." For detailed information on the epidemic in Rio de Janeiro, see Goulart, "Revisitando a Espanhola"; on the flu as portrayed in the Rio press, see Britto, "Dansarina." For an account of the emergency services organized by Carlos Chagas in the city of Rio, see Chagas Filho, *Carlos Chagas*, 147–58; on the epidemic in São Paulo, see Bertolli Filho, "Gripe Espanhola"; Bertucci, *Influenza*. On the Spanish flu in the city of Salvador, see Souza, *Gripe Espanhola*; in Porto Alegre, see Abrão, *Banalização da Morte*; and in Belo Horizonte, Anny Jackeline Torres, *Influenza Espanhola*. Disagreeing with the notion that the epidemic was democratic, Bertolli Filho shows that the death rate in poor neighborhoods was double that in more well-to-do ones.

73. Alves died on January 16, 1919. On Alves's illness and death, see A. A. de M. Franco, *Rodrigues Alves*, vol. 2. On the economic impact of World War I in South America, see Albert, *South America*. For a discussion of the political dynamics of the end of the Brás administration and the election and succession of Alves, see Bello, *História da República*, 316–22.

74. Afrânio de Melo Franco, minister of transportation and public works, lost his wife and son (Chagas Filho, *Carlos Chagas*; A. A. de M. Franco, *Rodrigues Alves*).

In São Paulo, both Mayor Washington Luis and state sanitation director Arthur Neiva fell ill (Bertucci, *Influenza*).

75. *ACD*, October, November 1918.

76. Unlike the heads of sanitation agencies, who lost prestige as a result of the epidemic (e.g., Carlos Seidl resigned after serving as head of the General Directorate for five years), physicians earned the respect of parliamentarians by volunteering at emergency health care sites in the DF, which were also staffed by professionals from other states who had traveled to Rio for a medical conference (Chagas, *Discurso*; Chagas Filho, *Carlos Chagas*; Fontenelle, "Higiene e Saúde Pública"). Senator Alfredo Ellis (SP) paid tribute in a speech to the more than fifty doctors who succumbed to the disease between October and November 1918 (*ACD*, November 18, 1918).

77. *ACD*, May 27, 1919.

78. Ibid., July 9, 1919.

79. For the Bahian medical tradition and how it helped stifle movements for scientific and institutional innovation in public health, see Castro Santos, "Power, Ideology, and Public Health," ch. 5; Castro Santos, "Origens da Reforma Sanitária"; Castro Santos, "Poder, Ideologias, e Saúde." For health conditions and services in First Republic Bahia, see Souza, *Gripe Espanhola*; Chaves, *História da Saúde*.

80. *ACD*, July 2, 1919.

81. Ibid., October 11, 1919.

82. Ibid.

83. T. Torres, "Últimos Redutos," 82–3.

84. Fontenelle, "Higiene e Saúde Pública," 55–56.

85. Duffy, "Social Impact of Disease"; Fraser, *Evolution*; Rosenberg, *Cholera Years*.

86. Epidemics spur tremendous distrust in government ability to protect society, as is evident in Brazil's parliamentary debate on the Spanish flu. Analyzing a smallpox epidemic in Milwaukee, Wisconsin, in 1894, by which time the disease could already be prevented through vaccination, Leavitt has shown that the social dissatisfaction and political reactions generated by an epidemic can lead to the curtailment of public health power. Milwaukee's municipal board of health fell into disgrace, and the smallpox epidemic effectively reversed the tendency to expand municipal authority ("Politics and Public Health," 553–54).

87. Brazil, *Coleção das Leis . . . 1919*, 2:393–97.

88. Labra, "Movimento Sanitarista," 119.

89. Fontenelle, "Higiene e Saúde Pública," 64.

90. Nonmedical members of the commission included Domingos da Silva Cunha, professor of sanitary engineering at the Polytechnic School (Escola Politécnica), and one jurist, Clóvis Beviláqua. Others appointed were Miguel Couto, president of the National Academy of Medicine; Carlos Chagas, director of the Oswaldo Cruz Institute; professors Rocha Faria (commission chair) and Afrânio

Peixoto; Aloísio de Castro, director of the Rio de Janeiro School of Medicine; and Teófilo Torres, federal health inspector and director of the General Directorate. See Couto, "Criação do Ministério"; Fontenelle, "Higiene e Saúde Pública."

91. Penna, "Organização Sanitária," 101-2.

92. On Pessoa's election as a "compromise formula" and on his term in office (1919-22), see Bello, *História da República*; Carone, *República Velha*. For the Pessoa government's economic and financial woes, see Fritsch, "Apogeu e Crise," 41-50. Sanitation policy enjoyed great national expansion under Pessoa, a development that had much to do with his tremendous drive to implement drought-mitigation works in the northeast from 1920 to 1922 (Buckley, "Drought in the Sertão"). Many of these projects involved the construction of dams, roads, and ports, and the U.S. companies hired to help with the projects found themselves grappling with yellow fever and malaria. According to Robert Levine, this was the only significant investment in public works in the region under the First Republic ("Pernambuco e Federação," 151).

93. Over the 1910s, the amount of space allocated to health and sanitation in presidential addresses grew from one or two paragraphs—dealing almost solely with yellow fever and sanitary conditions in the DF—to much longer, emphatic sections highlighting numerous health and sanitation topics, especially in the messages of Pessoa and Arthur Bernardes. See Brazil, Presidente, 1919-22, *Mensagens Presidenciais*; Brazil, Presidente, 1923-26, *Mensagens Presidenciais*.

94. *ACD*, September 24, 1919.

95. Ibid.

96. Ibid.

97. Ibid.

98. Ibid., October 14, 1919.

99. Ibid., October 22, 1919.

100. Ibid., November 18, 1919.

101. Ibid., November 29, 1919.

102. Ibid., November 11, 1919.

103. Ibid., November 18, 1919.

104. A reading of the *ACD* from 1916 on leaves no doubt about this shift: the diagnosis of Brazil's public health conditions was no longer controversial but represented an interpretation embraced by the majority of those in the federal legislature.

105. Under the approved bill, the National Department of Public Health would have an Office of the Director General (a physician appointed by the president) and three directorates: Inland Sanitation Services in the nation's capital; Maritime and River Sanitary Defense; and Rural Sanitation and Prophylaxis. The department would be responsible for hygiene services in the DF (general and specific prevention measures against communicable diseases); household hygiene measures; sanitary policing of housing, factories, repair and machine shops, schools, commercial establishments, hospitals, slaughterhouses, public spaces, hotels, and

so on; sanitation services at sea and river ports; rural prevention measures in the DF, the territory of Acre, and, under specific agreements, the states; scientific study and research into the nature, etiology, prevention, and treatment of communicable diseases; the provision of serums, vaccines, and medication to treat diseases and epidemics in any region of the country; oversight of the making of these products at private laboratories; provision of official medications through the Oswaldo Cruz Institute; chemical testing of nationally produced and imported foodstuffs; medical inspection of immigrants and passengers whose destination was a Brazilian port; assistance to the ill within the DF who had to be isolated; compilation and publication of demographic and health statistics; oversight of sewerage and new sewer networks in the DF; oversight of pharmaceuticals, serums, vaccines, and other biological products sold to the public; oversight of the practice of medicine, pharmacy, and dentistry; and the drafting of a national sanitary code, subject to congressional approval (Brazil, *Coleção das Leis . . . 1920*, 1:1–7).

106. Penna, *Defesa Sanitária*, 11; Penna, *Saneamento do Brasil*.

Chapter 4. Consciousness Converges with Interests: A National Public Health Policy

1. Dickens, "Nobody's Story."
2. See Wohl, *Endangered Lives*, 5–6.
3. T. Torres, "Saúde Pública em 1918," 34–35.
4. Fraga, *Introdução*, 9–10.
5. Jabert, "Formas de Administração."
6. In a number of countries, including the United States, leprosy was the first illness entrusted to centralized federal agencies, because states had problems isolating and treating the sick and lacked the will to do so. In the late 1910s, officials established a national leprosarium in Louisiana to house the sick and keep them from circulating about the country (Soviero, "Nationalization of a Disease"). Brazil saw heated debate on the subject, and the circulation of leprosy patients remained a serious problem in the late 1920s. Policymakers debated two solutions: constructing a large national leprosarium to isolate all carriers in one place (potentially on Ilha Grande, off the coast of Rio de Janeiro) or establishing isolation hospitals in various locations around the country, dividing the ill among "cities of Lazarus" (*lazarópolis*). Starting in the late 1910s, the federal government began implementing an approach somewhat akin to the second alternative as part of the drive to nationalize public health policy (Araújo, "Profilaxia da Lepra"; Sodré, *Trabalhos Parlamentares*, 39–43; Cabral, *Lepra, Medicina, e Políticas*).
7. Brazil, Ministério da Justiça e Negócios Interiores, *Relatório* (1923), 211. The issue of milk and meat safety had its own unique characteristics. With the growth of Brazil's main cities, barns and slaughterhouses moved to other municipalities,

which were generally less well equipped for oversight than the big centers. The cooperation problems found at the federal level haunted intermunicipal relations as well and constituted one of the reasons for entrusting health and hygiene initiatives to the states. But few states boasted the technical or financial resources needed for oversight or had the political power to take action in areas controlled by local bosses. In Brazil, the topic did not garner nationwide attention until the 1920s, and the situation subsequently changed slowly and unsteadily. The increased focus was visible mostly in the form of greater mention in executive messages and statements and grievances by federal agency leaders and doctors, and it never reached the same level of publicity as the demands lodged by the rural sanitation movement. For a history of eating habits in Brazil, see Carneiro, "Comida e Sociedade"; Jaime Rodrigues, *Alimentação, Vida Material, e Privacidade.* The Brazilian case differed substantially from that of the United States, where Congress passed food safety and oversight regulations in the form of the 1906 Food and Drug Act, assigning responsibility to the Department of Agriculture, even before other sanitation policies had been passed. The U.S. law was the by-product of a strong public opinion movement (including business interests) that urged federal regulation of interstate food commerce (Young, *Pure Food*).

8. T. Torres, "Últimos Redutos," 74.

9. *ACD*, May 27, 1919.

10. Barros, *Quatro Anos*, 27–28.

11. "Small-Pox: We All Must Have It to Accommodate the New-Yorkers." This exclamation of disgust was published in 1882 by a Chicago newspaper that sided with calls to establish a federal health agency charged with smallpox inspection nationwide, something New York authorities opposed. The residents of Chicago, living on the shores of Lake Michigan and thus a comfortable distance away from the main Atlantic seaports, complained about the onus they had to bear because negligent authorities in coastal cities let smallpox carriers come and go as they pleased (cited in Warner, "Local Control," 427–28 n. 60). The U.S. experience shows how perceptions of public health interdependence were not divided solely across geographic or economic lines. The juxtaposition was not, as had long been argued, merely between the more developed North and the more backward South; a distinction could also be made between cities in the heartland and those on the seaboard, which were viewed as having more public health problems and being less responsible and less willing to work cooperatively to reach a national solution (J. H. Ellis, *Yellow Fever*; Humphreys, *Yellow Fever*; Warner, "Local Control," 428 n. 60).

12. Penna, *Saneamento do Brasil*, 294; T. Torres, "Últimos Redutos."

13. Seidl, *Relatório*, 22.

14. Brazil, Ministério da Justiça e Negócios Interiores, *Relatório* (1923), 198–99.

15. In the United States, the federal government won greater power in the public health realm thanks to Supreme Court rulings and judicial reviews of congressional

decisions on interstate and international trade (pursuant to Article 1, Section 8, of the U.S. Constitution). Individual states enjoyed limited policing power in the realm of interstate action and could not impose quarantines or close their borders to stop the inflow and circulation of merchandise and people from suspected epidemic areas. Analogies were drawn between public health issues and their impacts (e.g., contagion) on the one hand and suprastate economic relations on the other, and the courts increasingly ascribed a greater regulatory role to the federal government in the health arena (Kagan, "Federal Public Health"; Tobey,*National Government*, 48–60).

16. See Santos, *Razões da Desordem*, 52.

17. Mueller, *Public Choice*, 9–15; Ostrom, *Meaning of American Federalism*, 164–66.

18. Ostrom, *Meaning of American Federalism*, 166–72.

19. Mueller, *Public Choice*, 11.

20. Ostrom, *Meaning of American Federalism*, 168–69.

21. Samuelson and Nordhaus, *Economia*, 886; Schwartz, *Public Health*, 125–26.

22. De Swaan, *Care of the State*; Olson, *Logic of Collective Action*.

23. Olson, *Logic of Collective Action*.

24. De Swaan, *Care of the State*.

25. Lessa, *Invenção Republicana*.

26. Mann, "Autonomous Power"; Mann, *Sources of Social Power*.

27. Santos, *Razões da Desordem*, 51–59.

28. Buchanan and Tullock, *Calculus of Consent*, 61.

29. Ibid., 45–46.

30. Ibid., 74–75.

31. Coase, "Nature of the Firm."

32. Buchanan and Tullock, *Calculus of Consent*, 113–15.

33. Brazil, *Coleção das Leis . . . 1918*, 2:533–35; Brazil, *Coleção das Leis . . . 1919*, 2:393–97.

34. *Saúde* 2 (1919): 173.

35. Article 1, Decree 13.538.

36. Souza Araújo, *Profilaxia Rural . . . Paraná*.

37. T. Torres, "Últimos Redutos," 82.

38. Article 9, Decree 13.538.

39. The state of Pernambuco had tried to organize campaigns to combat rural endemic diseases without federal government help. In 1919, the newly inaugurated state administration concluded that this strategy would not work. It then proposed a $140,000 agreement with the Rockefeller Foundation under which the U.S. philanthropic agency would direct state health and asked the federal government for the remainder of the needed resources. Two years later, under an accord with the International Health Board, six Pernambuco municipalities had health posts targeting hookworm and other parasitic worm diseases (*Folhetos de Hygiene* 64 [1922]: 42).

40. Souza Araújo, *Profilaxia Rural . . . Paraná*, 15.

41. Article 6, Decree 13.538.

42. Article 13, Decree 13.538.

43. Article 5, Decree 13.538.

44. Articles 11, 12, Decree 13.538. This same prerequisite had been applied during the federal commissions to fight yellow fever in the north of Brazil in the early 1910s (Frahia, *Oswaldo Cruz*, 35–36).

45. Article 14, Decree 13.538.

46. Souza Araújo, *Profilaxia Rural . . . Paraná*.

47. Ibid., 39–42.

48. Ibid., 44–45.

49. In practice, the federal appointment of the head of a state health agency was a matter of negotiation between the national authority and the governor, since this head would be directing the state's public health services. When possible, the appointee was supposed to be a native of the state or someone with close personal or political ties to it, helping to ease what was often a rather antagonistic relationship between federal agencies and local powers. Paraná serves as an example yet again: physician H. C. de Souza Araújo, who set up the rural agency there in 1918–19, was a Paraná native who worked for the Oswaldo Cruz Institute. On relations between federal and state agencies in Bahia starting at the dawn of the twentieth century, see Castro Santos, "Power, Ideology and Public Health."

50. *Saúde* 2 (August 20, 1918): 155. To Barreto's way of thinking, if São Paulo—which had already organized a state public health agency—so desired, it could easily shell out six thousand contos de réis for a Rural Prophylaxis Service and receive another third of this amount from federal coffers, whereas "states in the North" might not be able to invest even a meager two hundred contos de réis.

51. *Saúde* 2 (August 20, 1918): 158- 60.

52. Fontenelle, "Higiene e Saúde Pública," 55–56.

53. According to contemporary observers, the commissions began to be demobilized when federal sanitation agencies were reorganized during 1920–21 (Fontenelle, "Higiene e Saúde Pública"; Peryassu, "Profilaxia da Febre Amarela," 50–52). A new drive to combat yellow fever soon followed under the auspices of the federal rural agencies in northeastern states. In 1923, the Cooperative Yellow Fever Service was established, and the federal government and the Rockefeller Foundation entered into a major agreement under which the foundation received responsibility for efforts to eradicate yellow fever in the northeast (Benchimol, *Febre Amarela*, ch. 2; Cueto, "Ciclos de la Erradicación," 188–96; Faria, "Fase Pioneira," 117–19; Odair Franco, "História"; Lowy, *Vírus, Mosquitos, e Modernidade*, ch. 4).

54. Article 9, Decree 3.987 (January 2, 1920); Article 990, Decree 14.354 (September 15, 1920). See Brazil, *Coleção das Leis . . . 1920*, 1:1–7, 3:244–484.

55. Article 12, Decree 3.987.

56. Decree 14.354 was amended several times before Decree 16.300 (December

31, 1923) revised the law, which remained in effect through the end of the First Republic.

57. The law creating the National Department of Public Health was enacted on August 15, 1920, and the department began its operations on October 1. Rural health services did not begin operating in the states until 1921 (see Belisário Penna, director of the DSPR, to Carlos Chagas, director of the department, April 8, 1921, BRRJCOC BP 03-04, Arquivo Belisário Penna).

58. Brazil, Ministério da Justiça e Negócios Interiores, *Relatório* (1923); Brazil, Presidente, 1919–22, *Mensagens Presidenciais*; Brazil, Presidente, 1923–26, *Mensagens Presidenciais*; Fraga, "Saneamento Urbano e Rural," 529.

59. Leprosy and venereal disease, especially syphilis, had been drawing the attention of the general public, sanitarians, and philanthropists such as Eduardo Guinle, who had begun collaborating with the department to build hospitals and infirmaries in the DF (Araújo, "Profilaxia da Lepra"). On Guinle's philanthropy, see Sanglard, *Entre os Salões e o Laboratório*; on the Inspectorate for Leprosy and Venereal Disease Prophylaxis, see Cabral, *Lepra, Medicina, e Políticas*.

60. Articles 133, 134, Decree 14.354 (July 15, 1920).

61. Article 12, Decree 3.987 (January 2, 1920).

62. Articles 354–70, Decree 14.354.

63. As in the United States, leprosy was the first illness transferred into federal hands, no doubt in response to the problem of free riders.

64. *Folhetos de Hygiene* 54 (1922).

65. Article 1,104, Decree 14.354.

66. Brazil, Ministério da Justiça e Negócios Interiores, *Relatório* (1923); Brazil, Presidente, 1919–22, *Mensagens Presidenciais*; Brazil, Presidente, 1923–26, *Mensagens Presidenciais*.

67. Brazil, Ministério da Justiça e Negócios Interiores, *Relatório* (1923), 212.

68. Decree 16.300 (December 31, 1923); Article 317, Decree 16.300.

69. Articles 1,019–67, Decree 16.300.

70. The 1923 version of the administrative regulations stipulated through Decree 16.300 can be found in Brazil, *Coleção das Leis . . . 1923.*

71. Araújo, "Profilaxia da Lepra"; Brazil, Ministério da Justiça e Negócios Interiores, *Relatório* (1921); Brazil, Ministério da Justiça e Negócios Interiores, *Relatório* (1923); Brazil, Presidente, 1919–22, *Mensagens Presidenciais*; *Folhetos de Hygiene* 54 (1922); Arquivo Belisário Penna.

72. Faria, "Fase Pioneira," 117; *Folhetos de Hygiene* 54 (1922): 42.

73. Rural verminosis posts were not permanent facilities and did not constitute an alternative to federal, state, or municipal agencies. Such posts had limited goals and lacked the authority of other health posts but nevertheless constituted an additional resource for states in the fight against infestations of parasitic worms and the drive to educate the public about hygiene practices. In addition, they relieved

some pressure on the federal budget. According to the foundation, the objective of these efforts "is not to eradicate uncinariasis [hookworm], since [the foundation] of course lacks the authority to mandate the public to follow one of the vital prophylactic measures, which is to build latrines. . . . Its standard actions in this realm have been to: ascertain local infestation rates, thereby irrefutably demonstrating the dissemination of this malady; undertake mass treatment of rural populations with vermifuge so they will have an intimate notion of the value of health through the effects of cure; and awaken local and general administrations to these results" (*Folhetos de Hygiene* 54 [1922]: 40, 44).

74. Ibid., 44.

75. Faria, "Fase Pioneira," 105.

76. Souza Araújo, *Profilaxia Rural . . . Pará*, 22–25.

77. Ibid., 34–36.

78. Ibid., 36–38.

79. Ibid., 22–25.

80. Belisário Penna, typewritten comments concerning the budget for the DSPR, as approved by the Federal Chamber of Deputies for fiscal year 1922. Although his notes are not dated, they were probably written in the second half of 1921 (BRRJ-COC BP 03-04, Arquivo Belisário Penna, COC/Fiocruz). Some of this information was also included in the address Epitácio Pessoa delivered when he left office on November 15, 1922 (Brazil, Presidente, 1919–22, *Mensagens Presidenciais*).

81. Penna was worried about pressure on his budget and concerned that his agency would not be able to render the promised services, in part because fixed expenditures for the DF, under the exclusive jurisdiction of his agency, represented roughly 20 percent of its total budget (BRRJCOC BP 03-04, Arquivo Belisário Penna).

82. L. W. Hackett to W. Rose, October 15, 1920, RG 5/S112/B95/F1302, Rockefeller Archives Center. Hackett made this prediction fifteen days after the government began implementing the law that had created the National Department of Public Health. Belisário Penna to Carlos Chagas, April 8, 1921 (BRRJCOC BP 04-04, Arquivo Belisário Penna), was less optimistic about the federal government's ability to create such a fund. Even as more and more states were opting into these agreements, the government still did not know how to estimate how much it would collect, a problem that hampered planning.

83. Pena, "Surgimento do Imposto."

84. Reproduced in *Revista de Saúde Pública* 1, no. 4 (1925): 72–73, this agreement was mediated by Clementino Fraga, an influential Bahian doctor and federal deputy who signed on behalf of the state government. Fraga replaced Carlos Chagas as head of the National Department of Public Health in 1926 and held the post until 1930.

85. Brazil, Presidente, 1923–26, *Mensagens Presidenciais*, 32–36.

86. Ibid., 212. The years between 1922 and 1926 were a time of political turmoil,

when a constitutional reform augmented executive power vis-à-vis the states and the federal legislature (Bello, *História da República*; Carone, *República Velha*). The work of the sanitation agencies and even their presence were undoubtedly affected by the political rebellions and interventions that occurred in some states. There are also indications that federal financing of rural sanitation agencies hit snags and that the drought relief works initiated under the Pessoa administration were abandoned.

87. Official DSPR publications demonstrate that the rural agencies were located in the states and municipalities but did not belong to them (see, for example, Barros Barreto, *Serviços de Saneamento*; Brazil, Departamento Nacional de Saúde Pública/Diretoria de Saneamento e Profilaxia Rural /Serviço no Estado do Amazonas, *Ano de Campanha*; Souza Araújo, *Profilaxia Rural . . . Pará*; L. F. Torres, *Guia Sanitário*; BRRJCOC BP 03-04, Arquivo Belisário Penna).

88. Penna, *Defesa Sanitária*, 15-16.

89. This was one of the issues that prompted defections from the sanitary movement. Based on very general goals such as "the sanitation of Brazil," the movement's unity failed to withstand the personal, technical, and political clashes that surfaced as soon as its leaders were assigned to top posts in the National Department of Public Health in 1920. Penna left the DSPR on November 15, 1922. During 1921–22, his letters to Carlos Chagas, director of the department, and the letters he received from his subordinates in the states reveal clashes over matters such as budgets, the agency's general political orientation, and relations with state politicians. Penna had grown disillusioned with the political entanglements and bargaining that would have inevitably resulted in public policies distinct from those envisioned as scientific responses to the problems of nature (see Arquivo Belisário Penna and Arquivo Carlos Chagas).

90. Arquivo Belisário Penna; Barroso, "Relatório."

91. Some sources suggest that public health agencies and the army enjoyed amicable relations in certain places in the northeastern interior, with the military ceding property and infrastructure for agency facilities (see Arquivo Belisário Penna).

92. Sebastião Barroso to Belisário Penna, ca. October 1921, BRRJCOC BP 02-02, Arquivo Belisário Penna. Castro Santos analyzed the various challenges to establishing state health policies in Bahia, including the lack of unity among state elites and regional factionalism, which contrasted with the cohesiveness of the São Paulo elites, who facilitated the inauguration of public health policies ("Power, Ideology and Public Health," ch. 5). Souza, *Gripe Espanhola*, also analyzes factionalism in health in Bahia.

93. Araújo, "Profilaxia da Lepra"; Fraga, *Introdução*.

94. During 1926–27, fourteen of Brazil's twenty states spent more than 2 percent of their budgets on public health and assistance, a figure that the head of rural sanitation for Bahia deemed significant in comparison with the many previous years of total neglect (Barreto, "Orçamentos Estaduais"). The following states invested

4 percent or more, in ascending order: PR (4 percent), AM (4.1 percent), SP (4.4 percent), MT (4.5 percent), PE (6.4 percent), BA (6.6 percent), and RN (7.7 percent), while those who spent less than 2 percent were RS (1.9 percent), GO (1.7 percent), CE (1.3 percent), RJ (1.1 percent), ES (0.8 percent), SC (0.5 percent), and PI (0.4 percent). In absolute terms, the states that spent the most, in descending order, were SP, BA, MG, PE, RS, and PR. Total health expenditures by the latter six states represented nearly 90 percent of the total spent by all twenty states. São Paulo's outlay alone accounted for roughly 50 percent of this total and was equivalent to about 60 percent of the 1926 budget for federal services within the National Department of Public Health (Labra, "Movimento Sanitarista," 154). The smallest investments were made by PI, GO, SC, and CE (Barreto, "Orçamentos Estaduais," 122–23). While these data, which were zealously compiled and presented by Barreto, do prove his point that state governments were increasingly engaged in public health matters, the inequalities between the states are blatant.

95. Recurring outbreaks of smallpox and yellow fever in the DF from 1926 to 1928 were a warning sign to the federal government about the need for strict nationwide enforcement of the compulsory smallpox vaccine as well as the country's extreme vulnerability to yellow fever, targeted by the Rockefeller Foundation–led Yellow Fever Commission. The return of yellow fever had a major hand in undermining the prestige of the U.S. foundation (Barros Barreto, "Febre Amarela"; Benchimol, *Febre Amarela*; Cueto, "Ciclos de la Erradicación"; Odair Franco, "História"; Lowy, *Vírus, Mosquitos, e Modernidade*).

96. Treasury allocations to the department rose by about 180 percent from 1920 to 1925 and by around 50 percent from 1925 to 1930. These figures do not take into account extraordinary investments in combating epidemic outbreaks in a number of states (Labra, "Movimento Sanitarista," 154).

97. According to data from João de Barros Barreto, sanitation personnel in the states held 4,137 conferences from 1919 to 1926 (45 in 1919 and 2,189 in 1926) and distributed some 590,000 pieces of educational literature (see *Saneamento* 2, no. 3 [1927]). Free hygiene courses consisting of forty-two lessons were taught under the auspices of the DSPR (see *Saneamento* 1, no. 2 [1926]), and a number of conferences on hygiene were aired by the Rádio Clube do Brasil (Autran, *Conferências sobre Higiene*).

98. Brazil, Ministério da Justiça e Negócios Interiores, *Relatório* (1923); Faria, "Fase Pioneira"; Fraga, *Introdução*.

99. Brazil, Presidente, 1923–26, *Mensagens Presidenciais*, 628. The Rockefeller Foundation contributed to the training of public health physicians by awarding some seventy grants for study at Johns Hopkins University and establishing and organizing the Hygiene Institute at the São Paulo School of Medicine (Cueto, "Ciclos de la Erradicación"; Faria, "Fase Pioneira"; Faria, *Saúde e Política*; Farley, *To Cast Out Disease*; Labra, "Movimento Sanitarista").

100. The proposals put forth by the National Academy of Medicine and the

Pro-Sanitation League of Brazil from 1917 to 1920 urged that key posts be held by physicians. In 1929, attendees at the fifth Congress of the Brazilian Society of Hygiene (Sociedade Brasileira de Higiene) called for the establishment of a Ministry of Health, where only "professional sanitarians" would hold the posts of minister or director. Moreover, proponents of the idea felt that these doctors should be employed on a full-time basis, with the contractual obligation of working exclusively at public health agencies (*regime de dedicação exclusive em tempo integral*) (Barreto, "Como Organizar o Ministério").

101. Fraga, *Introdução*.

102. In England and the United States, the institutional and legal solidification of the field of vital statistics played an important role in the movement for greater governmental responsibility in health (Metz, "Social Thought"; Schwartz, *Public Health*, 8–20). In Brazil, however, the call to organize and standardize these statistics came only later, as a consequence of expanded public authority. In many states, demographic and health statistics were first compiled under agreements with the federal government.

103. See Rokkan, "Dimensions of State Formation."

104. See Skocpol, *Protecting Soldiers*.

Chapter 5. São Paulo Exceptionalism?
Political Autonomy and Public Health Interdependence

1. Neiva, "Serviço Sanitário," 25.

2. Blount, "Public Health Movement," 2.

3. This image has been attributed to Arthur Neiva, and he claimed authorship: "In point of fact, for some time now I have noted that São Paulo has courageously taken upon its shoulders the consciousness of its due responsibility toward Brazil. A while back, I said that São Paulo is the locomotive that hauls 20 cars, these being the states, whose passengers bellow and complain about the engine whenever it asks the central powers for fuel to haul the heavy wagons, panting as it drags them up a steep incline" (Neiva, "Serviço Sanitário," 26).

4. Love, *São Paulo*; Love, "Autonomia e Interdependência"; Reis, "Elites Agrárias"; Reis, "Poder Privado."

5. Love, *São Paulo*, xviii.

6. Ibid.; Wirth, "Minas e a Nação."

7. According to Love, "São Paulo's leaders in the years 1889–1937 tried to control federal financial and fiscal activity in areas where state action was impossible or inadequate—monetary and exchange policies, foreign loan guarantees, legislation on tariffs and immigration, and diplomatic representation relevant to financial and economic affairs. Paulista statesmen did not expect the public works and patronage concessions (entailing reciprocal obligations) that were central to the Mineiros'

strategy. São Paulo alone had the option of intervening in the economy at its own initiative" (*São Paulo*, 265).

8. Reis, "Elites Agrárias"; Reis, "Poder Privado."

9. This section of the book relies on secondary sources on São Paulo, especially the work of Blount ("Public Health Movement"; "Administração da Saúde Pública"); Castro Santos ("Power, Ideology, and Public Health"; "Reforma Sanitária 'Pelo Alto'"; "Poder, Ideologias e Saúde"); Mota (*Tropeços da Medicina Bandeirante*); and Ribeiro (*História Sem Fim*). Another source used in nearly all more recent studies is Mascarenhas, "Contribuição."

10. Merhy, *Capitalismo e a Saúde Pública*; Costa, *Lutas Urbanas*; Castro Santos, "Power, Ideology, and Public Health"; Castro Santos, "Reforma Sanitária 'Pelo Alto'"; Castro Santos, "Poder, Ideologias, e Saúde"; Ribeiro, *História Sem Fim*; Telarolli, *Poder e Saúde*. In addition to the influx of foreign laborers, Castro Santos underscores the importance of domestic migration to São Paulo ("Reforma Sanitária 'Pelo Alto,'" 364–65).

11. Lúcia Lippi de Oliveira, *Brasil dos Imigrantes*; Ribeiro, *História Sem Fim*; Telarolli, *Poder e Saúde*; Trento, *Outro Lado do Atlântico*.

12. Ribeiro, *História Sem Fim*, 21–63, 99–148.

13. Blount, "Public Health Movement."

14. Telarolli, *Poder e Saúde*.

15. Ibid. As the foundation of Brazilian federalism, local autonomy ran into legal trouble even in the state that was theoretically its biggest defender. The São Paulo state constitution gave its Congress express but not exclusive authority to legislate on public health within the state but was completely silent about municipal authority on the matter (Barroso, *Pela Saúde Pública*, 27).

16. Blount, "Public Health Movement," ch. 3.

17. Ibid., 97; Castro Santos, "Reforma Sanitária 'Pelo Alto,'" 381–86.

18. Bertucci, *Saúde*; Blount, "Public Health Movement," 92.

19. Blount, "Public Health Movement," 87–95.

20. During this period, the development of São Paulo state health services was also facilitated by the low turnover and longevity of agency directors. Emílio Ribas, who served from 1896 to 1917, and Arthur Neiva, who held the post from 1917 to 1920, ensured the uniformity and continuity of government action. Over most of the next decade, the agency had only two directors: Geraldo de Paula Souza (1922–27) and Waldomiro de Oliveira (1927–30).

21. Benchimol and Teixeira, *Cobras, Lagartos*; Blount, "Public Health Movement," 101–2, 106–7; Stepan, *Beginnings of Brazilian Science*, 65–67.

22. Blount, "Public Health Movement"; Stepan, *Beginnings of Brazilian Science*.

23. Almeida, *República dos Invisíveis*; Castro Santos, "Reforma Sanitária 'Pelo Alto,'" 378; Stepan, *Beginnings of Brazilian Science*, 134–56. On the Pasteur Institute, see Teixeira, *Ciência e Saúde*. On the Butantan Institute, see Benchimol

and Teixeira, *Cobras, Lagartos*. On the Biological Institute, established in 1927 for agricultural research and defense in the state of São Paulo, see Ribeiro, *História, Ciência, e Tecnologia*. For information on the International Health Board's role in disseminating experimental medicine in Brazil and strengthening public health teaching at medical schools through the Rockefeller Foundation–São Paulo, see Faria, "Fase Pioneira," 97–102, 127; Faria, *Saúde e Política*; Marinho, *Elites em Negociação*.

24. Almeida, *República dos Invisíveis*; Benchimol, *Febre Amarela*; Blount, "Administração da Saúde Pública," 42; Castro Santos, "Reforma Sanitária 'Pelo Alto,'" 117; McGrew, "Yellow Fever," 361–62; Stepan, *Beginnings of Brazilian Science*, 142–44.

25. Castro Santos, "Reforma Sanitária 'Pelo Alto,'" 127–29.

26. Blount, "Public Health Movement," 130.

27. Ibid., 134–37.

28. Ibid., 143–51; Castro Santos, "Reforma Sanitária 'Pelo Alto'"; Ribeiro, *História Sem Fim*.

29. Fontenelle, "Higiene e Saúde Pública," 51; Faria, "Fase Pioneira"; Faria, *Saúde e Política*; Marinho, *Elites em Negociação*.

30. Blount, "Public Health Movement," 141.

31. Ibid.; Blount, "Administração da Saúde Pública"; Castro Santos, "Reforma Sanitária 'Pelo Alto.'"

32. Castro Santos, "Reforma Sanitária 'Pelo Alto,'" 384.

33. Love, *São Paulo*, 20–22.

34. Blount, "Public Health Movement," 166–67.

35. Castro Santos, "Reforma Sanitária 'Pelo Alto'"; Ribeiro, *História Sem Fim*; Merhy, *Saúde Pública*.

36. N. Rodrigues, "Higiene Pública: A Organização do Serviço Sanitário," 445.

37. W. de Oliveira, "Profilaxia da Febre Amarela," 37.

38. Penna, *Saneamento do Brasil*, 30.

39. Neiva, "Programa Apresentado," 22.

40. Blount, "Public Health Movement"; Blount, "Administração da Saúde Pública"; Merhy, *Capitalismo e a Saúde Pública*; Merhy, *Saúde Pública*; Ribeiro, *História Sem Fim*; Telarolli, *Poder e Saúde*.

41. Iyda, *Cem Anos*; Merhy, *Capitalismo e a Saúde Pública*; Merhy, *Saúde Pública*; Ribeiro, *História Sem Fim*. In Merhy's opinion, São Paulo serves as a fine case because it was "a strategic place from which Brazilian society could move toward the development of capitalism in Brazil in the period from 1920 to 1945, grounded on the process of industrialization" (*Saúde Pública*, 24–25).

42. Costa, *Lutas Urbanas*, ch. 2; Labra, "Movimento Sanitarista," ch. 1; Iyda, *Cem Anos*, 33–53.

43. Iyda, *Cem Anos*; Merhy, *Capitalismo e a Saúde Pública*, 60–63; Merhy, *Saúde Pública*.

44. Blount, "Public Health Movement," 177–84.

45. Costa, *Lutas Urbanas*; Labra, "Movimento Sanitarista."

46. Benchimol and Teixeira, *Cobras, Lagartos*.

47. Ribeiro, *História Sem Fim*, 269–70.

48. Labra, "Movimento Sanitarista."

49. Blount, "Public Health Movement," esp. ch. 5; Blount, "Administração da Saúde Pública." Another, more specific criterion cited in favorable evaluations of the experience was the development of a complex of research and production institutions within the public health arena (Blount, "Public Health Movement"; Castro Santos, "Reforma Sanitária 'Pelo Alto'"; Ribeiro, *História, Ciência, e Tecnologia*; Stepan, *Beginnings of Brazilian Science*; Teixeira, *Ciência e Saúde*).

50. Castro Santos, "Power, Ideology, and Public Health," 223.

51. Ibid., 163–84.

52. Castro Santos, "Reforma Sanitária 'Pelo Alto,'" 361, 386–87.

53. Neiva, "Programa Apresentado."

54. Ibid., 2, 3.

55. Ibid., 1.

56. Ibid., 4–5. For a detailed discussion of port health services, see Rebelo, "Entre o *Carlo R.*"; Rebelo, Maio, and Hochman, "Princípio do Fim."

57. Neiva, "Programa Apresentado," 15–20.

58. Ibid., 7, 8.

59. Ibid., 8.

60. Ibid., 8. In an enthusiastic description of the work of the Neiva-led sanitation agencies in the interior of São Paulo, Lobato declared that work should be initiated by the state government—"already necessarily equipped"—and that the state should coordinate municipal actions. Lobato's approach reflected the common view that public health authority should first be organized at the center and later returned to municipalities, still considered legally competent to foster health and sanitation but financially unable to do so. Moreover, Lobato argued, municipalities were ruled by bosses (*coroneloides*) who damaged public health with "their personal opinions" (Lobato, *Mr. Slang*, 297–302).

61. Lobato, *Mr. Slang*, 302.

62. Blount, "Public Health Movement," 151; Castro Santos, "Reforma Sanitária 'Pelo Alto,'" 328.

63. Egas, *Galeria dos Presidentes*, 602–3.

64. Love, *São Paulo*, 202, points out that Mato Grosso and Paraná were economic satellites of São Paulo, a situation that likely influenced the sanitary defense initiatives along the state's western border.

65. See Santos, *Razões da Desordem*, 51–59.

66. Some analyses tend to view the IHB as an instrument of U.S. imperialism, while others place value on the philanthropic activities of the Rockefeller Foundation, which are seen as typical of U.S. culture. More recent scholars have

emphasized the Rockefeller Foundation's actions within the specific context of each country where it worked. For an assessment of this literature from a Latin American perspective, see Birn, *Marriage of Convenience*; Cueto, *Missionaries of Science*; Cueto, "Ciclos de la Erradicación"; Faria, "Fase Pioneira"; Palmer, *Launching Global Health*.

67. One example is a letter written by the director of public health in Bahia, Gonçalo Moniz, to the U.S. consul in the state, asking the diplomat to contact the Rockefeller Foundation medical mission about the matter of possible aid, since the state had found it impossible to implement any prevention measures against communicable disease in rural areas. A number of other invitations and requests for assistance were submitted to the Rockefeller Foundation by state governments from 1916 on. See RG5/305.3/S.1/B.28/F.441, Rockefeller Archives Center.

68. The mandatory inclusion of malaria within these agreements was a unilateral decision by the federal government that it imposed on the IHB, suggesting that the work of the Rockefeller Foundation was neither unrestricted nor based on autonomous decisions. In at least two letters to W. Rose, director of the IHB (which was headquartered in New York City), IHB-Brazil director L. Hackett described the frustrations and challenges his office faced in its efforts to comply with this legal requirement. See L. Hackett to W. Rose, April 28, August 1, 1919, RG5/S1.2/B78/F.1109, Rockefeller Archives Center.

69. Castro Santos, "Power, Ideology, and Public Health"; Cueto, *Missionaries of Science*; Cueto, "Ciclos de la Erradicación."

70. Castro Santos, "Power, Ideology, and Public Health"; Faria, "Fase Pioneira"; Faria, *Saúde e Política*; Marinho, *Elites em Negociação*.

71. See L. Hackett to W. Rose, April 28, 1917, RG5/305.20/S.1/B46/F695, Rockefeller Archives Center.

72. *Folhetos de Hygiene* 54 (1922). When São Paulo state agencies asked the Rockefeller Foundation for help, they were not just requesting assistance but also going through the philanthropic agency to demonstrate their capabilities and independence in conducting sanitation campaigns. Yet again, São Paulo was distinguishing itself from other states. It proposed two concurrent campaigns against hookworm in different locales, one led by state agencies and the other headed by the IHB-Brazil. As Hackett saw it, this approach was a kind of "friendly competition," whose goals included garnering more resources for the state, developing a competitive spirit among state personnel, and showing the federal government that São Paulo agencies could produce results independently and efficiently without outside help. See L. Hackett to W. Rose, April 28, 1917, RG5/S1.2/B78/F.1109, Rockefeller Archives Center.

73. Merhy, *Saúde Pública*, 78.

74. Love, *São Paulo*, xix; Love, "Brazilian Federal State."

75. Reis, "Elites Agrárias"; Reis, "Poder Privado."

Bibliography

Archives

Arquivo Arthur Neiva, Centro de Pesquisa e Documentação Histórica, Fundação Getúlio Vargas, São Paulo

Arquivo Belisário Penna, Casa de Oswaldo Cruz, Fundação Oswaldo Cruz, Rio de Janeiro

Arquivo Carlos Chagas, Casa de Oswaldo Cruz, Fundação Oswaldo Cruz, Rio de Janeiro

Arquivo Clementino Fraga, Casa de Oswaldo Cruz, Fundação Oswaldo Cruz, Rio de Janeiro

Arquivo Nacional, Rio de Janeiro

Arquivo Rockefeller, Banco de Dados, Universidade Estadual do Rio de Janeiro, Instituto de Medicina Social, Rio de Janeiro

Fundação Biblioteca Nacional, Rio de Janeiro

Rockefeller Archives Center, Sleepy Hollow, New York

Lusophone Journals and Newspapers

Arquivos de Higiene (Departamento Nacional de Saúde Pública, Rio de Janeiro)

Boletim Sanitário (Departamento Nacional de Saúde Pública, Rio de Janeiro)

Brasil-Médico (Rio de Janeiro)

Folhetos de Hygiene (Departamento Nacional de Saúde Pública, Rio de Janeiro)

Gazeta Médica da Bahia (Salvador)

A Profilaxia Rural (Diretoria de Saneamento e Profilaxia Rural, Rio de Janeiro)
Revista de Higiene e Saúde Pública (Rio de Janeiro)
Revista de Saúde Pública (Serviço Estadual da Bahia, Salvador)
Revista Médico-Cirúrgica do Brasil (Rio de Janeiro)
Saneamento (Serviço de Saneamento Rural, Rio de Janeiro)
Saúde (Liga Pró-Saneamento do Brasil, Rio de Janeiro)

Public Documents

Brazil. *Coleção das Leis da República dos Estados Unidos do Brasil de 1904: Atos do Poder Legislativo*. Rio de Janeiro: Imprensa Nacional, 1907.

——. *Coleção das Leis da República dos Estados Unidos do Brasil de 1914: Atos do Poder Executivo*. Rio de Janeiro: Imprensa Nacional, 1916.

——. *Coleção das Leis da República dos Estados Unidos do Brasil de 1918: Atos do Poder Executivo*. Rio de Janeiro: Imprensa Nacional, 1919.

——. *Coleção das Leis da República dos Estados Unidos do Brasil de 1919: Atos do Poder Executivo*. Rio de Janeiro: Imprensa Nacional, 1920.

——. *Coleção das Leis da República dos Estados Unidos do Brasil de 1920: Atos do Poder Legislativo*. Rio de Janeiro: Imprensa Nacional, 1921.

——. *Coleção das Leis da República dos Estados Unidos do Brasil de 1923: Atos do Poder Legislativo*. Rio de Janeiro: Imprensa Nacional, 1924.

——. *Coleção das Leis da República dos Estados Unidos do Brasil de 1926: Atos do Poder Executivo*. Rio de Janeiro: Imprensa Nacional, 1927.

Brazil. Departamento Nacional de Saúde Pública/Diretoria de Saneamento e Profilaxia Rural/Serviço no Estado do Amazonas. *Um Ano de Campanha*. Manaus: A Semana/Casa Editora, 1922.

Brazil. Ministério da Justiça e Negócios Interiores. *Relatório do Ministério da Justiça e Negócios Interiores: Introdução*. Rio de Janeiro: Imprensa Nacional, 1921.

——. *Relatório do Ministério da Justiça e Negócios Interiores (Departamento Nacional de Saúde Pública)*. Rio de Janeiro: Imprensa Nacional, 1923.

Brazil. Câmara dos Deputados. *Anais da Câmara dos Deputados*. 14 vols. Rio de Janeiro: Imprensa Nacional, 1917.

——. *Anais da Câmara dos Deputados*. 14 vols. Rio de Janeiro: Imprensa Nacional, 1918.

——. *Anais da Câmara dos Deputados*. 14 vols. Rio de Janeiro: Imprensa Nacional, 1919.

——. *Anais da Câmara dos Deputados*. 15 vols. Rio de Janeiro: Imprensa Nacional, 1920.

Brazil. Presidente. *Mensagem Apresentada ao Congresso Nacional na Abertura da 8ª Legislatura pelo Presidente Marechal Hermes Rodrigues da Fonseca*. Rio de Janeiro: Imprensa Nacional, 1912.

Brazil. Presidente, 1915–18 [W. Bráz]. *Mensagens Presidenciais: Presidência Wenceslau Bráz, 1915–1918.* Brasilia: Câmara dos Deputados, 1978.

Brazil. Presidente, 1919–22 [D. Moreira e E. Pessoa]. *Mensagens Presidenciais: Presidência Delfim Moreira, 1919, e Presidência Epitácio Pessoa, 1920–1922.* Brasilia: Câmara dos Deputados, 1978.

Brazil. Presidente, 1923–26 [A. Bernardes]. *Mensagens Presidenciais: Presidência Arthur Bernardes, 1923–1926.* Brasilia: Câmara dos Deputados, 1978.

Brazil. Presidente, 1927–30 [W. Luís]. *Mensagens Presidenciais: Presidência Washington Luís, 1927–1930.* Brasilia: Câmara dos Deputados, 1978.

Brazilian Documents, Texts, and Reports, 1890–1940

Abranches, J. D. de. *Governos e Congressos da República dos Estados Unidos do Brasil: Apontamentos Biográficos sobre Todos os Presidentes e Vice-Presidentes da República, Ministros de Estado, e Senadores e Deputados ao Congresso Nacional, 1889 a 1917.* São Paulo: Abranches, 1918.

Araújo, O. de S. "A Profilaxia da Lepra e das Doenças Venéreas no Brasil e a Atuação do Departamento Nacional de Saúde Pública." *Arquivos de Higiene* 1, no. 11 (1927): 193–253.

Autran, H. *Conferências sobre Higiene . . . Irradiadas pela Estação Rádio Club do Brasil.* Rio de Janeiro: Inspetoria de Demografia Sanitária/Departamento Nacional de Saúde Pública, 1926.

Barbosa, P. "Pequena História da Febre Amarela no Brasil." *Arquivos de Higiene* 3, no. 1 (1929): 5–25.

Barbosa, P., and C. B. Rezende. *Os Serviços de Saúde Pública no Brasil, Especialmente na Cidade do Rio de Janeiro: 1808–1907 (Esboço Histórico e Legislativo).* Rio de Janeiro: Imprensa Nacional, 1909.

Barreto, A. L. C. A. de B. "Como Organizar o Ministério de Saúde e Assistência Pública no Brasil." In *Anais do Quinto Congresso Brasileiro de Higiene, Recife 17 a 22 de outubro de 1929,* 2:63–85. Rio de Janeiro: Oficinas Gráficas da Inspetoria de Demografia Sanitária, 1929.

———. "Orçamentos Estaduais e Serviços Sanitários." *Arquivos de Higiene* 1, no. 1 (1927): 121–24.

Barros, G. de. *Quatro Anos de Administração Sanitária.* Recife: Imprensa Industrial, 1920.

Barros Barreto, J. de. "Febre Amarela, Dificuldades de Campanha." *Arquivos de Higiene* 3, no. 1 (1929): 433–49.

———. *Serviços de Saneamento e Profilaxia no Paraná, em 1922.* Curitiba: Empresa Gráfica Paranaense, 1923.

Barroso, S. M. *Doenças que Pegam: Meios de Evitá-las.* São Paulo: Melhoramentos, 1938.

———. *Pela Saúde Pública.* Rio de Janeiro: Imprensa Nacional, 1919.

————. "Relatório: Serviços de Saneamento e Profilaxia Rural do Estado da Bahia no Ano de 1922." Salvador: n.p., 1923.

Bello, José Maria. "Um Problema Nacional." In *Saneamento do Brasil*, ed. B. Penna, iii–v. Rio de Janeiro: Revista dos Tribunais, 1918.

Castro, A. O., and A. S. Castagnino. *O Senado Federal de 1890 a 1927: Relação dos Senadores desde a Constituinte até a 13a.* Rio de Janeiro: n.p., 1927.

Cavalcanti, P. "A Canaan Sertaneja." *Saúde* 1, nos. 4–6 (1918): 265–81.

Chagas, C. *Discurso do Dr. Carlos Chagas no Banquete Oferecido pela Classe Médica do Rio de Janeiro, no Edifício do Derby-Club, em Homenagem aos Médicos Bahianos, em 9 de Dezembro de 1918.* Rio de Janeiro: Tipografia do Jornal do Comércio, 1919.

Couto, M. "A Criação do Ministério da Saúde Pública." *Revista Médico-Cirúrgica do Brasil* 27, no. 9 (1919): 383–87.

————. "O Ministério da Saúde Pública: Sessão Magna de 3 de Junho de 1917." In *As Alocuções do Presidente da Academia de Medicina*, 35–38. Rio de Janeiro: Tipografia Besnard Frères, 1923.

————. "O Saneamento Rural: Homenagem ao Presidente da República Dr. Wenceslau Bráz. Sessão Magna de 30 de Junho de 1918." In *As Alocuções do Presidente da Academia de Medicina*, 41–45. Rio de Janeiro: Tipografia Besnard Frères, 1923.

Diniz, Almáquio. *O Estado, o Direito, e a Saúde Pública.* Rio de Janeiro: n.p., 1929.

Egas, E. *Galeria dos Presidentes de São Paulo: Período Republicano, 1889–1920.* São Paulo: O Estado de S. Paulo, 1927.

Fontenelle, J. P. "Higiene e Saúde Pública." In *Dicionário Histórico, Geográfico, e Etnográfico do Brasil: Comemorativo do Primeiro Centenário da Independência*, 1–101. Rio de Janeiro: Imprensa Nacional, 1922.

————. *A Saúde Pública no Rio de Janeiro: Distrito Federal, 1935–1936: Relatório do Serviço de Saúde do Distrito Federal.* Rio de Janeiro: n.p., 1937.

Fraga, C. "Saneamento Urbano e Rural." In *Livro do Centenário da Câmara dos Deputados*, 521–35. Rio de Janeiro: Imprensa do Brasil, 1926.

————. *Introdução ao Relatório dos Serviços do DNSP (1927) pelo Prof. Clementino Fraga.* Rio de Janeiro: Inspetoria de Demografia Sanitária, Departamento Nacional de Saúde Pública, 1928.

Leão, P., et al., eds. *Afrânio versus Afrânio.* Niterói: Tipografia Jeronimo Silva, 1922.

Lobato, Monteiro. *Mr. Slang e o Brasil e o Problema Vital.* 1918. São Paulo: Brasiliense, 1956.

Neiva, A. *Discursos-Pronunciados no Banquete que Lhe Foi Oferecido a 18 de Novembro de 1916 no Rio de Janeiro.* Rio de Janeiro: Tipografia Besnard Frères, 1917.

————. "Programa Apresentado pelo Dr. Arthur Neiva ao Conselheiro Rodrigues Alves para a Reforma da Higiene no Brasil, por Ocasião do Convite que Daquele Estadista Recebeu para Diretor da Saúde Pública, e por Ele Aprovado Integralmente." In Arquivo Arthur Neiva, CPDOC/FGV, 1918.

————. "Serviço Sanitário de S. Paulo: Despedidas: Discurso Proferido pelo Sr.

Dr. Arthur Neiva e Publicado no *O Estado de S. Paulo* em 10 de Maio de 1920." In *Coletânea*, ed. A. Neiva, 25-27. 1920. Rio de Janeiro: n.p., 1940.

Neiva, A., and B. Penna. "Viagem Científica pelo Norte da Bahia, Sudoeste de Pernambuco, Sul do Piauí, e de Norte a Sul de Goiás." *Memórias do Instituto Oswaldo Cruz* 8, no. 30 (1916): 74-224.

Oliveira, W. de. "Profilaxia da Febre Amarela no Estado de São Paulo." *Arquivos de Higiene* 3, no. 3 (1928): 37-57.

Peixoto, A. "Discurso Pronunciado no Banquete Oferecido ao Prof. Miguel Pereira, em 19 de Maio de 1918." In *Afrânio versus Afrânio*, ed. P. Leão et al., 29-37. Niterói: Tipografia Jeronimo Silva, 1922.

———. *Higiene*. 2nd ed. Rio de Janeiro: Francisco Alves, 1917.

Penna, Belisário. *Defesa Sanitária do Brasil*. Rio de Janeiro: Tipografia Revista dos Tribunais, 1922.

———. "Discurso Pronunciado pelo Dr. Belisário Penna na Sede da Sociedade Nacional de Agricultura, a 11 de Fevereiro de 1919, em Sessão Comemorativa do 1° Aniversário da Fundação da Liga Pró-Saneamento do Brasil." *Saúde* 2, no. 2 (1919): 218-30.

———. *Minas e Rio Grande do Sul: Estado da Doença, Estado da Saúde*. Rio de Janeiro: Tipografia Revista dos Tribunais, 1918.

———. "Organização Sanitária Nacional." *Saúde* 2, no. 2 (1919): 101-2.

———. *O Saneamento do Brasil*. 1918. Rio de Janeiro: Editora dos Tribunais, 1923.

———. "A Vitória do Saneamento: Conferência Realizada na Sociedade Nacional de Agricultura do Rio, pelo Dr. Belisário Penna, no Dia 12 de Fevereiro de 1920." In *Afrânio versus Afrânio*, ed. P. Leão et al., 7-28. Niterói: Tipografia Jeronimo Silva, 1922.

Pereira, M. "O Brasil É Ainda um Imenso Hospital: Discurso Pronunciado pelo Professor Miguel Pereira por Ocasião do Regresso do Professor Aloysio de Castro, da República Argentina, em Outubro de 1916." *Revista de Medicina* 7, no. 21 (1922): 3-7.

Peryassu, A. G. "Profilaxia da Febre Amarela no Brasil." *Arquivos de Higiene* 1, no. 2 (1927): 49-74.

Rodrigues, N. "Higiene Pública: A Classe Médica e a Administração Sanitária no Brasil e nos Estados Unidos." *Gazeta Médica da Bahia* 24, no. 10 (1892): 420-25.

———. "Higiene Pública: A Organização do Serviço Sanitário no Brasil." *Brasil-Médico*, November 8, 1891, 331-32; November 15, 1891, 336-38.

———. "Higiene Pública: O Serviço de Higiene Pública nos Estados Brasileiros." *Gazeta Médica da Bahia* 24, no. 10 (1892): 441-45.

———. "Inspetoria Geral de Higiene." *Gazeta Médica da Bahia* 23, no. 1 (1891): 46-47.

Sá, C. *O Serviço de Saneamento Rural no Estado do Rio de Janeiro em 1924*. N.p.: Departamento Nacional de Saúde Pública, 1925.

Seidl, C. P. "Função Governamental em Matéria de Higiene: Conferência Lida na Biblioteca Nacional a 28 de Novembro de 1913." In *Anais da Biblioteca Na-*

cional do Rio de Janeiro, 43–71. Rio de Janeiro: Oficinas Gráficas da Biblioteca Nacional, 1916.

———. *Relatório da Diretoria Geral de Saúde Pública Apresentado ao Exmo. Sr. Dr. Carlos Maximiliano Pereira dos Santos, Ministro da Justiça e Negócios Interiores, Ano de 1916*. Rio de Janeiro: Imprensa Nacional, 1917.

Sodré, A. "O Novo Inspetor de Higiene." *Brasil-Médico*, June 8, 1891, 152.

———. "A Propósito da Nomeação do Inspetor Geral de Higiene." *Brasil-Médico*, August 22, 1891, 252.

———. *Saneamento do Brasil: Discursos*. Rio de Janeiro: Tipografia Besnard Frères, 1918.

———. *Trabalhos Parlamentares: Discursos e Pareceres*. Rio de Janeiro: Imprensa Nacional, 1920.

Souza Araújo, H. C. de. *O Impaludismo no Norte do Paraná e sua Profilaxia: Apresentado ao Dr. Alfonso Alves de Camargo, Presidente do Paraná, em 31 de Julho de 1917 e Lido perante a Sociedade de Medicina do Paraná, em 6 de Agosto de 1917*. Rio de Janeiro: n.p., 1917.

———. *A Profilaxia Rural no Estado do Pará*. Belém: Tipografia da Livraria Gillet, 1922.

———. *A Profilaxia Rural no Estado do Paraná: Esboço de Geografia Médica*. Curitiba: Livraria Econômica, 1919.

Torres, L. F. *Guia Sanitário do Chefe de Posto*. Niterói: Departamento Nacional de Saúde Pública, Serviço de Saneamento Rural no Estado do Rio de Janeiro, 1924.

Torres, T. "Relatório dos Serviços Efetuados pela Comissão Sanitária Federal no Estado do Espírito Santo Apresentado ao Exmo Sr. Diretor Geral de Saúde Pública." In *Relatório da Diretoria Geral de Saúde Pública Apresentado ao Exmo. Sr. Dr. Carlos Maximiliano Pereira dos Santos, Ministro da Justiça e Negócios Interiores, ano de 1917*, 41–66. Rio de Janeiro: Imprensa Nacional, 1919.

———. "A Saúde Pública em 1918: Relatório do Dr. Theophilo Torres, Diretor Geral de Saúde Pública." *Revista Médico-Cirúrgica do Brasil* 27, no. 2 (1919): 29–54.

———. "Serviço Sanitário Federal em Manaus: Relatório Apresentado em 3 de Janeiro de 1916." In *Relatório da Diretoria Geral de Saúde Pública Apresentado ao Exmo. Sr. Dr. Carlos Maximiliano Pereira dos Santos, Ministro da Justiça e Negócios Interiores, Ano de 1916*, 207–25. Rio de Janeiro: Imprensa Nacional, 1917.

———. "Os Últimos Redutos da Febre Amarela: Comunicação Feita ao VIII Congresso Brasileiro de Medicina." *Revista Médico-Cirúrgica do Brasil* 27, no. 3 (1919): 65–67.

Secondary Sources

Abrão, Janete Silveira. *Banalização da Morte na Cidade Calada: A Hespanhola em Porto Alegre, 1918*. Porto Alegre: EDIPUCRS, 1998.

Bibliography

Ackerknecht, E. H. "Anticontagionism between 1821 and 1867." *Bulletin of the History of Medicine* 22, no. 5 (1948): 562–93.

Albert, Bill. *South America and the First World War: The Impact of the War on Brazil, Argentina, Peru, and Chile.* Cambridge: Cambridge University Press, 2002.

Albuquerque, M., et al. *A Ciência Vai à Roça: Imagens das Expedições do Instituto Oswaldo Cruz (1911–1913).* Rio de Janeiro: Casa de Oswaldo Cruz/Fiocruz, 1991.

Almeida, Marta de. *República dos Invisíveis: Emílio Ribas, Microbiologia, e Saúde Pública em São Paulo, 1898–1917.* Bragança Paulista: Editora da Universidade São Francisco, 2003.

Amado, Janaina, "Região, Sertão, Nação." *Estudos Históricos* 15 (1995): 145–51.

Ashford, Douglas E. *History and Context in Comparative Public Policy.* Pittsburgh: University of Pittsburgh Press, 1992.

Baldwin, Peter. *Contagion and the State in Europe, 1830–1930.* Cambridge: Cambridge University Press, 2005.

Bello, José Maria. *História da República 1889–1945 (Adenda 1945–1954).* São Paulo: Editora Nacional, 1956.

Benchimol, Jaime, ed. *Febre Amarela: A Doença e a Vacina, uma História Inacabada.* Rio de Janeiro: Editora Fiocruz/Bio-Manguinhos, 2001.

———, ed. *Manguinhos: Do Sonho à Vida—A Ciência na Belle Époque.* Rio de Janeiro: Casa de Oswaldo Cruz/Fiocruz, 1990.

———. *Dos Micróbios aos Mosquitos: Febre Amarela e a Revolução Pasteuriana no Brasil.* Rio de Janeiro: Editora Fiocruz/Editora UFRJ, 1999.

———. *Pereira Passos: Um Haussmann Tropical.* Rio de Janeiro: Secretaria Municipal de Cultura, Turismo, e Esportes, 1990.

———. "Reforma Urbana e Revolta da Vacina na Cidade do Rio de Janeiro." In *O Brasil Republicano*, vol. 1, *O tempo do Liberalismo Excludente: Da Proclamação da República à Revolução de 1930*, ed. Jorge Ferreira and Lucilia de Almeida Neves, 231–86. Rio de Janeiro: Editora Civilização Brasileira, 2003.

Benchimol, Jaime, and Luiz A. Teixeira. *Cobras, Lagartos, e Outros Bichos: Uma História Comparada dos Institutos Oswaldo Cruz e Butantan.* Rio de Janeiro: Editora UFRJ, 1993.

Berge, A. F. L. *Mission and Method: The Early Nineteenth-Century French Public Health Movement.* Cambridge: Cambridge University Press, 1992.

Bertolli Filho, C. "A Gripe Espanhola em São Paulo." *Ciência Hoje* 10, no. 58 (1989): 31–41.

Bertucci, Liane Maria. *Influenza, a Medicina Enferma.* Campinas: Editora Unicamp, 2004.

———. *Saúde: Arma Revolucionária, São Paulo, 1891–1925.* Campinas: Centro de Memória/Universidade de Campinas, 1997.

Birn, Anne-Emanuelle. *Marriage of Convenience: Rockefeller International Health and Revolutionary Mexico.* Rochester: University of Rochester Press, 2006.

Blount, J. A. "A Administração da Saúde Pública no Estado de São Paulo: O

Serviço Sanitário, 1892–1918." *Revista de Administração de Empresas* 12, no. 4 (1972): 40–48.

———. "The Public Health Movement in São Paulo, Brazil: A History of the Sanitary Service, 1892–1918." PhD diss., Tulane University, 1971.

Boccaccio, M. "Ground Itch and Dew Poison: The Rockefeller Sanitary Commission, 1909–14." *Journal of the History of Medicine and Allied Sciences* 27, no. 1 (1972): 30–53.

Breeden, J. O. "Disease as a Factor in Southern Distinctiveness." In *Disease and Distinctiveness in the American South*, ed. T. Savitt and H. Young, 1–28. Knoxville: University of Tennessee Press, 1988.

Briggs, A. "Cholera and Society in the Nineteenth Century." *Past and Present* 19, no. 1 (1961): 76–96.

Britto, N. A. "La Dansarina: A Gripe Espanhola e o Cotidiano na Cidade do Rio de Janeiro." *História, Ciências, Saúde–Manguinhos* 4, no. 1 (1997): 11–30.

———. *Oswaldo Cruz: A Construção de um Mito na Ciência Brasileira*. Rio de Janeiro: Editora Fiocruz, 1995.

Buchanan, J. M., and G. Tullock. *The Calculus of Consent: Logical Foundations of Constitutional Democracy*. Ann Arbor: University of Michigan Press, 1965.

Buckley, Eve Elizabeth. "Drought in the Sertão as a Natural or Social Phenomenon: Establishing the Inspetoria Federal de Obras Contra as Secas, 1909–1923." *Boletim do Museu Paraense Emilio Goeldi, Ciências Humanas* 5, no. 2 (2010): 379–98.

Cabral, Dilma. *Lepra, Medicina, e Políticas de Saúde no Brasil (1894–1934)*. Rio de Janeiro: Editora Fiocruz, 2013.

Campos, A. L. V. *A República do Picapau Amarelo: Uma Leitura de Monteiro Lobato*. São Paulo: Martins Fontes, 1985.

Carneiro, Henrique. "Comida e Sociedade: Significados Sociais na História da Alimentação." *História: Questões e Debates* 42, no. 1 (2005): 71–80.

Carone, E. *A República Velha II: Evolução Política (1889–1930)*. 2nd ed. São Paulo: Difel, 1974.

Carvalho, J. M. de. *Os Bestializados: O Rio de Janeiro e a República que Não Foi*. São Paulo: Companhia das Letras, 1987.

———. "As Forças Armadas na Primeira República: O Poder Desestabilizador." In *O Brasil Republicano: Sociedade e Instituições (1889–1930)*, 3rd ed., ed. B. Fausto, 183–234. São Paulo: Difel, 1985.

Cassedy, J. H. "The 'Germ of Laziness' in the South, 1900–1915: Charles Wardell Stiles and the Progressive Paradox." *Bulletin of the History of Medicine* 47, no. 2 (1971): 159–69.

Castro Santos, Luiz Antonio de. "Estado e Saúde Pública no Brasil (1889–1930)." *Dados-Revista de Ciências Sociais* 23, no. 2 (1980): 237–50.

———. "As Origens da Reforma Sanitária e da Modernização Conservadora na Bahia durante a Primeira República." *Dados-Revista de Ciências Sociais* 41, no. 3 (1998): 593–633.

———. "O Pensamento Sanitarista na Primeira República: Uma Ideologia de Construção da Nacionalidade." *Dados-Revista de Ciências Sociais* 28, no. 2 (1985): 193–210.

———. "Poder, Ideologias, e Saúde no Brasil da Primeira República: Ensaio de Sociologia Histórica." In *Cuidar, Controlar, Curar: Ensaios Históricos sobre Saúde e Doença na América Latina e no Caribe*, ed. Gilberto Hochman and Diego Armus, 249–93. Rio de Janeiro: Editora Fiocruz, 2004.

———. "Power, Ideology, and Public Health in Brazil (1889–1930)." PhD diss., Harvard University, 1987.

———. "A Reforma Sanitária 'Pelo Alto': O Pioneirismo Paulista no Início do Século XX." *Dados-Revista de Ciências Sociais* 36, no. 3 (1993): 361–92.

Chagas Filho, C. *Carlos Chagas, Meu Pai*. Rio de Janeiro: Casa de Oswaldo Cruz/Fiocruz, 1993.

Chalhoub, Sidney. *Cidade Febril: Cortiços e Epidemias na Corte Imperial*. São Paulo: Companhia das Letras, 1996.

Chaves, Cleide de Lima. *História da Saúde e das Doenças no Interior da Bahia: Séculos XIX e XX*. Vitória da Conquista: Edições Uesb, 2013.

———. "Poder e Saúde na América do Sul: Os Congressos Sanitários Internacionais, 1870–1889." *História, Ciências, Saúde–Manguinhos* 20, no. 2 (2013): 411–34.

———. "Políticas Internacionais de Saúde: O Primeiro Acordo Sanitário Internacional da América (Montevidéu, 1873)." *Locus: Revista de História* 15, no. 2 (2009): 9–27.

Coase, Ronald Harry. "The Nature of the Firm." *Economica*, n.s., 4, no. 16 (1937): 386–405.

Cooper, D. B. "Brazil's Long Fight against Epidemic Disease, 1849–1917, with Special Emphasis on Yellow Fever." *Bulletin of the New York Academy of Medicine* 51, no. 5 (1975): 672–96.

———. "Oswaldo Cruz and the Impact of Yellow Fever on Brazilian History." *Bulletin of the Tulane Medical Faculty* 26, no. 1 (1967): 49–52.

Cooper, D. B., and K. Kiple. "Yellow Fever." In *The Cambridge World History of Human Disease*, ed. K. Kiple, 1100–1107. Cambridge: Cambridge University Press, 1993.

Costa, N. do R. *Lutas Urbanas e Controle Sanitário: Origens das Políticas de Saúde no Brasil*. Petrópolis: Vozes-Abrasco, 1985.

Crosby, A. W. *America's Forgotten Pandemic: The Influenza of 1918*. Cambridge: Cambridge University Press, 1989.

Cueto, Marcos. "Los Ciclos de la Erradicación: La Fundación Rockefeller y la Salud Pública Latinoamericana, 1918–1940." In *Salud, Cultura, y Sociedad en América Latina: Nuevas Perspectivas Históricas*, ed. M. Cueto, 179–202. Lima: IEP-OPS, 1996.

———. *Missionaries of Science: The Rockefeller Foundation and Latin America*. Bloomington: Indiana University Press, 1994.

———. *The Value of Health: A History of the Pan American Health Organization.* Washington, D.C.: Pan American Health Organization, 2007.

Cunha, E. da. *Rebellion in the Backlands.* Trans. Samuel Putnam. Chicago: University of Chicago Press, 1944.

———. *Os Sertões: Campanha de Canudos.* 1902. Brasilia: Editora UNB, 1963.

De Swaan, A. *In Care of the State: Health Care, Education, and Welfare in Europe in the Modern Era.* Cambridge, Mass.: Polity, 1990.

Dickens, C. "Nobody's Story." In *Christmas Stories*, 61–66. London: Oxford University Press, 1971.

Duffy, J. *The Sanitarians: A History of American Public Health.* Urbana: University of Illinois Press, 1990.

———. "Social Impact of Disease in the Late Nineteenth Century." *Bulletin of the New York Academy of Medicine* 47, no. 7 (1971): 797–810.

Dwork, D. "Contagion." In *Macmillan Dictionary of the History of Science*, 2nd ed., ed. W. F. Bynum, E. J. Browne, and R. Porter, 75–77. London: Macmillan, 1988.

Edson, C. "The Microbe as a Social Leveler." *North American Review* 161 (1895): 421–6.

Elias, Norbert. *Introdução à Sociologia.* Lisbon: Edições 70, 1980.

———. *O Processo Civilizador: Formação do Estado e Civilização.* Rio de Janeiro: Jorge Zahar Editor, 1993.

———. *State Formation and Civilization: The Civilizing Process.* Vol. 2. Trans. Edmund Jephcott. Oxford: Blackwell, 1982.

———. *What Is Sociology?* Trans. Stephen Mennell and Grace Morrissey. New York: Columbia University Press, 1978.

Ellis, J. D. *The Physician-Legislators: Medicine in the Early Third Republic, 1870–1914.* Cambridge: Cambridge University Press, 1990.

Ellis, J. H. *Yellow Fever and Public Health in the New South.* Lexington: University Press of Kentucky, 1992.

Ettling, J. *The Germ of Laziness: The Rockefeller Philanthropy and Public Health in the New South.* Cambridge: Harvard University Press, 1981.

Faria, Lina Rodrigues de. "A Fase Pioneira da Reforma Sanitária Brasileira no Brasil: A Atuação da Fundação Rockefeller (1915/1930)." Master's thesis, Instituto de Medicina Social/Universidade do Estado do Rio de Janeiro, 1994.

———. *Saúde e Política: A Fundação Rockefeller e Seus Parceiros em São Paulo.* Rio de Janeiro: Editora Fiocruz, 2007.

Farley, John. *To Cast Out Disease: A History of the International Health Division of the Rockefeller Foundation (1913–1951).* Oxford: Oxford University Press, 2004.

Fernandes, Tania Maria Dias. *Vacina Antivariólica: Ciência, Técnica, e o Poder dos Homens (1808–1920).* 2nd ed. Rio de Janeiro: Fiocruz, 2010.

Frahia, H. *Oswaldo Cruz e a Febre Amarela no Pará.* Belém: Conselho Estadual de Cultura, 1972.

Bibliography

Franco, A. A. de M. *Rodrigues Alves: Apogeu e Declínio da Democracia*. 2 vols. Rio de Janeiro: José Olympio, 1973.

Franco, Odair. "História da Febre Amarela no Brasil." *Revista Brasileira de Malariologia e Doenças Tropicais* 21, no. 4 (1969): 315–520.

Fraser, D. *The Evolution of the British Welfare State*. London: Macmillan, 1984.

Fritsch, W. "Apogeu e Crise na Primeira República." In *A Ordem do Progresso: Cem Anos de Política Econômica Republicana (1889–1989)*, ed. M. de P. Abreu, 31–72. Rio de Janeiro: Editora Campus, 1989.

Fundação Casa de Rui Barbosa. *O Governo Presidencial do Brasil, 1889–1930 (Guia Administrativo do Poder Executivo no Período da República Velha)*. Brasilia: Fundação Casa de Rui Barbosa/Senado Federal/Pró-Memória, 1985.

Goulart, Adriana da Costa. "Revisitando a Espanhola: A Gripe Pandêmica de 1918 no Rio de Janeiro." *História, Ciências, Saúde–Manguinhos* 12, no. 1 (2005): 101–42.

Hall, J. A., and G. J. Ikenberry. *O Estado*. Lisbon: Estampa, 1990.

———. *The State*. Minneapolis: University of Minnesota Press, 1989.

Hall, Peter A., and Rosemary C. R. Taylor. "Political Science and the Three New Institutionalisms." *Political Studies* 44, no. 5 (1996): 936–57.

Hamlin, Christopher. "Commentary: Ackerknecht and Anticontagionism: A Tale of Two Dichotomies." *International Journal of Epidemiology* 38, no. 1 (2009): 22–27.

———. *Public Health and Social Justice in the Age of Chadwick: Britain, 1800–1854*. Cambridge: Cambridge University Press, 1998.

Hannaway, C. "Environment and Miasmata." In *Companion Encyclopedia of the History of Medicine*, ed. W. F. Bynum and R. Porter, 292–308. London: Routledge, 1993.

Harrison, Mark. "Disease, Diplomacy, and International Commerce: The Origins of International Sanitary Regulation in the Nineteenth Century." *Journal of Global History* 1, no. 2 (2006): 197–217.

Hintze, Otto. "Calvinism and Raison d'État in Early Seventeenth-Century Brandenburg." In *The Historical Essays of Otto Hintze*, ed. Felix Gilbert, 88–154. New York: Oxford University Press, 1975.

Hobsbawm, E. *Nations and Nationalism since 1780: Programme, Myth, Reality*. 2nd ed. Cambridge: Cambridge University Press, 1992.

Hochman, Gilberto. "Priority, Invisibility, and Eradication: The History of Smallpox and the Brazilian Public Health Agenda." *Medical History* 53, no. 2 (2009): 229–52.

Hochman, Gilberto, and N. Azevedo. "Oswaldo Cruz." In *Dictionary of Medical Biography*, ed. William F. Bynum and Helen Bynum, 4:378–80. Westport, Conn.: Greenwood, 2007.

Hochman, Gilberto, Nísia Trindade Lima, and Marcos C. Maio. "The Path of

Eugenics in Brazil: Dilemmas of Miscegenation." In *The Oxford Handbook of the History of Eugenics*, ed. Alison Bashford and Philippa Levine, 493–510. New York: Oxford University Press, 2010.

Hochman, Gilberto, Maria Teresa V. B. Mello, and Paulo R. Elian Santos. "A Malária em Foto: Imagens de Campanhas e Ações no Brasil da Primeira Metade do Século XX." *História, Ciências, Saúde–Manguinhos* 9, supp. (2002): 233–73.

Hollanda, C. B. *Modos de Representação Política: O Experimento da Primeira República Brasileira*. Belo Horizonte: Editora UFMG, 2009.

Humphreys, M. *Yellow Fever and the South*. New Brunswick, N.J.: Rutgers University Press, 1992.

Immergut, E. M. *Health Politics: Interests and Institutions in Western Europe*. Cambridge: Cambridge University Press, 1992.

Iyda, M. *Cem Anos de Saúde Pública: A Cidadania Negada*. São Paulo: Editora Unesp, 1994.

Jabert, Alexander. "Formas de Administração da Loucura na Primeira República: O Caso do Estado do Espírito Santo." *História, Ciências, Saúde–Manguinhos* 12, no. 3 (2005): 693–716.

Joll, J. *A Europa desde 1870*. Lisbon: Publicações Dom Quixote, 1982.

Kagan, M. "Federal Public Health: A Reflection of a Changing Constitution." *Journal of the History of Medicine and Allied Sciences* 16, no. 3 (1961): 256–79.

Kramer, H. D. "The Germ Theory and the Early Public Health Program in the United States." *Bulletin of the History of Medicine* 22, no. 3 (1948): 233–47.

Kropf, Simone Petraglia. *Doença de Chagas, Doença do Brasil: Ciência, Saúde, e Nação (1909–1962)*. Rio de Janeiro: Editora Fiocruz, 2009.

Kunitz, S. J. "Explanations and Ideologies of Mortality Patterns." *Population and Development Review* 13, no. 3 (1987): 379–408.

———. "Hookworm and Pellagra: Exemplary Diseases in the New South." *Journal of Health and Social Behavior* 29, no. 2 (1988): 139–48.

Labra, M. E. "O Movimento Sanitarista dos Anos 20: Da Conexão Sanitária Internacional à Especialidade em Saúde Pública no Brasil." Master's thesis, Escola Brasileira de Administração Pública/Fundação Getúlio Vargas, 1985.

Leavitt, J. W. "Politics and Public Health: Smallpox in Milwaukee, 1894–1895." *Bulletin of the History of Medicine* 50, no. 4 (1976): 553–68.

Leite Neto, L. *Catálogo Biográfico dos Senadores Brasileiros, 1826–1986*. Brasilia: Senado Federal, 1986.

Lessa, R. *A Invenção Republicana: Campos Sales, as Bases, e a Decadência da Primeira República Brasileira*. São Paulo: Vértice-Iuperj, 1988.

Levine, R. "Pernambuco e Federação Brasileira, 1889–1937." In *O Brasil Republicano: Estrutura de Poder e Economia (1889–1930)*, 4th ed., ed. B. Fausto, 122–51. São Paulo: Difel, 1985.

Lima, Nísia Trindade. "Uma Brasiliana Médica: O Brasil Central na Expedição

Científica de Arthur Neiva e Belisário Penna e na Viagem ao Tocantins de Julio Paternostro." *História, Ciências, Saúde–Manguinhos* 16, supp. 1 (2009): 229–48.

———. "Doctors, Social Scientists, and Backlands Peoples: Continuity and Change in Representations of Brazil's Rural World." *Canadian Journal of Latin American and Caribbean Studies* 35, no. 69 (2010): 39–66.

———. "Public Health and Social Ideas in Modern Brazil." *American Journal of Public Health* 97, no. 7 (2007): 1209–15.

———. *Um Sertão Chamado Brasil.* 2nd ed. São Paulo: Hucitec Editora, 2013.

Lima, Nísia Trindade, and N. A. Britto. *A Campanha do Saneamento Rural na Imprensa do Rio de Janeiro.* Rio de Janeiro: Casa de Oswaldo Cruz/Fiocruz, 1991.

———. "Salud y Nación: Propuesta para el Saneamento Rural: Un Estudio de la Revista *Saúde* (1918–1919)." In *Salud, Cultura, y Sociedad en América Latina: Nuevas Perspectivas Históricas*, ed. M. Cueto, 135–58. Lima: IEP-OPS, 1996.

Lima, Nísia Trindade, and Gilberto Hochman. "Condenado pela Raça, Absolvido pela Medicina: O Brasil Descoberto pelo Movimento Sanitarista da Primeira República." In *Raça, Ciência, e Sociedade*, ed. Marcos C. Maio and R. Santos, 23–40. Rio de Janeiro: Fundação Cultural Banco do Brasil/Editora Fiocruz, 1996.

Link, W. A. "Privies, Progressivism, and Public Schools: Health Reform and Education in the Rural South, 1909–1920." *Journal of Southern History* 54, no. 4 (1988): 623–42.

Lobato, Monteiro. *Urupês.* 1914. São Paulo: Brasiliense, 1957.

Love, Joseph. "Autonomia e Interdependência: São Paulo e a Federação Brasileira, 1889–1937." In *O Brasil Republicano: Estrutura de Poder e Economia (1889–1930)*, 4th ed., ed. B. Fausto, 53–76. São Paulo: Difel, 1985.

———. "The Brazilian Federal State in the Old Republic (1889–1930): Did Regime Change Make a Difference?" In *State and Nation Making in Latin America and Spain: Republics of the Possible*, ed. Miguel A. Centeno and Agustin E. Ferraro, 100–115. Cambridge: Cambridge University Press, 2013.

———. *São Paulo in the Brazilian Federation, 1889–1937.* Stanford: Stanford University Press, 1980.

Lowy, Ilana. *Vírus, Mosquitos, e Modernidade: A Febre Amarela no Brasil entre Ciência e Política.* Rio de Janeiro: Editora Fiocruz, 2006.

Luz, M. T. *Medicina e Ordem Política Brasileira.* Rio de Janeiro: Graal, 1982.

Mann, Michael. "The Autonomous Power of the State: Its Origins, Mechanisms, and Results." *European Journal of Sociology* 25, no. 2 (1984): 185–213.

———. *The Sources of Social Power: The Rise of Classes and Nation-States, 1760–1914.* Cambridge: Cambridge University Press, 1993.

Marcus, A. I. "Disease Prevention in America: From a Local to a National Outlook, 1880–1910." *Bulletin of the History of Medicine* 53, no. 2 (1979): 184–203.

———. "Physicians Open a Can of Worms: American Nationality and Hookworm in the United States, 1893–1909." *American Studies* 30, no. 2 (1989): 103–19.

———. "The South's Native Foreigners: Hookworm as a Factor in Southern Distinctiveness." In *Disease and Distinctiveness in the American South*, ed. T. Savitt and H. Young, 79–99. Knoxville: University of Tennessee Press, 1988.

Marinho, Maria Gabriela S. M. C. *Elites em Negociação: Breve História dos Acordos entre a Fundação Rockefeller e a Faculdade de Medicina de São Paulo (1916–1931)*. Bragança Paulista: Editora Universidade São Francisco, 2003.

Mascarenhas, R. de S. "Contribuição para o Estudo da Administração Sanitária Estadual em São Paulo." Livre Docência, Faculdade de Higiene e Saúde Pública, Universidade de São Paulo, 1949.

McClary, A. "Germs Are Everywhere: The Germ Threat as Seen in Magazine Articles, 1890–1920." *Journal of American Culture* 3, no. 1 (1990): 33–46.

McGrew, R. "Contagion." In *Encyclopedia of Medical History*, ed. R. McGrew, 77–79. New York: McGraw-Hill, 1985.

———. "Yellow Fever." In *Encyclopedia of Medical History*, ed. R. McGrew, 356–64. New York: McGraw-Hill, 1985.

Meade, Teresa. *"Civilizing" Rio: Reform and Resistance in a Brazilian City, 1889–1930*. University Park: Pennsylvania State University Press, 1997.

———. "'Civilizing Rio de Janeiro': Public Health Campaign and the Riot of 1904." *Journal of Social History* 20, no. 2 (1986): 301–22.

Mendonça, Sônia R. *O Ruralismo Brasileiro*. São Paulo: Hucitec Editora, 1997.

Merhy, Emerson Elias. *O Capitalismo e a Saúde Pública: A Emergência das Práticas Sanitárias no Estado de São Paulo*. Campinas: Papirus, 1985.

———. *A Saúde Pública como Política: Um Estudo de Formuladores de Políticas*. São Paulo: Hucitec, 1992.

Metz, K. H. "Social Thought and Social Statistics in the Early Nineteenth Century: The Case of Sanitary Statistics in England." *International Review of Social History* 29, no. 2 (1984): 254–73.

Mishra, R. *Society and Social Policy*. London: Macmillan, 1982.

Mosby's Medical Dictionary. 9th ed. St. Louis: Elsevier/Mosby, 2009.

Mota, André. *Tropeços da Medicina Bandeirante: Medicina Paulista entre 1892 e 1920*. São Paulo: Edusp, 2005.

Mueller, D. C. *Public Choice II*. Cambridge: Cambridge University Press, 1989.

Murard, L., and P. Zylberman. "La Raison de l'Éxpert ou l'Hygiène comme Science Appliqué." *European Archives of Sociology* 26, no. 1 (1985): 58–89.

Nettl, J. P. "The State as Conceptual Variable." *World Politics* 22, no. 4 (1968): 559–92.

Oliveira, Lúcia Lippi de. *O Brasil dos Imigrantes*. Rio de Janeiro: Jorge Zahar Editor, 2001.

———. *A Questão Nacional na Primeira República*. São Paulo: Brasiliense/CNPq, 1990.

Olson, M., Jr. *The Logic of Collective Action: Public Goods and Theory of Goods*. Cambridge: Harvard University Press, 1965.

Ostrom, V. *The Meaning of American Federalism*. San Francisco: ICS, 1991.

Palmer, Steven. *Launching Global Health: The Caribbean Odyssey of the Rockefeller Foundation.* Ann Arbor: University of Michigan Press, 2010.

Patterson, K. D., and G. F. Pyle. "The Geography and Mortality of the 1918 Influenza Pandemic." *Bulletin of the History of Medicine* 65, no. 1 (1991): 4–21.

Pelling, M. "Contagion/Germ Theory/Specificity." In *Companion Encyclopedia of the History of Medicine,* ed. W. F. Bynum and R. Porter, 309–34. London: Routledge, 1993.

Pena, M. V. J. "O Surgimento do Imposto de Renda: Um Estudo sobre a Relação entre Estado e Mercado no Brasil." *Dados-Revista de Ciências Sociais* 35, no. 3 (1992): 337–70.

Pernick, M. S. "Politics, Parties, and Pestilence: Epidemic Yellow Fever in Philadelphia and the Rise of the First Party System." In *Sickness and Health in America: Readings in the History of Medicine and Public Health,* 2nd ed., ed. J. W. Leavitt and R. Numbers, 356–71. Madison: University of Wisconsin Press, 1985.

Pierson, P. "When Effect Becomes Cause: Policy Feedback and Political Change." *World Politics* 45, no. 4 (1993): 595–628.

Porter, D. "Enemies of the Race: Biologism, Environmentalism, and Public Health in Edwardian England." *Victorian Studies* 34, no. 2 (1991): 159–78.

———. "Public Health." In *Companion Encyclopedia of the History of Medicine,* ed. W. F. Bynum and R. Porter, 1231–61. London: Routledge, 1993.

Rebelo, Fernanda. "Entre o *Carlo R.* e o *Orleannais*: A Saúde Publica e a Profilaxia Marítima no Relato de Dois Casos de Navios de Imigrantes no Porto do Rio de Janeiro, 1893–1907." *História, Ciências, Saúde–Manguinhos* 20, no. 3 (2013): 765–96.

Rebelo, Fernanda, Marcos C. Maio, and Gilberto Hochman. "O Princípio do Fim: O 'Torna-Viagem,' a Imigração, e a Saúde Pública no Porto do Rio de Janeiro em Tempos de Cólera." *Estudos Históricos* 24, no. 47 (2011): 69–87.

Reis, E. P. "The Agrarian Roots of Authoritarian Modernization in Brasil, 1880–1930." PhD diss., Massachusetts Institute of Technology, 1979.

———. "Elites Agrárias, State Building, e Autoritarismo." *Dados-Revista de Ciências Sociais* 25, no. 3 (1982): 331–48.

———. "Poder Privado e Construção de Estado na Primeira República." In *Corporativismo e Desigualdade: A Construção do Espaço Público no Brasil,* ed. R. Boschi, 43–68. Rio de Janeiro: Editora Rio Fundo/Iuperj, 1991.

Ribeiro, Maria Alice Rosa. *História, Ciência, e Tecnologia: 70 Anos do Instituto Biológico de São Paulo na Defesa da Agricultura, 1927–1997.* São Paulo: Instituto Biológico de São Paulo, 1997.

———. *História Sem Fim . . . Inventário da Saúde Pública: São Paulo, 1880–1930.* São Paulo: Editora Unesp, 1993.

Richmond, P. A. "American Attitudes toward the Germ Theory of Disease (1860–1880)." *Journal of the History of Medicine and Allied Sciences* 9, no. 4 (1954): 428–54.

Rio, João do. "A Peste." In *Dentro da Noite*, 59–62. 1910. Rio de Janeiro: Ministério da Cultura/Biblioteca Nacional/Departamento Nacional do Livro, 1978.

Rodrigues, Jaime. *Alimentação, Vida Material, e Privacidade: Uma História Social de Trabalhadores em São Paulo nas Décadas de 1920 a 1960*. São Paulo: Alameda, 2011.

Rokkan, S. "Dimensions of State Formation and Nation-Building: A Possible Paradigm for Research on Variations within Europe." In *The Formation of National States in Western Europe*, ed. C. Tilly, 562–600. Princeton: Princeton University Press, 1975.

Rosen, G. *A History of Public Health*. 2nd ed. Baltimore: Johns Hopkins University Press, 1993.

Rosenberg, C. *The Cholera Years: The United States in 1832, 1849, and 1866*. 1962. Chicago: University of Chicago Press, 1987.

Sá, Dominichi Miranda de. "Uma Interpretação do Brasil como Doença e Rotina: A Repercussão do Relatório Médico de Arthur Neiva e Belisário Penna." *História, Ciências, Saúde–Manguinhos* 16, supp. 1 (2009): 183–203.

———. "A Voz do Brasil: Miguel Pereira e o Discurso Sobre o 'Imenso Hospital.'" *História, Ciências, Saúde–Manguinhos* 16, supp. 1 (2009): 333–48.

Samuelson, P. A., and W. D. Nordhaus. *Economia*. São Paulo: McGraw-Hill, 1993.

———. *Economics*. New York: McGraw-Hill, 2010.

Sanglard, Gisele. *Entre os Salões e o Laboratório: Guilherme Guinle, a Saúde, e a Ciência no Rio de Janeiro, 1920–1940*. Rio de Janeiro: Editora Fiocruz, 2008.

Santos, Wanderley G. dos. *Razões da Desordem*. Rio de Janeiro: Rocco, 1993.

Schwartz, J. I. "Public Health: Case Studies on the Origins of Government Responsibility for Health Services in the United States." Ithaca: Environmental Health Planning Training Program/Cornell University, 1977.

Schwartzman, Simon. *Formação da Comunidade Científica no Brasil*. São Paulo: Companhia Editora Nacional, 1979.

Schweickardt, Júlio César, and Nísia Trindade Lima. "Do 'Inferno Florido' à Esperança do Saneamento: Ciência, Natureza, e Saúde no Estado do Amazonas durante a Primeira República (1890–1930)." *Boletim do Museu Paraense Emílio Goeldi, Ciências Humanas* 5, no. 2 (2010): 399–416.

Sevcenko, N. *A Revolta da Vacina: Mentes Insanas em Corpos Rebeldes*. São Paulo: Brasiliense, 1984.

Shakespeare, William. *William Shakespeare: The Complete Works*. Oxford: Oxford University Press, 1988.

Shapiro, A. L. "Private Rights, Public Interest, and Professional Jurisdiction: The French Public Health Law of 1902." *Bulletin of the History of Medicine* 54, no. 1 (1980): 4–22.

Shryock, R. H. *Medicine in America: Historical Essays*. Baltimore: Johns Hopkins University Press, 1972.

Skidmore, Thomas E. *Black into White: Race and Nationality in Brazilian Thought.* Durham: Duke University Press, 1993.

———. "Racial Ideas and Social Policy in Brazil, 1870–1940." In *The Idea of Race in Latin America, 1870–1940,* ed. Richard Graham, 7–36. Austin: University of Texas Press, 1990.

Skocpol, T. *Protecting Soldiers and Mothers: The Political Origins of Social Policy in the United States.* Cambridge: Harvard University Press, 1992.

Skocpol, T., and E. Amenta. "State and Social Policies." *Annual Review of Sociology* 12 (1986): 131–37.

Souza, Christiane Maria Cruz de. *A Gripe Espanhola na Bahia: Saúde, Política, e Medicina em Tempos de Epidemia.* Salvador: Editora da Universidade Federal da Bahia /Editora Fiocruz, 2009.

Soviero, D. J. "The Nationalization of a Disease: A Paradigm?" *Public Health Reports* 101, no. 4 (1986): 399–404.

Stepan, N. *Beginnings of Brazilian Science: Oswaldo Cruz, Medical Research, and Policy, 1890–1920.* New York: Science History, 1976.

Stern, Alexandra Minna, and Howard Markel. "Commentary: Disease Etiology and Political Ideology: Revisiting Erwin H. Ackerknecht's Classic 1948 Essay 'Anticontagionism between 1821 and 1867.'" *International Journal of Epidemiology* 38, no. 1 (2009): 31–33.

Sullivan, M. *Our Times: The United States, 1900–1925.* Vol. 3. New York: Scribner's, 1930.

Teixeira, Luiz A. *Ciência e Saúde na Terra dos Bandeirantes: A Trajetória do Instituto Pasteur de São Paulo no Período de 1903–1916.* Rio de Janeiro: Editora Fiocruz, 1995.

Telarolli, R., Jr. *Poder e Saúde: As Epidemias e a Formação dos Serviços de Saúde em São Paulo.* São Paulo: Editora Unesp, 1996.

Temkin, O. "An Historical Analysis of the Concept of Infection." In *Studies in Intellectual History,* 123–47. Baltimore: Johns Hopkins University Press, 1953.

Thelen, K., and S. Steinmo. "Historical Institutionalism in Comparative Politics." In *Structuring Politics: Historical Institutionalism in Comparative Analysis,* ed. S. Steinmo, K. Thelen, and F. Longstreth, 1–32. Cambridge: Cambridge University Press, 1992.

Tilly, C. "Reflections on the History of European State-Making." In *The Formation of National States in Western Europe,* ed. C. Tilly, 3–83. Princeton: Princeton University Press, 1975.

Tobey, J. A. *The National Government and Public Health.* 1926. New York: Arno, 1978.

Tomes, N. "The Private Side of Public Health: Sanitary Science, Domestic Hygiene, and the Germ Theory, 1870–1900." *Bulletin of the History of Medicine* 64, no. 4 (1990): 509–39.

Tomkins, S. M. "The Failure of Expertise: Public Health Policy in Britain during the 1918–19 Influenza Epidemic." *Social History of Medicine* 5, no. 1 (1992): 435–54.

Torres, Anny Jackeline. *A Influenza Espanhola numa Capital Planejada—Belo Horizonte, 1918*. Belo Horizonte: Argvmentvm, 2007.

Trento, Angelo. *Do Outro Lado do Atlântico: Um Século de Imigração Italiana no Brasil*. São Paulo: Studio Nobel, 1989.

Viscardi, C. *O Teatro das Oligarquias: Uma Revisão da "Política do Café com Leite,"* 4th ed. Belo Horizonte: Fino Traço, 2012.

Warner, M. "Local Control versus National Interest: The Debate over Southern Public Health, 1878–1884." *Journal of Southern History* 50, no. 3 (1984): 407–28.

Waserman, M. "The Quest for a National Health Department in the Progressive Era." *Bulletin of the History of Medicine* 49, no. 3 (1975): 353–80.

Weber, M. *Economía y Sociedad*. Mexico City: Fondo de Cultura Económica, 1964.

Wirth, J. "Minas e a Nação: Um Estudo de Poder e Dependência Regional, 1889–1937." In *O Brasil Republicano: Estrutura de Poder e Economia (1889–1930)*, 4th ed., ed. B. Fausto, 76–99. São Paulo: Difel, 1985.

Wohl, A. S. *Endangered Lives: Public Health in Victorian Britain*. Cambridge: Harvard University Press, 1983.

Young, J. H. *Pure Food: Securing the Federal Food and Drug Act of 1906*. Princeton: Princeton University Press, 1989.

Index

GILBERTO HOCHMAN is a researcher and professor at the
Casa de Oswaldo Cruz, Fundação Oswaldo Cruz. His other
books include *Cuidar, Controlar, Curar*; *Políticas Públicas
no Brasil*; and *Médicos Intérpretes do Brasil*.

DIANE GROSKLAUS WHITTY's translations include *The
Devil and the Land of the Holy Cross: Witchcraft, Slavery,
and Popular Religion in Colonial Brazil*.

The University of Illinois Press
is a founding member of the
Association of American University Presses.

Composed in 11/13 Bulmer
by Jim Proefrock
at the University of Illinois Press
Cover designed by Jim Proefrock
Cover illustration courtesy of
Casa de Oswaldo Cruz
Manufactured by Sheridan Books, Inc.

University of Illinois Press
1325 South Oak Street
Champaign, IL 61820-6903
www.press.uillinois.edu